EXPERT ADVISOR

Microsoft® Word™ 5.0

FOR THE IBM® PC

E X P E R T   A D V I S O R

Microsoft® Word™ 5.0

FOR THE IBM® PC

Paul E. Hoffman

Addison-Wesley Publishing Company, Inc.

Reading, Massachusetts   Menlo Park, California   New York
Don Mills, Ontario   Wokingham, England   Amsterdam   Bonn
Sydney   Singapore   Tokyo   Madrid   San Juan

Many of the designations used by manufacturers and sellers to
distinguish their products are claimed as trademarks. Where those
designations appear in this book and Addison-Wesley was aware of
a trademark claim, the designations have been printed in initial
capital letters (i.e., Microsoft).

Library of Congress Cataloging-in-Publication Data
Hoffman, Paul E., 1957–
    Expert advisor: Microsoft Word 5.0 for the IBM PC / Paul E. Hoffman.
        p.   cm.
    Includes index.
    ISBN 0-201-14698-3
    1. Microsoft Word (Computer program)   2. IBM Personal
Computer — Programming.   3. Word processing.   I. Title.
Z52.5.M52H627 1989
652.5 — dc20   89-33772

Series Editor: Carole McClendon
Cover design by Corey & Company: Designers
Text design by Joyce Weston
Technical reviewer: Stephen Owades
Set in 10.5-point Palatino by Publication Services, Inc.

ISBN 0-201-14698-3
ABCDEFGHIJ - HA - 89
First printing, September 1989

Contents

Acknowledgments   vii

Introduction   ix

Alphabetical Entries   1

Appendices   247

Index   265

Acknowledgments

This book would not be possible without all the wonderful people at Addison-Wesley who helped see it through the publishing process. I am especially indebted to Carole McClendon and Rachel Guichard. Stephen Owades did a wonderful job of reviewing the technical aspects of the manuscript.

Special thanks go to John Barlow and Robert Hunter for general inspiration.

Introduction

This book is a complete reference to Microsoft Word version 5.0 for the IBM PC. Any Word user will find this book helpful and easy to use. Beginners who are somewhat familiar with Word will find that the topics in this book provide a good overview of Word's features and commands. Intermediate users will find that Word has many features that allow a great deal of flexibility in their work. Advanced Word users will find many hints and tricks as well as examples for new and interesting ways to use some of Word's basic features. For any level user, this book demonstrates how different Word commands interact, how to take advantage of many of Word's little-known secrets, and how to avoid some of Word's traps.

Since many topics in Word relate to more than one command or keyboard action, this book is organized alphabetically by subject, rather than by command name. Since many of Word's commands have names that do not clearly reflect their use (such as **Library Table** to create a table of contents), this encyclopedic organization lets you quickly find the command or commands that relate to the topics described. The book is heavily cross-referenced so that you can see which topics relate to other topics. A separate index organized by Word command name provides additional assistance.

Each Word entry has the following format:

Overview   The Overview section explains in simple terms what the command or feature does and also gives an idea of the scope of the entry. If the topic relates to others in the book, these topics are discussed here as well.

Procedure   The Procedure section provides the exact method or methods for using the command or feature. Any shortcuts (such as keyboard equivalents) are listed here. If features require the use of a combination of commands to realize the full use of a feature, these command combinations are explained in detail.

Examples   People who use only some of Word's features in their normal writing might overlook other features that do not seem to apply to their work. The Examples section affords an opportunity to get new ideas for using the feature. These examples often use the same documents that are used elsewhere in the book. This approach allows the user to understand how to apply many ideas to the same piece of work.

Warnings   Of course, not every Word command is completely straightforward. The Warnings section lists ways in which using the feature can cause confusion, create unpleasant side effects, or result in the partial or total loss of documents. This section notes potential problems associated with the command.

Tips   You must go well beyond the Microsoft manual if you want to maximize Word's potential. The Tips section shows you how to increase the power of commands, sometimes by using a small variant. These tips will help you write more efficiently.

How to Use This Book

This book covers version 5 of Microsoft Word and is also helpful for people using version 4. Features new to version 5 are indicated in the headings. See the entry "Versions of Word" for a list of the improvements in version 5. Call Microsoft at 800/426-9400 for more information on updating your copy of Word.

Word was one of the first programs to allow extensive use of a mouse. Many Word users consider the mouse to be an integral part of Word, and they perform most of their tasks with the mouse; other users never use the mouse. This book accommodates both types of users by explaining all actions in terms of both mouse and keyboard use, though emphasis is given to either the mouse or keyboard in situations where one technique is easier to use (for example, it is much easier to split the screen with the mouse, but it is faster to save the current file with the keyboard).

Word's menus are not always easy to use from the keyboard since you cannot simply type the first character of the command to use it. In cases where two or more commands have the same first letter, only one of them is activated by typing that letter. For example, in the format menu three commands — running-head, replace, and revision-marks — start with the letter R.

Word uses capital letters to indicate the letters to type on the screen. This book uses boldface capital letters so that you can clearly see which letter you must type. Thus, the three Format commands are **F**ormat **R**unning-head, **F**ormat rep**L**ace, and **F**ormat revision-**M**arks; in each command, you can easily see the letters that you will type to activate the command.

As you read this book, remember that what you print might look quite different from what you see in the screen shots or the samples of printed output. There is a wide variety of printers available for the PC, and each printer has different capabilities and output quality. Some printers support boldface characters, while others do not. Some printers let you choose many different fonts, while most let you choose only one or two. If you use more than one printer in your work, it is especially important that you use Word's style sheets for setting the formatting characteristics of your documents. This allows you to maximize each printer's capabilities.

This book has three appendices. Appendix A contains a chart of all of Word's menus and may be used to get an overview of how the program is set up and its conceptual organization. Appendix B is a chart of gallery commands. Appendix C is a set of quick reference charts for many features of Word and the PC.

Expert Advisor: Microsoft Word 5.0 for the IBM PC is much more than a reference to Word. You will find that it is a solution-oriented guide to all of Word's features. It is full of examples and ideas for expanding your use of Word and for creating more attractive documents with less effort. We hope that this book will help you take advantage of Word's many capabilities.

Alphabetical
Entries

Annotations

Overview

Adding comments and notes to your work is often useful. For example, you may want to leave notes to yourself about material that you want to write about later. Or people reviewing a document in Word might want to add comments. Ideally, you might want to be able to make the annotations disappear so that you can see how the document looks without notes, but then be able to make the annotations reappear when you edit.

Word has two methods of adding annotations. The primary method uses the Format Annotation command (new in version 5), which puts the annotations with the footnotes at the end of your document and acts very much like Word's Format Footnote command. (See Footnotes.) The second method of adding annotations is to use styles with hidden text. This technique places the annotations next to the text on which you are commenting. Unfortunately, these annotations are more difficult to remove than the version 5 annotations.

Procedure

Format Annotation Command (Version 5 Only)   To add an annotation in your text, select the character to which you want to anchor the annotation and give the Format Annotation command. Enter the annotation type (maximum 28 characters) in the *mark* field and press Enter. Word automatically jumps you to the end of the document where the footnote and annotation text is kept. Each person annotating a document may use his or her name as an annotation mark.

Annotations are marked in the text with a number in the footnote numbering sequence and the specified annotation mark. The annotation text is preceded by the same number and mark. You can also specify that the date and time when the annotation was created be included in the annotation. These items can be edited or removed if desired.

Give the Window Split Footnote command to view annotations in their own window. This command lets you see both the regular text and annotations simultaneously. Since you usually want the annotation window to be smaller than the regular window, enter a number such as 17 in the *at line* field in the Window Split Footnote command. The footnote and annotation window scroll as you scroll through your main text to show you the footnotes and annotations closest to the main text you are viewing.

3

To jump back and forth between the main text and the annotations, use the Jump Annotation command. This command has three possible points to jump to, depending on what is selected when you give the command.

SELECTED	WORD JUMPS TO
Annotation mark in main text	That annotation at the end of the document
Annotation text at the end of the document	Annotation mark for that text
Some text in main text	Next annotation mark in main text

To remove an annotation, simply delete its annotation mark; Word will delete the associated annotation text.

An especially handy feature of the **Format Annotation** command is its ability to use a macro to merge annotations from different people into one document. For example, if three people are to separately annotate a document, you can copy the document three times, give the copies different names, and give each person a copy. Each person then adds annotations (but no other edits) and returns the annotated copies. To begin, load the glossary file called MACRO.GLY that came with Word with the **Transfer Glossary Load** command. Press Ctrl AM to run the "annot_merge.mac" macro. The macro prompts you for the name of the original document into which you want the annotations added, then asks for the name of the first document. Word then merges in the annotations. Repeat this for each copy, and your document will then have all the reviewers' annotations. If you are on a network, you can use copies of the file that reside on different disks in the network.

You can also list annotations into another file to look at them separately from the main document. (This is useful when you want a summary of a note but do not want to see the associated text.) To begin, load the glossary file called MACRO.GLY that came with Word with the **Transfer Glossary Load** command. Press Ctrl AC to run the "annot_collect.mac" macro. The macro prompts you for the name of the destination document where you want the annotations listed. You can then choose whether to give the name of each document individually or use Word's document retrieval feature to select the documents. (See Retrieving Documents.) Each entry in that file contains the page number, line number, annotation mark, and annotation text, formatted so you can view and sort the annotations easily.

Hidden Text   Word allows you to create one or more styles for annotations, depending on the type of annotation involved. (See Styles.) If all of your annotations are paragraphs, create paragraph styles; if the annotations appear in the same line with other text, create character styles.

Seeing annotations in a different character format is helpful. In the gallery, give the **F**ormat command, and set the *boldface* field to *Yes*. Now give the **E**xit command to return to your document. Any annotations that you format with that style will show in boldface.

To make the annotations disappear (for example, when you repaginate), add the hidden character format to the annotation's style. Give the **G**allery command and select the style you want to change. Give the **F**ormat command, and select *Yes* for the *hidden* field. The annotations will disappear from the screen when you give the **E**xit command. When you want to see the annotations, use the gallery to turn off the hidden formatting. You can also turn on *show hidden text* in the **O**ptions command to make the annotations reappear.

To remove an annotation, use the **W**indow **O**ptions command (version 4) or the **O**ptions command (version 5) to show hidden text, then search for the styles with the **F**ormat s**E**arch command to find each occurrence of the style. You can then delete the annotations in the same way you delete any text. (See Deleting Text.)

Examples   **Format Annotation Command (Version 5 Only)**   Assume that you have two people, Chris and Terry, reviewing a document called REPORT that you have just finished editing. In DOS, make two copies of REPORT.DOC called CREPORT.DOC and TREPORT.DOC, and give them to Chris and Terry.

After they have added annotations and given you back the copies, run Word and load the MACRO.GLY glossary. Press Ctrl AM to run the "annot_merge.mac" macro, and enter REPORT.DOC for the name of the original document. When prompted for the first file, enter CREPORT.DOC, and then enter TREPORT.DOC at the next prompt. Finally, enter n since you have entered all the documents you want to merge. You now have both sets of annotations in one file.

If you want to see all the annotations by themselves, use the "annot_collect.mac" macro. Create REPORTAN.DOC, part of which looks like Figure 1. If you wish, you can sort this list by selecting a column and using the **L**ibrary **A**utosort command. (See Columns.)

Hidden Text   Assume that you are leaving notes just for yourself in a document and, thus, need only one character style of annotation. Give the Gallery command, and in the gallery, give the **Insert** command to create the new style. Type AN to name the key code, select *Character* for the *usage*, and enter Annotation for the remark. Press Enter to add this new entry to the style sheet. You will see an entry similar to Figure 2.

   If you have many reviewers, create a style sheet that contains a style for each person who will comment. That style sheet might look like Figure 3.

Page 1:

   Terry I'll have Sandy check the quote with Roger.

   Terry They're not going to like this...

   Chris Nice way of stating this.

   Chris Check this quote with Roger.

   Chris What about gross sales?

   Chris Can't we get a strong lead sentence?

Page 2:

   Terry "Changeover" or "Transition"?

Figure 1

```
1   AN Character 1                         Annotation
       Palatino (roman k) 12 Hidden.
2   FR Character Footnote reference        Normal footnote reference
       NewCentSchlbk (roman j) 10 Superscript.
3   ND Division Standard                   Normal division
       Page break. Page length 11"; width 8.5". Page # format Arabic. Top margin 1";
       bottom 1"; left 1"; right 1". Top running head at 0.5". Bottom running head
       at 0.5". Footnotes on same page.
4   NP Paragraph Standard                  Normal paragraph
       Palatino (roman k) 12/14. Flush left, space after 1 li. Tabs at: 3" (left
       flush).
◆
```

Figure 2

```
1    TE Character 2                    Annotations from Terry
        Palatino (roman k) 12 Hidden.
2    CH Character 1                    Annotations from Chris
        Palatino (roman k) 12 Hidden.
```

Figure 3

Warnings   If a division has footnotes or annotations, the *Continuous* choice in the Format Division Layout command does not work. Word will always go to a new page if there is a footnote or annotation.

Tips   You will benefit by having different types of annotations to yourself. For example, you might classify your comments into categories such as "question," "weak point," "check citation," "get quotation permission," and so on. Use different words or phrases in your annotation mark names or style names.

Version 5 annotations are remembered when you cut or copy text that includes them to the scrap. Thus, any annotations in that text will be preserved if you use the scrap to hold text that is being moved.

If you are using the hidden text, you can merge these style sheets into a current style sheet with the Transfer Merge command in the gallery. When you want to hide the annotation styles, be sure that Word is not showing hidden text. If you can still see an annotation after formatting it as hidden, use the Window Options command (version 4) or the Options command (version 5) to prevent Word from showing hidden text in that window.

ASCII Files.   *See* Importing and Exporting Files

Autosave   [Version 5 Only]

Overview   Many operating systems are tolerant of power failures and secure from events that cause the computer to stop. Unfortunately, MS-DOS does not fit this description. Thus, you should save your work to disk every few minutes; if the power fails or another program causes Word or MS-DOS to stop, you will lose only the work done after your last save.

Word's autosave feature allows you to tell Word to save your work automatically at predefined intervals. If you use this feature, Word saves temporary files for any open file that has been changed, including documents, style sheets, and glossaries. If you wish, Word can ask whether it should save the temporary file. If saving on your system takes a long time, you can skip over an automatic save and continue working.

The autosave feature is designed to be efficient and unobtrusive. After the first automatic save, the autosave feature saves only the changes you have made in the file rather than saving the entire document. When you save the document you are working on with the **Transfer Save** command or when quitting, Word saves all changes as normal to the document. Since saving only the changes is much faster than saving the whole document, the autosave feature does not take as much time as full saves.

If you are making many changes to a file, Word waits until it is idle before starting the autosave, thereby allowing you to work without distraction. Since the autosave feature saves to a temporary file instead of to your document's file, you can decide to quit without saving your changes just as you can without autosave.

Word will never attempt an autosave while you are running a macro. If you have autosave set on and Word runs low on memory and displays the blinking *SAVE* light, it will autosave immediately.

It is easy to recover if a failure occurs while you are editing a file. Rename the temporary file that was saved by the autosave command, open it up, and immediately save it with the **Transfer Save** command. Word will process the changes it made to the temporary file and create a complete fresh file.

Procedure   **Setting Autosave**   Use the **O**ptions command to turn on autosaving. In the *autosave* field, enter the number of minutes you want between saves. If you do not want to use autosaving, set the *autosave* field to 0. Generally, setting autosave to 5 is a reasonable balance between safety and convenience.

If you want Word to ask you whether to save files when autosaving, set the *autosave confirm* field to *Yes*. Although this can help save time, it can also be annoying, so you may want to leave *autosave confirm* set to *No*.

Recovering From a Failure With Autosave   Autosave files are stored in the same directory as the Word program. Documents are saved with the extension .SVD, style sheets with .SVS, and glossaries with .SVG. If you have files that were never named before the failure occurred, they are stored with names such as UNTITLED.

Word prompts "Autosave backup files exist. Enter Y to recover files, or Esc to ignore." If you enter Y, Word recovers the files and deletes the autosave files. If you do not recover, Word keeps the autosave files on disk unless you edit the unrecovered files, in which case it will delete the autosave backups.

Recovering From a Failure Without Autosave   Word saves the temporary files in the same directory from which Word was run. The files are listed below.

FILE NAME	HOLDS
MWDOCn.TMP	Document in window n. For example, MWDOC1.TMP is the document that is in window 1.
MWSTYn.TMP	Style sheets for the documents. If you have a style sheet that you are working on in the gallery that is not attached to any document, it is called MWSTY9.TMP.
MWGLY.TMP	The glossary.

If you have a failure, follow these steps:

1. Use the MS-DOS RENAME command to rename the document on which you were working to a different name. You may want to refer back to this version of the document later.
2. Use the MS-DOS RENAME command to rename the temporary file to the name of the document.
3. Start Word and load the renamed temporary file.
4. Immediately save the file with the **T**ransfer **S**ave command.

Warnings   Because Word stores the temporary files from the autosaving on the Word program directory, autosaving is of little use if you are starting Word from a RAM disk. Word does not look at the TMP or TEMP environment variables when saving temporary files since this might cause it to write them to a RAM disk. As long as you start Word from a floppy disk, hard disk, or over the network, you can recover your temporary files and therefore recover your work.

If you are running on a network, Word stores the temporary files on the directory from which you started Word. Thus, if you run Word on a RAM disk in a network environment, your temporary files will be lost if the system crashes.

Autosaving is often not useful if you have only floppy drives and no hard disk. Since Word saves the temporary files on the same disk as regular Word files, you might run out of disk space quickly. Being on a slow network will compound the problem.

Bookmarks

[Version 5 Only]

Overview

When you read nonfiction, you often want to mark places in the book for future reference. Even if the book's table of contents and index are very good, there are often places that you want to remember and be able to thumb to quickly.

Word's bookmark feature allows you to place markers throughout a document so that you can flip to them at a later time. These bookmarks are more convenient than standard physical bookmarks since they mark a range of text, not just a page. Also, since you can assign a name to each bookmark, you can easily locate a particular section of text.

Bookmarks are also used in Word's cross-referencing feature. (See Cross-Referencing.)

Procedure

To create a bookmark, select the text you want and give the Format bookmarK command. Enter the desired name in the *name* field. Bookmark names have a maximum of 31 characters (letters, numbers, periods, hyphens, and underscores, but not spaces).

The Jump bookmarK command lets you go to the bookmark you name. When you give the Jump bookmarK command, Word selects the entire range.

The bookmark is "anchored" to the first and last characters in the range. As long as that first character is in your document, the bookmark is valid. If you move the text in that range, the bookmark will refer correctly to the range wherever you move it. However, if you delete some of the text in the range (but keep the first character), the bookmark will be valid and will include the same number of characters as you originally specified. Thus, if your range was 90 characters long, the bookmark continues to refer to the same first character and the 89 characters after it even if you delete 50 characters from the middle of the original range.

If you copy text with a bookmark in it and place it in the same document, the bookmark is not copied since you cannot have two bookmarks with the same name. If you copy the text to another document and that document does not already have a bookmark with that name, the bookmark will be copied as well.

To change a bookmark name, select the first character and give the Format bookmarK command. Word fills in the *name* field with the current name; simply delete this and enter the new name you want. To remove a bookmark without deleting the anchor character, select the anchor character and give the Format bookmarK command, clear the bookmark name from the entry field, and press Enter. When Word prompts you to confirm the loss of the bookmark, press Y.

Bookmarks are also used with the Library Link Document command. This command lets you bring part or all of another Word document or ASCII file into your document when you print. The command prompts you for a file name and a bookmark in that file. If you do not include a bookmark name (such as for an ASCII file), Word links in the entire file.

Tips Bookmarks work well with macros. You can make macros that give the Jump bookmarK command and name a bookmark. This lets you create single-key macros that jump to specific parts of your document, such as the first page of each chapter or to certain tables that you update frequently.

You may want to put the same bookmarks in many of your documents. For example, you might mark the beginning of the table of contents and index in each document with bookmarks that have the same name. You can then use the same macros to jump to these bookmarks in every document.

Bookmarks are remembered when you cut or copy text that includes
them to the scrap. Thus, any bookmarks in that text are preserved if you
use the scrap to hold text that is being moved.

Borders and Boxes

Overview   Word has many methods of adding horizontal and vertical lines to documents. These capabilities let you create forms with check boxes, highlighted headings or important information, or simply make your documents more distinctive. When combined with Word's style sheets, borders
and boxes give you powerful features usually found only in desktop publishing software.

Boxes surround an entire paragraph; borders are lines that appear
along one side of the paragraph. You can specify more than one border for
a paragraph (for example, you can specify a left and top border together).
Boxes and borders are formats associated with paragraphs, so they automatically shrink and expand if you change other paragraph indents.
Thus, if you have a box around a paragraph and change the indentation of
both sides to make the paragraph smaller, the sides of the box automatically shrink. If you add text to a paragraph in a box, the bottom of the box
automatically moves down as you type in the box.

Boxes and borders go from the left indent to the right indent; however,
if you have a negative measurement for the first line (such as for an outdented paragraph) the box or border aligns with the first line in the paragraph. There are four line styles for boxes and borders: normal, bold,
double, and thick (the thick style is new in version 5).

Note that Word's boxes and borders feature is very different than
Word's line drawing feature. Line drawing lets you use the cursor control
keys to draw lines on the screen, but the lines do not change when you
reformat text. (See Line Drawing.)

The Format Border command also lets you add shading to a paragraph.
(See Shading.)

Procedure   To enclose a paragraph in a box, select any part of the paragraph, give the
Format Border command, and set the *type* field to *Box*. You can select a *line*

12

style of *Normal, Bold, Double,* or *Thick.* Figure 4 shows the options available in the **Format** **B**order command.

If you have two adjacent paragraphs with boxes, the bottom of the upper box is joined with the top of the lower box. However, if the line styles are different (for example, if the upper box is normal and the lower box is double) the boxes are not joined. If you have two side-by-side paragraphs with boxes and the right indent of the first box is at the same position as the left indent of the second box, the common border will be joined.

Use the **Format** **B**order command to add lines above, below, to the left, or to the right of a paragraph. To add lines above and below a paragraph, give the **Format** **B**order command, change the *type* to *Lines,* and select *Yes* for both *above* and *below.*

Examples   Figure 5 shows how a centered, boxed headline stands out from the rest of the text. This paragraph is formatted in two steps. Select the paragraph,

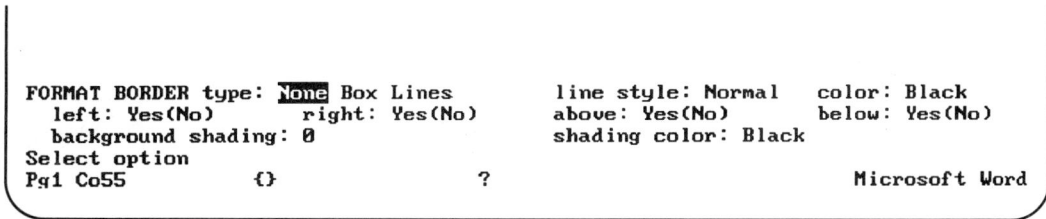

Figure 4

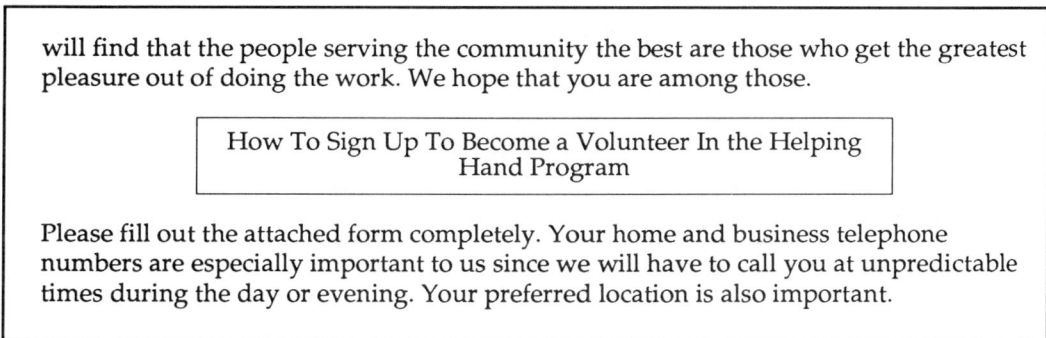

Figure 5

give the **Format P**aragraph command, change the *alignment* field to *Centered*, enter 1 in for *left indent*, and enter 1 in for *right indent*. Next, give the **Format B**order command and change the *type* to *Box*.

Warnings   The appearance of the borders and boxes in your documents depends to a large extent on the capabilities of your printer since printers vary in their ability to handle certain tasks. For example, some printers can print bold borders better than others; on PostScript printers, boxes appear closer to the text than on other printers. If you switch between printers, you may see a significant formatting difference when using borders and boxes.

Tips   Since a bottom border goes from the left indent to the right indent, it is sometimes used for the top of a table. Since the border takes up a line by itself, you may prefer using the underlining character format instead.

If your printer prints incorrect characters for borders and boxes, you may have to change the printer driver. (See Printer Drivers.)

Using left and right borders is sometimes a good way of highlighting text without making it stand out too much. A comparison of the visual impact of the two paragraphs in Figure 6 illustrates this point.

Boxes can be created around groups of paragraphs with combinations of lines above, below, left, and right. Avoid space above and below paragraphs when you are using this type of multi-paragraph box.

Please fill out the attached form completely. Your home and business telephone numbers are especially important to us since we will have to call you at unpredictable times during the day or evening. Your preferred location is also important.

Please fill out the attached form completely. Your home and business telephone numbers are especially important to us since we will have to call you at unpredictable times during the day or evening. Your preferred location is also important.

Figure 6

Changing. *See* **Replacing**

Character Formatting

Overview   You can apply character formats to any text or graphics in Word. Word's wide variety of character formats allows you to give your documents a distinctive style by adding flair and embellishment. Character styles are also used to add emphasis and clarity to specific words in your documents.

Word's character formatting can be divided into three categories: character display, fonts, and placement. See Fonts for more information on how Word lets you choose fonts and font sizes; see Subscripts and Superscripts for more information on character placement.

Procedure   To add formatting to a group of characters or a style, select the characters or style and give the Format Character command. If only a single character is selected and you are using the Alt key combinations, you must give the command twice. Figure 7 shows the available choices. Select *Yes* or *No* for each character display type. You can have as many character formats as you want on any character.

```
FORMAT CHARACTER bold: Yes No        italic: Yes No          underline: Yes No
            strikethrough: Yes No    uppercase: Yes No       small caps: Yes No
            double underline: Yes No position: Normal Superscript Subscript
            font name:               font size:              font color:
            hidden: Yes No
Select option
Pg1 Co55            {}               ?                       Microsoft Word
```

Figure 7

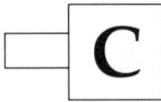

Adding character formatting to selected characters is faster with the Alt key. The following list shows the keys you can use.

FORMAT	KEY
Bold	Alt B
Double underline	Alt D
Hidden	Alt E
Italic	Alt I
Small caps	Alt K
Strikethrough	Alt S
Subscript	Alt -
Superscript	Alt +
Underline	Alt U

In version 4, if you have a style sheet attached to your document, you must use Alt X before the above keys. In version 5, if any styles attached to your document begin with these characters, you must press Alt X instead and the letter for the keyboard equivalents. For example, if you have a style with the name BG, to make the selection bold you must type Alt XB.

There are two ways to remove a character format from a character after you have selected it: you can use the **F**ormat **C**haracter command and select *No* for the format, or you can use the Alt Space Bar to remove all character formatting from the selected characters.

Hidden formatting is used for special purposes in Word. If you are creating a table of contents or index, hidden characters are used to flag the entries. (See Indexes and Table of Contents.) You can also use hidden text to leave messages for yourself in your documents. (See Annotations.) If you are including spreadsheets or graphics files, you format the file information in hidden text. (See Spreadsheets and Graphics.)

To see hidden text, set the *show hidden text* field in the **W**indow **O**ptions command (version 4) or the **O**ptions command (version 5) to *Yes*. To see where the text is but not see the text, set the *visible* field in the **O**ptions command (version 4) or the *show non-printing symbols* field (version 5) to *Partial* or *Complete*.

Examples Figure 8 shows samples of each character format as well as some examples of mixing formats.

Text with single character formats:
Bold
Italic
<u>Underline</u>
~~Strikethrough~~
UPPERCASE
SMALL CAPS
<u>Double underline</u>

Good combinations include ***bold and italic*** and <u>SMALL CAPS WITH UNDERLINE</u>.

Figure 8

Warnings   Using the strikethrough format can be dangerous if you also use revision marks. (See Revision Marks.) When you remove revision marks, Word deletes all text in strikethrough format. Thus, you should never use strikethrough in any document in which you might use revision marks unless you intend for all text in strikethrough to be deleted.

Word will not format capital letters in either small caps or uppercase. To use either the small caps or uppercase formats, you must select lowercase characters. The small caps format is almost useless in style sheets since capital letters will appear larger than lowercase letters. Note that this is different than the Control F4 key, which toggles the case of the letters as an editing command.

Some printers cannot print in all character formats. For example, some laser printers cannot print boldface or italic characters, and many dot matrix printers cannot print italic characters.

Depending on your display, you may be able to see all the character formats on screen. Monochrome screens with no graphics will show bold-face characters in bold, characters formatted with the uppercase format in reverse video, and all other formats in underline. Color screens with no graphics will show each character format in a different color, up to the maximum number of colors available on the screen. Hercules monochrome graphics boards can display many character styles directly.

Tips   Remember to use style sheets for character formatting. (See Styles.) Since you can create character styles in Word, you can make styles for almost any purpose for which you would use direct character formatting. For example, you might have a style for emphasis and a different style for book titles. If you change from a printer that does not have many capabilities to one that does, you can easily make all the formatting in your document match the capabilities of the new printer. This becomes more difficult if you use direct character formatting.

Most character formats can be added to each other (for example, characters can be both bold and italic), but version 5 does not permit an underline and double underline on the same characters. If you select underlined characters and press Alt D to make them double underlined, Word removes the underline format. Likewise, if you have selected double underlined characters and press Alt U to make them underlined, Word removes the double underline format.

Combining character formats and fonts in your printing can make a strong visual impact. However, you should avoid using too many in a document since the effect can be garish and distracting. In general, the boldface font and underline format will fill most of your needs.

Many style manuals warn against using character formatting for emphasis in sentences. A different character format within a sentence certainly stands out, but the reader may not understand how much you want to emphasize the emphasized word. Use emphatic words rather than character formatting to make your meaning clear.

Columns

Overview

Most common business correspondence such as letters and reports are printed in a single column. However, Word can also prepare documents such as newsletters that are often presented in several columns. This feature is sometimes called *newspaper columns*.

Defining columns is easy since Word requires equal-sized columns. Simply specify the number of columns you want in the current division and the amount of space between the columns. Word then determines the column width and placement on the page. Note that version 5 allows different numbers of columns in different sections of a page.

A new feature in Word version 5 is its ability to show columns on the screen as they will be printed out. (Earlier versions of Word let you see only one long column and the column breaks.) Although this feature slows down Word's performance, its advantages are obvious. (See Layout for more information on this feature.)

Procedure

Specify the number of columns for each division. If your document has only one division, the number you specify will be valid for the entire document. Use the Format Division Layout command to tell Word how many columns you want and how much space you want between the columns. Figure 9 shows the options available in the Format Division Layout command.

To see the columns on the screen as they will be printed, tell Word that you want to see the layout. Give the Options command and set *show layout* to *Yes*. (See Layout.)

You can wrap the text in two columns around a picture by placing the picture on the page with the Format pOsition command. (See Paragraph Placement.) The columns will position themselves around the picture in the same way a single column positions itself.

To force Word to go to a new column in version 5, enter a column break by pressing Alt Ctrl Enter. This will ensure that the next column begins with a heading. In version 4, you must put a division marker at the position you want the new column, then use the Format Division Layout command to specify that the new division starts in a new column (by setting the *division break* field to *Column*).

*Examples
(Version 5
Only)*

Figure 10 shows some of what Word can do with columns. The top half of the page was formatted as two columns, the middle rule as a single column, and the bottom half of the page as three columns.

To create a page like this, start with the text as one division. Move the cursor to the first letter that will appear in the bottom half of the page, and press Ctrl Enter twice to put in two division marks. Press Up Arrow to

```
FORMAT DIVISION LAYOUT footnotes: Same-page End
          number of columns: 1          space between columns: 0.5"
              division break:(Page)Continuous Column Even Odd
      Select option
      Pg1 Co1              {}                    ?                    Microsoft Word
```

Figure 9

Although last quarter was a weak one for our clients, Industrial Refrigeration's sales increased over the same quarter last year. Due to our strong technology and new models, we were able to introduce significant new products to new customers and increase our main-line sales at the same time. With net sales of over $7.3M, this quarter's results indicate that Industrial Refrigeration will finish the fiscal year with a healthy profit.

The restaurant-building market continues to have difficulties, and we scaled back our efforts in the super-restaurant refrigeration units in response. As we did this, we started a new marketing campaign for our smallest cold-storage units aimed at the construction industry. The results were phenomenal, and we were able to increase production of the IR200 series to meet the new demand generated by the marketing campaign.

Management feels strongly about the future of Industrial Refrigeration. President Roger Eisenstadt says, "We are very excited about the new IR800 series. The flexible ventilation system and the easily-removed racks should give us a big advantage in markets with stringent health inspectors. In addition, the development on our laboratory line is almost complete. We will have significant announcements in the coming quarter about a complete scientific refrigeration system that can be installed in new buildings and be retrofitted in rebuilding projects."

Earnings from continuing operations were down slightly due to the process of scaling back the manufacturing of the IR500 series. There was no loss of personnel since the employees were able to move easily to the increased IR200 production. The short-term changeover cost was $120,000 and was easily made up for by the increased sales of the IR200 models.

Research costs were up sharply in the quarter as Industrial Refrigeration finished the development of the IR800 series. The costs were mostly in ventilation fabrication and design, since the IR800 has a very different structure than other models. Research costs for the IRLAB series of laboratory units also increased last quarter, and will continue to increase this quarter as final design and revision is made to the series.

Sales increased by $1.2M over the same quarter last year. Due to a strong marketing push for the IR200 series and advance orders for the IR800, the Industrial Refrigeration sales team both broadened our customer base (especially in the West) and had increased sales to our established customers. According to Joe Guiliani, Director of Sales, "We are having a steadily increasing influence with our customers. After GCL, one of our biggest competitors, was acquired in a hostile takeover in April, we were able to get many new clients from previous GCL accounts. Our goal is to not only keep those new

Figure 10

move the cursor up one line, and press Enter to add a blank paragraph between the paragraphs. Give the **Format Border** command and set the *type* field to *Lines* and *below* field to *Yes*. Give the **Format Division Layout** command and set *division break* to *Continuous*.

Next, move the cursor up to any text in the first division, and give the **Format Division Layout** command. Set the *number of columns* field to 2, *space between columns* to .5 in, and *division break* to *Continuous*. Move the cursor down to any text in the third division, and give the **Format Division Layout** command. Set *number of columns* to 3, *space between columns* to .3 in, and *division break* to *Continuous*.

Tips

Depending on your printer, it may be difficult to read text that is in thin columns. With high quality printers, columns can be as narrow as 2.5 inches. With other printers, the columns should be at least 3.5 inches wide. Check your printout carefully to make sure that the narrow columns are easy to read.

If your printer uses fixed spacing for letters, right-justified paragraphs are hard to read in multi-column printout because there are more extra spaces per line than in single-column lines. This is not as noticeable in printers with proportional spacing or microjustification. Before finalizing a design for a multi-column layout, experiment with both justified and left-aligned paragraphs.

Copy Command

Overview

The **Copy** command puts a copy of the selected text in the scrap or creates a glossary entry. If you use the **Copy** command to put text in the scrap when there is already text in the scrap, the new text will replace whatever was there. (See Scrap and Glossaries.)

Procedure

To put text in the scrap, select the text you want, give the **Copy** command, and press Enter at the prompt; or, simply press Alt F3. To make a glossary entry, select the text, give the **Copy** command, enter the name for the glossary entry, and press Enter.

Copying Formats

Overview   Since adding formats to text can require many steps, Word provides an easy way to copy the formats from some already-formatted text to unformatted text. Thus, you can apply the formatting once and make the same changes to other text.

Procedure   There are many ways to copy formats. The simplest method is to use the repeat action key, F4. Select the first unformatted text, give the **Format Character** command or the **Format Paragraph** command, enter the formatting you want, and press Enter. Select the next unformatted text and press F4. This performs the same operation, which is the application of the format. The mouse equivalent of the F4 key is pointing at *COMMAND* at the left of the bottom of the screen and clicking the left button.

You can also use the mouse to copy formats. Format some text with character formatting and move the selection to the unformatted text. Point at the formatted text, hold down the Alt key, and click the left button to copy the character formatting. This method can also be used to copy character style formatting.

Copying paragraph formats with the mouse is similar. Format a paragraph with paragraph formatting and move the selection to any characters in the unformatted text. Point in the selection bar next to the formatted text, hold down the Alt key, and click the right button to copy the paragraph formatting. This is especially handy for copying styles.

The following display summarizes character and paragraph formatting procedures.

TO COPY	SELECT THE TEXT TO BE FORMATTED AND POINT AT	THEN PRESS THE ALT KEY AND
Character formatting	The formatted characters	Click the left button
Paragraph formatting	The selection bar next to the formatted paragraph	Click the right button

Tips   You may want to add the same formatting to many sets of characters throughout a document. Even with a mouse, however, the above procedures can become tedious. Using a macro to define the formatting you want is a better solution. (See Macros.) An even better solution is to use character styles. (See Styles.)

Copying Text

Overview　　Word provides two methods for copying text. In the first method, the scrap lets you hold a piece of text and insert it in another location in the document or in a different document. In the second method, the mouse copies text without affecting the contents of the scrap (Microsoft calls this *speed copying*). (See Moving Text.)

Procedure　　Use the **C**opy command to copy the scrap. (See Copy Command.) Word prompts {} as the destination of the copy. Since this is what you want, simply press Enter. Once text is in the scrap, you can insert the contents of the scrap in another location in your document or in a different document, select the location you want to copy, and give the Insert command. The keyboard equivalent of this is Alt F3; the mouse equivalent is clicking on the **C**opy command with the right button.

To use the mouse to speed copy text without affecting the contents of the scrap, select the text you want to copy, point to the location you want to insert the text, hold down the Shift key, and click the left mouse button. You can also tell Word that you want the text to appear before different blocks of text. The following list shows how this is done.

TO INSERT IN FRONT OF	POINT AT	HOLD DOWN THE SHIFT KEY AND CLICK THE MOUSE BUTTON
Character	Text	Left
Word	Text	Right
Sentence	Text	Both
Line	Selection bar	Left
Paragraph	Selection bar	Right
Beginning of document	Selection bar	Both

You can use either the scrap or speed copying to copy text from one window to another. Word treats the text as if it were being copied from within the document. Thus, if you have different style sheets attached to the two documents, the copied text may be formatted differently in the destination document.

Tips　　If you use a mouse, speed copying usually works better than the scrap. It is also much faster if you are using a floppy-based system with no hard disk.

Cross-Referencing [Version 5 Only]

Overview

Reports often contain related information in many places. For example, the beginning sections of a long report might include summary details of other sections in the report. Usually you refer to the later section by name (for example, "See *Financial Standing* for more detail"). However, this method is cumbersome in a long report because the reader must turn to the table of contents to find the page number before going to the new section.

Word's cross-referencing feature lets you imbed the page number with the reference (for example, "See *Financial Standing* on page 54 for more detail"). Using cross-referencing for pages removes the necessity of keeping track of page numbers that might change as you edit your document or as you change printers.

Cross-referencing is also very convenient with Word's sequence feature. (See Sequences.) Instead of cross-referencing to a figure or table by its number, you can refer to it by name. Thus, the printed output will have the correct figure or table number even if you have added a new figure or table.

Word evaluates the cross-reference when you print your document. Thus, you do not put a "fixed" page number or figure sequence number in your document; instead, you include a reference to it. When you print, Word formats your document, looks for all references, fills them in, and prints the document with the correct numbers. Cross-references can be to pages or sequences before or after the reference.

Cross-references to pages and to sequences refer to bookmarks. The values at those bookmarks are evaluated when you print page numbers. (See Bookmarks.)

Procedure

To cross-reference an item on a page, you must first mark the item with a bookmark. Select the beginning of what you want to refer to (such as the first letter of a title), give the **F**ormat bookmar**K** command, and enter a bookmark name in the *name* field. To refer to the page of that bookmark in your document, type page: followed by the bookmark name, and press F3. Word displays this in parentheses to indicate that it is a special mark, similar to the special glossary marks.

If you wish to refer to a sequence holder, that holder must be immediately followed by a bookmark. To refer to that holder, type the sequence name, a colon, and the bookmark name, then press F3. For instance, if you are referring to a figure whose bookmark is called "assets," and the sequence name for figures is "fig," you would enter `fig:assets`.

Examples   Assume that you want to refer to the page that the bookmark called "order-entry-program" is on. Type the preceding text, such as `For more information, see page` followed by a space. Next, create a reference to that page. Type `page:order-entry-program` and press F3. Word displays this as *For more information, see page (page:order-entry-program)* and will print the cross-reference as a number when you print your document. This output is shown in Figure 11.

Next, assume that you want to refer to a figure number. Go to the caption that contains the sequence holder. Figure 12 shows such a caption.

Move the cursor to the period after *(figure.number)* and give the Format bookmar**K** command. Enter `New.Building.Plans` for the bookmark name and press Enter.

Now move to the place where you want to refer to the figure. Type `This is shown in Figure figure.number:New.Building.Plans` and press F3. Word puts the reference in parentheses. When the document is printed, it appears with the figure number, as shown in Figure 13.

For more information, see page 32

Figure 11

```
      .G.D:\NEWBUILD.PCX;5.5";2.468";PCX
Figure (figure.number:). New Building Plans for the
Proposed Site.
```

Figure 12

This is shown in Figure 4

Figure 13

Tips　　　　You can increase the clarity of your writing if you refer to both figure numbers and page numbers for figures that appear in other parts of the document. For example, it would make the reader's job easier if you included the page number with the figure number shown above. This would appear on the screen as `This is shown in Figure (figure.number:New.Building.Plans) on page (page:New.Building.Plans)`. This saves the reader from going back to the table of figures to find the page number for the figure.

Delete Command

Overview　　The **Delete** command removes the selected text from your document and puts a copy of it in the scrap or creates a glossary entry. If you use the **Delete** command to put text in the scrap when there is already text in the scrap, the new text replaces whatever was there. (See Scrap and Glossaries.)

Procedure　　To remove text from your document and put it in the scrap, select the text you want, give the **Delete** command, and press Enter at the prompt; or, simply press the Delete key. To remove the text and make a glossary entry, select the text, give the **Delete** command, enter the name for the glossary entry, and press Enter.

Deleting Text

Overview　　Word allows you to delete text to the scrap or to remove it without affecting the contents of the scrap. (See Scrap.) You can, of course, also delete text by putting the cursor to the right of the text and pressing Backspace. If you use overtype mode (by pressing F5), each character you type over is deleted.

Procedure　　Use the **Delete** command or the Delete key to put the selection in the scrap. This replaces the contents of the scrap with the selected text and removes the selected text from your document. To delete text without putting it in the scrap, select it and press Shift Delete. In either case, you can reverse the effect of the action with the **Undo** command.

D

Division Formatting

Overview Word uses divisions to break up a document into sections. You add a division mark to separate two parts of your text if you want to have different division formatting in the two sections. If you also work with Microsoft Word on the Macintosh, note that divisions in that program are called "sections."

Division formatting includes margins (see Margins), headers and footers (see Headers and Footers), page numbers (see Page Numbers), placement of footnotes (see Footnotes), number of columns (see Columns), and line numbers (see Line Numbering). This formatting can be applied to any division in a document.

Procedure Each new document starts off as a single division. To split a division into two divisions, move the cursor to the position at which you want to split and press Ctrl Enter. The two divisions will have the same division formatting as the previous single division.

The initial division formatting is the same as the formatting that is applied in the style sheet to the style entry that contains the "Standard" division variant. (See Styles.) If you change the settings in that style, documents will use those settings as the base division formatting.

Place the cursor in the division you want to format and give the Format Division command to change the division formatting. You can change the formatting of adjacent divisions by selecting text in each division and using the Format Division command.

The effects of the various Format Division commands are discussed in other sections of this book. One effect you should note, however, is how the division starts. In the Format Division Layout command, you can specify what the division break means. Your choices for *division break* are *Page, Continuous, Column, Even*, and *Odd*. These choices and their actions are shown below.

CHOICE	ACTION
Page	Start the division on a new page
Continuous	Continue the layout directly after the previous division
Column	Start the division at the top of the next column
Even	Start the division at the top of the next even-numbered page
Odd	Start the division at the top of the next odd-numbered page

Your choice for *division break* depends on your reason for splitting the division. If you split it to begin a new chapter and you are preparing a report or book that will eventually be printed on both sides of a page, you will probably want to set *division break* to *Odd*. If you have a page with one column across the top and many columns on the page, you should set *division break* to *Continuous*.

F1 Enumeration

Overview   Word dialogs often have fields in which you can type settings. This is true for all fields that accept file names, or that have many choices, or that have choices that change based on settings in other fields. You can get a list of possible choices in the field by selecting it and pressing F1 or pointing at it with the mouse and pressing the right button; this is the process of enumeration.

The fields that can be enumerated are listed below.

COMMAND	FIELD	CHOICES
Copy	*to*	Name of glossary to which to copy; { } for the scrap
Delete	*to*	Name of glossary to which to copy after deleting; { } for the scrap
Format Character	*font name*	Names of fonts; depends on the *printer* and *model* fields in the **Print Options** command
Format Character	*font size*	Size of font; depends on font selected in *font name* field
Format Tabs Set	*position*	Allows you to move the cursor on the ruler to select a position or to enter a number
Format Tabs Clear	*position*	Allows you to move the cursor on the ruler to select a position or to enter a number
Format Stylesheet Attach		Name of style sheet
Format Stylesheet Record	*variant*	Type of variant; depends on *usage* field
Format sEarch Character	*font name*	Names of fonts; depends on the *printer* and *model* fields in the **Print Options** command

28

F

COMMAND	FIELD	CHOICES
Format sEarch Character	*font size*	Size of font; depends on font selected in *font name* field
Format repLace Character	*font name*	Names of fonts; depends on the *printer* and *model* fields in the **P**rint **O**ptions command
Format repLace Character	*font size*	Size of font; depends on font selected in *font name* field
Format pOsition	*frame position horizontal*	Types of absolute horizontal positions (version 5 only)
Format pOsition	*frame position vertical*	Types of absolute vertical positions (version 5 only)
Format bookmarK	*name*	Names of bookmarks (version 5 only)
Insert	*from*	Name of glossary to which to copy after deleting; { } for the scrap
Jump bookmarK	*name*	Names of bookmarks (version 5 only)
Library Link Document	*filename*	Name of document (version 5 only)
Library Link Document	*bookmark*	Bookmark name (version 5 only)
Library Link Graphics	*filename*	Name of graphics file
Library Link Graphics	*file format*	Format of graphics file (version 5 only)
Library Link Graphics	*alignment in frame*	Type of alignment (version 5 only)
Library Link Graphics	*graphics width*	Width of the graphic when printed
Library Link Graphics	*graphics height*	Height of the graphic when printed
Library Link Spreadsheet	*filename*	Name of spreadsheet file
Library Link Spreadsheet	*area*	Named range to select
Options	*colors*	Colors available for display adapter
Options	*linedraw character*	Linedraw character sets and individual characters

29

COMMAND	FIELD	CHOICES
Options	*display mode*	Graphics mode
Options	*speller path*	Location of spelling module
Print Options	*printer*	Name of printer driver
Print Options	*setup*	Port to which printer is attached
Print Options	*model*	Model of your printer
Print Options	*graphics resolution*	Graphics resolutions available for your printer (version 5 only)
Print Options	*paper feed*	Type of feed for paper
Transfer Load	*filename*	Name of file to load
Transfer Delete	*filename*	Name of file to delete
Transfer Merge	*filename*	Name of file to merge into current document
Transfer Rename	*filename*	Name of file to rename
Transfer Glossary Merge	*filename*	Name of glossary to merge with current glossary
Transfer Glossary Clear	*names*	Names of glossary entries to remove
Transfer Glossary Load	*filename*	Name of glossary to load

Procedure   Press F1 with the field blank to get a list of files that you can open in any field that opens files (such as in the **Transfer Load** command). You can also add a partial path name to the field before pressing F1 to have Word look at a directory other than the one given in the **Transfer O**ptions command. For example, if you want to open one of the files in the D:\MANUALS\NEW directory but are not sure which file you want, enter the path in the *filename* field and press F1; you can then select the file from the list. You can also narrow the list by specifying part of the file name (such as "D:\MANUALS\NEW\S*.DOC" for documents in that directory that begin with the letter "S"). The commands on which this method works are **Format Stylesheet Attach, Library Link Document, Library Link Graph**ics**, Library Link Spreadsheet, Print Options, Transfer Load, Transfer Delete, Transfer Merge, Transfer Rename, Transfer Glossary Merge**, and **Transfer Glossary Load**.

Word version 5 makes enumerated file lists much more useful because it allows you to navigate through the tree structure of your file directory in those lists. Instead of simply listing files, Word also lists the names of the other directories and drives available, including the parent directory. The additional drives and parent directory have square brackets around their names. Figure 14 shows an example with the other drives and the parent directory listed.

To move to a directory in square brackets, select that directory and press F1 or Enter, or point at it and click the right button. Word then shows the selection in that directory. In the example, if you want to see what was in the subdirectory called OLD, select *[OLD]* and press Enter. Note that the directories shown contain only files that match the original file specification; you can, however, change that specification and press F1 to see the new listing.

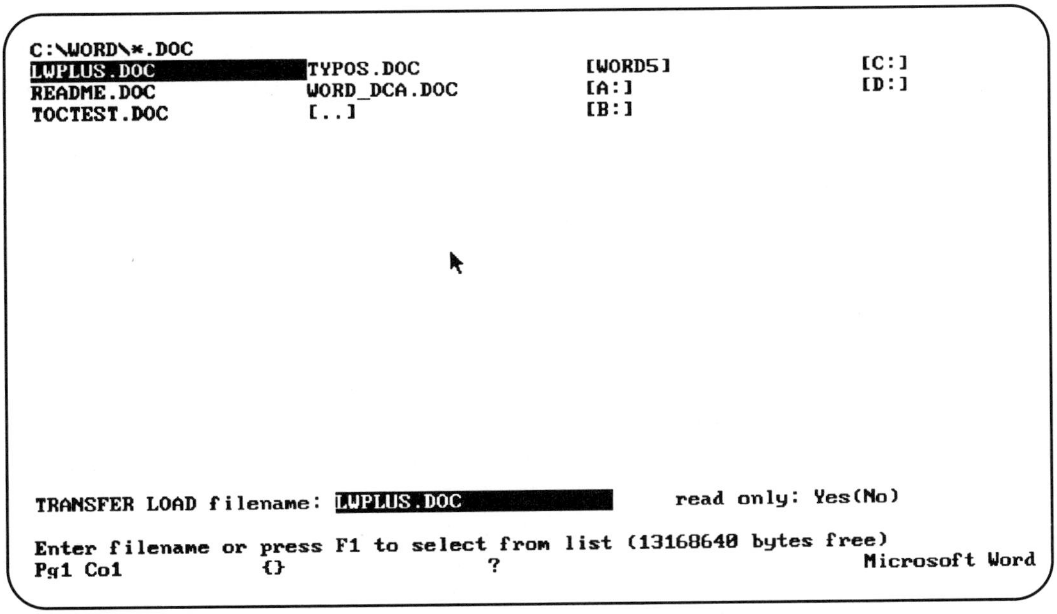

```
C:\WORD\*.DOC
LWPLUS.DOC            TYPOS.DOC          [WORD5]              [C:]
README.DOC           WORD_DCA.DOC       [A:]                 [D:]
TOCTEST.DOC          [..]               [B:]




                              ▸




TRANSFER LOAD filename: LWPLUS.DOC                 read only: Yes(No)

Enter filename or press F1 to select from list (13168648 bytes free)
Pg1 Co1              {}                    ?                Microsoft Word
```

Figure 14

31

Finding. *See* Searching

Fonts

Overview   Most advanced printers allow selection of fonts for printing. Some dot matrix printers use font cartridges, and most letter-quality printers allow you to change the print wheel to change fonts. Almost every laser printer has built-in fonts and accepts font cartridges, downloadable fonts, or both.

Documents that use different fonts for particular items often look more attractive and professional than documents in a single font. You can also use fonts to add clarity. For instance, this book uses `monospace` font for information that the user types in.

If you use more than one printer with Word, you can specify fonts that are unique to one printer and still print your documents on another printer. If the font you have named is not available on the printer you are using, Word will substitute a similar font if it can. Thus, if you use an advanced printer such as the Apple LaserWriter for final output but a dot-matrix printer for drafts, you should still set the fonts for the LaserWriter.

The fonts available for use are controlled by the printer driver with which you are printing. Word comes with dozens of printer drivers for the most popular printers. In addition, Microsoft has drivers to dozens of other printers that are less popular. (See Printer Drivers.) Printers based on the PostScript page description language (such as the Apple LaserWriter) handle fonts differently than other laser printers. (See PostScript Printers.)

Word has two types of font names. Each printer has printer-specific font names, even if the printer only prints in one font. Word also has generic font names, which are families of fonts. When you enter a font name, you can use either a specific name or a generic name. The generic names consist of a family name and a letter such as "Roman b." The generic names of Word fonts and their descriptions are as follows.

FAMILY	LETTERS	DESCRIPTION
Modern	a-p (16)	These fonts have uniform line width, such as simple dot-matrix or daisywheel fonts. The fonts may be sans serif or have serifs of the same line width. Word's default font is Modern a.
Roman	a-p (16)	Fonts in this family have a classical design with varying line widths. A common example of a Roman font is Times Roman, which is used by many newspapers for body type.
Script	a-h (8)	These fonts are slanted or italic characters. Many printers cannot make italic characters from other fonts. In such cases, Word tries to use a script font.
Foreign	a-h (8)	Some specialty fonts contain characters not used in English writing. For example, a font may contain Greek, Hindi, or Japanese characters. Fonts that simply expand the English character set to include more characters or diacritical marks (such as for European languages) do not fall in this category.
Decor	a-h (8)	These fonts are most commonly used in headlines or for specialty design.
Symbol	a-h (8)	These fonts have non-alphabetic characters such as math symbols and printers' symbols.

Word's generic font names provide printing flexibility. If you specify a generic name and the printer on which you are printing has a font in that family, Word uses that printer font. Even if you use a specific name, Word can determine from the font number associated with the name which family the font belongs in and use a similar font. If you are using a daisywheel printer, Word prompts you *Enter Y after mounting font* for each font change and waits for you to press Y.

In the **Format Character** command, you can type either a generic name or a specific name in the *font name* field. Word always lets you enter a generic name. If you enter a specific name for a font and that font is not supported by the printer currently selected in the **Print Options** command, Word will not accept the font name.

Procedure   Use the **Format Character** command to name the font you want to use. Enter the name in the *font name* field or press F1 to get a list of all fonts for the currently selected printer and model. You can have Word give the Format Character command and select the *font name* field automatically by pressing Alt F8.

You must also select a font size. Although most printers have fixed-size fonts, Word lets you enter any font size. The font size is specified in points; most printers are set to either 10 or 12 points for their fonts. If you specify a large font size, you will not see larger characters on the screen, but you can see the larger lines when you use the **Print preView** command.

Downloadable Fonts Many laser printers use *downloadable* fonts, which reside on disk and are loaded into the printer by software on your computer. Downloadable fonts take up space in the laser printer's memory, leaving less space for the material you are printing. On printers with smaller memories, you must decide which fonts you need to download for each document you print so that you do not waste printer memory space on unused fonts.

If you specify a printer that has downloadable fonts when you set up Word with the SETUP program, SETUP copies the printer driver, a special data file, and the DOWN.EXE program to your Word directory. When you print a document that names downloaded fonts, Word runs the DOWN program that downloads the necessary fonts. If you do not run SETUP, you must copy the data file (whose extension is .DAT) with the same name as the printer driver (.PRD file). You must also be sure that the DOWN.EXE program is loaded on your system.

When you give the **Print Printer** command for a file that requires downloadable fonts, Word prompts *Enter Y to download fonts, press N to skip, Esc to cancel.* Press Y to run the DOWN program. If you have already downloaded the font or fonts to the printer (such as with a commercial downloading program), press N.

Tips If you have a Hewlett-Packard LaserJet Plus or LaserJet II, you can buy downloadable fonts from many manufacturers. These fonts also work with many of the laser printers that are compatible with the LaserJet II. These font packages usually include programs that download the fonts outside of Word so that you need not use Word's downloader. Some companies that sell downloadable fonts are as follows.

COMPANY	PRODUCT
Hewlett-Packard 800/367-4772	*Soft Fonts* — Fonts for Hewlett-Packard laser printers
SoftCraft, Inc. 16 N. Carroll Street, Suite 500 Madison, WI 53703	*Fancy Word* — Fonts that give high-quality output on dot-matrix printers. *Laser Fonts* — A variety of commercial fonts for laser printers
SWFTE International, Ltd. PO Box 219 Rockland, DE 19732	*Glyphix* — Fonts and font editor for laser printers
Image Processing Software 6409 Appalachian Way PO Box 5016 Madison, WI 53705	*Turbofonts* — Fonts for dot-matrix and laser printers

Warnings   Combining fonts and character formats in your printing can make a strong visual impact. However, you should avoid using too many in a document since the effect can be garish and distracting. In general, boldface font and underline format will fill most of your needs.

If a true italic is available on your printer, it is a better choice than underscoring. Italics are hard to read on some dot-matrix printers, but they are much better than underscoring on most laser printers.

Footers.   *See* **Running Heads**

Footnotes

Overview   Word's footnoting features allow much flexibility in displaying and editing footnotes. Although footnotes are more common in academic papers than in business, many financial reports use footnotes for highlighting details of numbers and trends.

One problem that many word processing programs have with footnotes is that the user must renumber all the footnotes if a new note is added in the middle of a document. Word, on the other hand, automatically numbers footnotes for you; thus, adding and deleting footnotes is quite easy. Word ensures that the footnote number in your text (the *footnote reference*) always matches the numbers on the footnote text.

Word lets you view your footnotes as you scroll through your text. If you open the footnote window, Word shows the footnote for the text in the main window. The footnote window always shows the footnote for the text currently on the screen.

There are two types of footnotes: numbered (or *enumerated*) and simple marks (such as asterisks). Most people use numbered footnotes since there is less ambiguity about which footnote reference is associated with each footnote. Also, few printers can produce any standard footnote marks other than the asterisk.

You can have Word place the footnotes at the bottom of the page or at the end of the division. If you choose to have the footnotes at the end of the division, it is likely that you want your document to be one long division. If you have more than one division or want to put the footnotes somewhere other than the end of the document (such as before an index), you must manually copy the footnotes before you print, as described below. Most business documents show the footnotes at the bottom of the page.

Footnotes work closely with Word's style sheets. There are default styles for the footnote reference character and for footnote paragraphs; you can modify these in the gallery. However, if you are using footnotes in a document, style sheets simplify the process of formatting the footnotes and references.

Procedure   Use the Format Footnote command to create a footnote. Word prompts you for the *reference mark*. For numbered footnotes, simply press Enter; if you are using footnote symbols, type the symbol (such as an asterisk) at the prompt. Word determines the correct number for the footnote mark and inserts it in your text. This mark is special because the footnote is associated with the mark. If you delete the footnote mark, Word also deletes the corresponding footnote. When Word adds a footnote in the middle of a document, it renumbers footnotes that follow the new one.

Word then opens the footnote window unless you already have it open or are near the end of the file where the footnotes are shown. If you are using many footnotes, it is usually convenient to leave the footnote window open at the bottom of the screen. To open the footnote window when you are not creating a footnote, use the **Window S**plit **F**ootnote command. A footnote window five or six lines tall is usually sufficient for most short footnotes. If you are going to leave the footnote window open while you work, you may want to use the **O**ptions command to save space by removing the screen borders and menu. Figure 15 shows you a screen split for footnotes.

Once the footnote window is open, you can enter any text you wish for the footnote. Footnotes can be any length. When you are finished with the footnote, you can close the window with the **W**indow **C**lose command or jump back to the text with the **J**ump **F**ootnote command. You also use the **J**ump **F**ootnote command to go from the document window to the footnote window if you want to edit text in the footnote.

Use the **F**ormat **D**ivision **L**ayout command to tell Word where the footnotes should appear when printed. Unfortunately, you cannot specify the characters used to make the line between the text and the footnotes at the bottom of the page; Word just uses a line. When you print, Word makes sure that any footnotes referenced in the text on the page appear on the page as well. This is not always possible if the footnote appears near the bottom of the page and the associated text is long. Figure 16 shows an example of how Word prints footnotes.

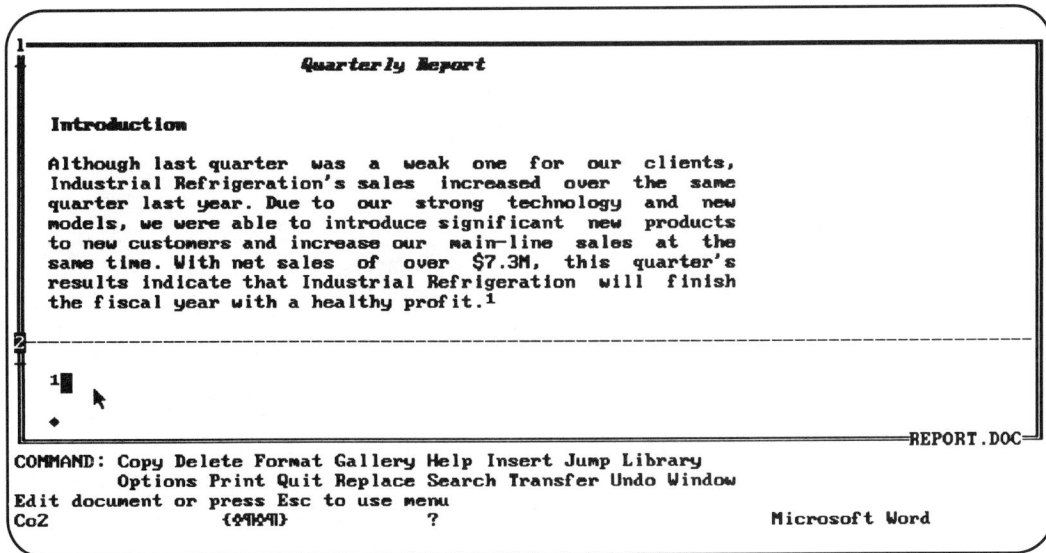

Figure 15

Quarterly Report

Introduction

Although last quarter was a weak one for our clients, Industrial Refrigeration's sales increased over the same quarter last year. Due to our strong technology and new models, we were able to introduce significant new products to new customers and increase our main-line sales at the same time. With net sales of over $7.3M, this quarter's results indicate that Industrial Refrigeration will finish the fiscal year with a healthy profit.[1]

The restaurant-building market continues to have difficulties, and we scaled back our efforts in the super-restaurant refrigeration units in response. As we did this, we started a new marketing campaign for our smallest cold-storage units aimed at the construction industry. The results were phenomenal, and we were able to increase production of the IR200 series to meet the new demand generated by the marketing campaign.

Management feels strongly about the future of Industrial Refrigeration. President Roger Eisenstadt says, "We are very excited about the new IR800 series. The flexible ventilation system and the easily-removed racks should give us a big advantage in markets with stringent health inspectors. In addition, the development on our laboratory line is almost complete. We will have significant announcements in the coming quarter about a complete scientific refrigeration system that can be installed in new buildings and be retrofitted in rebuilding projects."

Report to Stockholders

Earnings from continuing operations were down slightly due to the process of scaling back the manufacturing of the IR500 series. There was no loss of personnel since the employees were able to move easily to the increased IR200 production. The short-term changeover cost was $120,000 and was easily made up for by the increased sales of the IR200 models.

Research costs were up sharply in the quarter as Industrial Refrigeration finished the development of the IR800 series. The costs were mostly in ventilation fabrication and design, since the IR800 has a very different structure than other models. Research costs for the IRLAB series of laboratory units also increased last quarter, and will continue to increase this quarter as final design and revision is made to the series.

Sales increased by $1.2M over the same quarter last year. Due to a strong marketing push for the IR200 series and advance orders for the IR800, the Industrial Refrigeration sales team both broadened our customer base

---

[1]We believe that the profits from this year will increase next year due to the better market outlook and lower costs to us for manufactured goods.

Figure 16

Warnings   If a division has footnotes or annotations, the *Continuous* choice in the Format Division Layout command does not work. Word will always go to a new page if there is a footnote or annotation.

Tips   If you are creating a short document that will only have a few footnotes, you may want to restructure the document so that the footnotes appear as parenthetical comments in the text. Some readers find footnotes distracting, especially in shorter documents.

Annotations are a special type of footnote. They have footnote numbers in the same number series as ordinary footnotes, and they receive numbers in the same sequence as footnotes. If both annotations and footnotes are present in one document, you may want to remove the annotations, rather than make them hidden before printing, to avoid gaps in the footnote number sequence.

You can move text that has footnotes attached by cutting the text from the main part of the document to the scrap with the **Delete** command. When you pull the text from the scrap with the Insert command, the footnotes attached to it will come as well, and the footnotes following the text will be renumbered.

You can also attach footnotes to material in a glossary entry; the footnote will appear when you insert the entry in another portion of your text. This is an easy way to enter repetitive footnotes, such as multiple references to one title.

Foreign Characters.   *See* **Inserting Text**

Form Letters

Overview   Most businesses send form letters to their customers and clients. Many of these form letters—even those personalized with the recipient's name and address—are ignored. Word's merge feature lets you create form letters that are much more personalized than normal form letters. Instead of simply having a name and address at the top of the letter, you can include information in the letter that talks specifically about the recipient. For example, if you are sending letters thanking people for their contributions to a fund-raising drive, you can include the amount contributed so that the letter appears to have been written for that person only. If you have relevant information about the donor in a data base, you can include that information in a way that gives the form letter a personal touch.

Procedure   Creating form letters in Word is similar to creating normal documents. The text of the letter is stored in the *main document*, and the text that varies (such as the nam and address of each recipient) is stored in the *data document*. When you use the **Print Merge Printer** command, Word prints a version of the main document for each paragraph in the data document. Each paragraph is called a *record*. If you want to print your form letters to a file instead of to the printer, use the **Print Merge Document** command. The files produced by the **Print Merge Document** command have the merged information but none of the printer codes.

The main document has *fields* marked so that Word knows where to put the information from the data document. Each paragraph in the data document has information for the named fields. You can select the records you want to print out of the data document with the **Print Merge Options** command. To specify fewer than all the records in the entire data document, set the *range* field to *Records* and enter the record numbers desired in the *record numbers* field. You can list individual records or ranges of records; a range can be indicated by a colon or hyphen. For example, to merge records 1, 3, 5, and 10 through 20, enter 1,3,5,10-20.

Main Document   A field in the main document is marked by surrounding it with chevrons (the « and » symbols). These symbols are entered by typing Ctrl [and Ctrl], respectively. Do not confuse two less-than or greater-than symbols for the chevrons. (As you can see, « is different than <<.) A field called "address" would be marked in the document as «address». Field names can be a maximum of 64 letters and numbers but cannot contain periods or spaces.

The main document also contains *merge instructions* that are also surrounded by chevrons. A merge instruction tells Word what actions you want the **Print Merge** command to take. Every main document must start with the DATA instruction as its first paragraph. The DATA instruction tells Word the name of the data document. For example, if the data document is called AWARDS.DOC, enter «DATA AWARDS.DOC». Other merge instructions will follow.

«DATA CUST.DAT»

March 19, 1989

«name»
«address»
«city», «state» «zip»

Dear «name»:

Thank you for your interest in our <u>U. S. Blues</u> discount paint promotion. Enclosed please find a brochure containing complete information on the promotion and a list of participating dealers in «state».

Sincerely,

William Teague
Director of Marketing

Figure 17

The rest of the main document has normal text and field names. You can insert a field wherever appropriate in a main document. You do not need to use each field that is named in the data document, nor do you need to use the fields in the same order in which they appear in the data document. For example, if your data document has fields for first name and last name called "first_name" and "last_name," include two fields in the address at the top of the letter, and include the first name again (such as "Dear «first_name»") in the greeting. Figure 17 shows a sample main document. Note that you cannot use underscores in names in version 4, but that they are allowed in version 5.

Data Document The structure of the data document is also quite simple. Microsoft refers to the paragraphs in the data document as *records*. The first paragraph contains the *header record*, which is a list of the names of the fields in the order in which they appear in the other records. The field names in the header record are separated by either a comma or a Tab character unless you set the decimal character to a comma. (See Options.)

Because of the way in which Word handles commas, quotes, and semicolons in the data document, using Tab characters as separators is the better method, although the screen display is messy. Version 5 allows a maximum of 256 fields in each record, which should be sufficient for almost any application.

All the records after the header record hold the data used in merging. Each record is a single paragraph (don't worry about how the lines in a record wrap; Word ignores this). The fields in each record must appear in the same order as in the header record. As in the header record, the fields are separated by commas or Tab characters; again, using Tab characters is preferred. Each data record must have the same number of fields as the header record.

Each piece of data can be any length, but it must be present. If you want to leave a particular data item blank, you must still enter the separator character for its position, but you need not enter any data. For example, if one of your fields is "date _ of _ birth" and you do not know that information for each person in the data document, just leave the field blank and enter the two Tab characters. Rules for special characters in your data are described below. Figure 18 shows an example of the data document for the main document shown in Figure 17. This data document uses tabs as separators.

Merging   Since Word can send output to the printer or create a new document, the **Print Merge** command has three choices: **Printer**, **Document**, and **Options**. If you use the **Print Merge Document** command

name	address	city	state	zip
Randall Percy	3322 Alona Blvd.	Grand Forks	ND	58210
George Travenall	16625 San Bruno St.	Victorville	CA	92392
Sharon Bennet	41 Tigertail Lane	New Haven	CT	06505
Andrew Smith	1992 Industrial Way	Flagstaff	AZ	86010

Figure 18

when creating a main document and data document, you will not waste paper on experiments since you can view the results in the new document and make changes accordingly.

Type in the same main document and data document. If you wish, use split windows so that you can see the names in the main document when typing in the header record in the data document. You should display paragraph breaks when you type and edit the data document to guard against accidentally ending a record prematurely. Set *show non-printing symbols* to *partial* or *all* in the **O**ptions command.

Make the window for the main document the active window, and give the **Print Merge Printer** command. You must be in the main document when you give the command so that Word knows which file to use as the main document. Word will then print a page for each record in the data document. The first two records are shown in Figure 19.

As Word processes the document, it displays messages such as *Merging* and *Formatting*. To stop the merging process, press Escape. The **Print Merge** command also has its own error messages for the two circumstances discussed below.

MESSAGE	MEANING
Not a valid file	The data document named in the DATA instruction is missing. Either you typed the file name incorrectly, or the file does not reside in the same directory as the main document.
Unknown field name	The name of a field in the main document does not match the names in the header record of the data document. This is usually caused by a misspelling or slight difference between the fields in the two documents (such as "address_1" and "address1," which are different to Word) or by an invalid field name.

As you look at the printed output from the command, check that the fields are in the correct places; if they are not, your data document may have a record that is not in the proper order.

You need not make versions for every record in the data document. The **Print Merge O**ptions command lets you specify the record numbers you want to merge. To do so, change *range* to *Records* and enter the records you want to merge in the *record numbers* field. You can list individual records as a list separated by commas (such as "3,7,14") and list series of records with a colon or hyphen (such as "10-20" or "5:15").

March 19, 1989

Randall Percy
3322 Alona Blvd.
Grand Forks, ND   58210

Dear Randall Percy:

Thank you for your interest in our <u>U. S. Blues</u> discount paint promotion. Enclosed please find a brochure containing complete information on the promotion and a list of participating dealers in ND.

Sincerely,

William Teague
Director of Marketing

March 19, 1989

George Travenall
16625 San Bruno St.
Victorville, CA   92392

Dear George Travenall:

Thank you for your interest in our <u>U. S. Blues</u> discount paint promotion. Enclosed please find a brochure containing complete information on the promotion and a list of participating dealers in CA.

Sincerely,

William Teague
Director of Marketing

Figure 19

Header Documents   The data document does not need to be created by Word. In fact, most people who use Word's form letter capabilities create their data documents from data base management programs. Since these programs usually cannot generate the required header record in the data file, Word allows you to have a separate *header document*. The header document contains one paragraph, the header record.

To use a header document, the DATA instruction in your main document must contain the name of the header document, a comma, and the name of the data document. For example, if your header document is called SALE-SHD.DOC and your data document is called SALES.DAT, the DATA instruction in the main document would be "«DATA SALESHD.DOC, SALES.DAT»."

Merge Instructions   The DATA instruction is the only required merge instruction. However, the other merge instructions are very useful for creating complex or changing documents. You can use these instructions in your main document to help control the merge process and the text that appears in the merged documents. The additional merge instructions and their uses are listed below.

MERGE INSTRUCTION	USE
IF and ELSE	Prints text in merged version based on conditions in the text
SKIP	Skips over the record in the data document if a condition in the text is true
SET	Prompts you on the screen to enter a field value that will appear in all printed documents
ASK	Prompts you on the screen to enter a field value that will change in each printed document
INCLUDE	Prints the contents of another document in the current document
NEXT	Prints many records in one merged document

The IF instruction is the most powerful of these instructions and is the most frequently used. The IF instruction lets you control what goes into a merged document. You always use the IF instruction with the ENDIF instruction, and you sometimes use the IF instruction with the ELSE instruction and the ENDIF instruction.

The IF instruction has a test. If that test proves true for the current record, the text between the IF instruction and the ENDIF instruction is included in the merged version; if the test proves false, the text is ignored. For example, look at the paragraph in Figure 20. If the value in the "amount" field is greater than 1000, Word includes the sentence "Your prize qualifies you for our second drawing" in the merged document. If the value in the "amount" field is less than 1000, the sentence is ignored. In the printed output, Word properly wraps all lines based on the text included or excluded.

The IF instruction's test can be for numbers or for text. If you are comparing a number (as in the previous example), you can use =, <, < =, >, > =, and < > (not equal to). All of these operators can be used with text. The = and < > operators are commonly used with text fields to check for equivalence or difference between two fields. Figure 21 shows a test for the "city" field.

You can also easily test if a field is blank by using the IF instruction and the field name without any test. For example, to determine if the "middle _ initial" field is blank, use «IF middle _ initial».

The ELSE instruction gives increased flexibility when used with the IF instruction. Instead of simply choosing whether to include one section of text, the ELSE instruction lets you choose between two. Figure 22 shows an example of using the IF and ELSE instructions.

The SKIP instruction works with the IF instruction to let you choose which records to print. If the SKIP instruction is executed, Word skips that

---

We hope that you are as excited about winning as we are about giving you the prize. «IF amount > 1000»Your prize qualifies you for our second drawing.«ENDIF»Again, thank you for joining our raffle and enjoy the cash.

Figure 20

We have sales offices all over the United States, so you can easily get help with any problems you might have. «IF city = "New York"»Since you live in New York, you can simply call our main headquarters.«ENDIF» Please call if you have any questions.

Figure 21

We have sales offices all over the United States, so you can easily get help with any problems you might have. «IF city = "New York"»Since you live in New York, you can simply call our main headquarters.«ELSE»The list of sales offices is on the last page of your instruction manual.«ENDIF» Please call if you have any questions.

Figure 22

record when merging. Thus, you use the SKIP instruction as part of an IF instruction such as "«IF state = "California"»«SKIP»«ENDIF»." You can use the SKIP instruction as a convenient selection method for determining which data to use during a merge operation.

The SET and ASK instructions let you enter data in the merged documents at the time you print. These instructions let you fill in the values for fields; these are the only fields that are not filled in from the data document. With either command, Word prompts you for the value of the field after you give the **Print Merge** command. The difference between the two instructions is that the SET command prompts you only once, but the ASK instruction prompts you for the value for each record being printed. It is likely that you will use the SET instruction much more often than the ASK instruction.

Normally, the SET instruction appears at the beginning of the main document, immediately after the DATA instruction. There are three forms of the instruction. The first form uses Word's prompt for the information, the second lets you specify the prompting text, and the third form does not prompt you at all.

The most common use of the SET command is to fill in the date on letters. For example, the top of your document might look like Figure 23. When you give the **Print Merge** command, Word finds the data file and then prompts "Enter text" and "VALUE: " at the bottom of the screen. Type in the date exactly as you want it to appear in the text and press Enter. Word then substitutes the text you typed for the "today" field in all the letters.

Since the "Enter text" prompt is not very friendly, you might want to include your own prompt text. Figure 24 shows a SET instruction with the prompt message included.

«DATA CUST.DAT»«SET today = ?»
«today»

Figure 23

«DATA CUST.DAT»«SET today = ?Enter the date»
«today»

Figure 24

Although Word's prompting in the SET instruction is helpful, you might not need it. The third form of the SET instruction simply sets a field directly with no prompt. For example, if you have the line "«SET closing = Sincerely yours»" in a file, Word does not prompt for the value of the "closing" field.

The ASK instruction prompts for information at the beginning of each record. However, this prompt is not very useful since you do not know the contents of the record for which it is prompting.

The INCLUDE instruction lets you take information from another Word document or ASCII file and put it into your merged output. When Word finds an INCLUDE instruction during the merge process, it brings in all of the text from that particular document. This capability is helpful if you want to use information from another file that is updated by someone else. Figure 25 shows how the INCLUDE instruction operates.

Note that the INCLUDE statement works only with merged documents. Thus, unfortunately, you cannot include documents in other documents unless you use the **Print Merge** command.

The NEXT instruction allows you to put more than one record from the data document into the merged document. This is rarely used for regular form letters, but can be very useful when working with mailing labels. (See Mailing Labels.)

We have found that the market for «product» is weak at this point but that we would like to talk further with you about licensing rights.

«INCLUDE E:\NORMAN\RIGHTS\CLOSING.DOC»

I will call you soon to find out how we can work together on finding a market for «product».

Sincerely,

Terry Chen

Figure 25

Calculated Fields Because Word can perform mathematical operations when it merges, you can create *calculated fields* in your main document. A calculated field is a field in which Word performs some math on the values in fields before printing the results. You can use $+$, $-$, $*$, $/$, or $\%$ symbols in your calculated fields. (See Math.) For example, if you have a field called "amount" and a field called "tax," you might include a sentence like: "The total is «amount» plus «tax», which comes to «amount + tax»." You might also have something like: "Please be sure not to spend more than «limit*1.25»."

Calculated fields are especially useful when combined with the IF and SKIP instructions. You can use the calculation to determine what to say in a letter, or even whether to print the letter at all. For example, if you want to send a letter only to people who have sold more than a certain quantity, you might have a line such as "«IF sales < 10000»«SKIP»."

You can use the AND, OR, and NOT instructions to combine logical evaluations in the IF instruction. Simply put the AND or OR instruction between two sets for logical expressions, such as "«IF sales > 1000 AND sales < 2500»«SKIP»." Use the NOT instruction before a logical evaluation.

Examples   The IF instruction can be used in many ways in form letters. Figure 26 shows a main document with many IF instructions.

«DATA MAILING.DAT»«SET date = ?Enter the date»
«date»

«name»
«address1»
«IF address2»«address2»
«ENDIF»«city», «state» «zip»

Dear «name»:

Our reputation is quite important to us, and I am very sorry that you found our «product_com» unsatisfactory. «IF product_com = "cleaner" OR product_com = "soap"»We will certainly replace the package that you bought.«ELSE»We will certainly send you a refund.«ENDIF». Please understand that your dissatisfaction with our «product» is rare and we hope that this «IF product_com = "cleaner" OR product_com = "soap"»replacement«ELSE»refund«ENDIF» clears up this matter.

Figure 26

Warnings

Using Tab characters as separators in the data document reduces the number of problems you are likely to encounter when using form letters. Regardless of the separator you use, you must watch for special characters in your data document. Any data item that contains a quotation mark must be quoted entirely, and the quotation mark must be doubled, as shown in Figure 27.

If you are using commas as separators, you must follow the above rule about quotation marks; you must also look out for commas in your data. For example, many addresses contain commas (such as "4140 Sunset Blvd., Suite 7A"). Any field that contains a comma must also be quoted, as shown in Figure 28.

If you use Word's **O**ptions command to change the decimal character to a comma (such as for European formats), the fields in the data document must be separated by a Tab or a semicolon rather than a comma.

name	address	city	state	zip
Randall Percy	3322 Alona Blvd.	Grand Forks	ND	58210
George Travenall	16625 San Bruno St.	Victorville	CA	92392
Sharon Bennet	41 Tigertail Lane	New Haven	CT	06505
"Andrew ""Andy"" Smith"	1992 Industrial Way	Flagstaff	AZ	86010

Figure 27

name, address, city, state, zip

Randall Percy, "3322 Alona Blvd., Suite 2B", Grand Forks, ND, 58210

George Travenall, 16625 San Bruno St., Victorville, CA, 92392

Sharon Bennet, 41 Tigertail Lane, New Haven, CT, 06505

"Andrew ""Andy"" Smith", 1992 Industrial Way, Flagstaff, AZ, 86010

Figure 28

You cannot generate an accurate table of contents or index for main documents. For example, if you are using the INCLUDE instruction and your included documents have entries for the table of contents, they will be ignored. Since the Library Table and Library Index commands do not even read the included files, the space they take up in your output is not accounted for in the table of contents or index. Thus, the INCLUDE instruction is not useful for documents that need an accurate table of contents or index. Also note that your main document cannot refer to bookmarks that are in included files. Microsoft has partially addressed these problems with some of the sample macros included with Word. These macros allow you to build a document on the fly (with the **Transfer Merge** command) and make the table of contents and index in a separate file.

Tips To have character formatting on text in a field, give at least the first letter of the field name the desired formatting. For example, format the "a" in "amount" in bold to print the field "amount" in boldface.

You can move quickly from field to field in your main document. Press Ctrl > to go to the next field and Ctrl < to go to the previous field. Word goes to the first field if you press Ctrl > at the end of the document.

If you are printing mailing labels for letters, you can often save postage by sorting the letters in zip code order. In order to sort by a field other than the first field, use tab separators instead of commas in your data document. You can then select the entire data document, adjust the tabs so that all fields fit within the tabs, select the column with the zip codes, and sort. (See Sorting.)

The merge instructions can make printing mailing labels easy. (See Mailing Labels.)

Formatting

Overview Word allows formatting on three levels: characters, paragraphs, and divisions. Although there are many other choices in the Format command, all formatting ultimately applies to one of these three document elements. See Character Formatting, Division Formatting, and Paragraph Formatting for more detail on these three types of formatting.

The subcommands of the Format command are listed below.

- Character
- Paragraph
- Tab
- Border
- Footnote
- Division
- Running-head
- Stylesheet
- sEarch
- repLace
- revision-Marks
- pOsition (version 5 only)
- Annotation (version 5 only)
- bookmarK (version 5 only)

These subcommands can be grouped into the four types listed below.

- Character — Character
- Paragraph — Paragraph, Tab, Border, pOsition
- Division — Division, Running-head
- Other — Footnote, Stylesheet, sEarch, repLace, revision-Marks, Annotation, bookmarK

All character formatting is attached directly to the characters. Paragraph formatting, however, is attached to the mark at the end of each paragraph, which is invisible unless you have set *show non-printing symbols* to *Partial* or *All* in the Options command. Thus, tab settings, borders, and positional information are stored in the invisible mark. Division formatting is stored in the division mark (the row of colons) at the end of each division.

If you select text that has consistent formatting (such as all boldface or all paragraphs aligned the same way), the Format commands will show all settings. If any settings differ, however, the commands will show nothing set and no defaults. You can still add formatting with the commands, and Word will add the formats you choose to the entire selection. For example, if you select an entire document and give the Format Character command, Word might show no settings. If you enter a font name in the *font* field, Word changes all the text to that font but does not change any other character formatting. This method is also useful for changing the line spacing throughout the document.

The Format Footnote command does not really belong in the Format menu since you use it to insert rather than to format footnotes. The Format Stylesheet command lets you add styles to selected text; this command can affect characters, paragraphs, or sections. The Format sEarch and Format repLace commands let you search or change formats. Like the Format Footnote command, the Format revision-Marks, Format Annotation, and Format bookmarK commands do not really belong in the Format menu since you use them to add information to rather than to format the document. However, after version 3 was released, Microsoft attempted to maintain the appearance of the main menu. As a result, these features are included in the Format menu.

When you think about formatting your documents, you should usually think in terms of using style sheets. (See Styles.) Although they are more work initially, style sheets will facilitate format revisions. Since style sheets can have styles for character, paragraph, and section formatting, you can do anything with styles that you can with plain formatting.

Gallery Command.   *See* Styles

Galley Mode.   *See* Layout

Glossaries

Overview   No one enjoys retyping the same words, phrases, or paragraphs. Of course, Word lets you use the scrap to save yourself from retyping, but even the scrap is of little use if the text you are reentering is in another document or if you have many repetitive phrases. Word's glossary feature lets you store in one spot all the words, phrases, and paragraphs that you would normally have to retype. Recalling them is quick and easy.

Each entry in the glossary consists of a name and the associated text. You can have as many entries in a glossary as you wish, and each entry can be of any length. You can also keep as many glossaries on disk as you wish and load them selectively. For example, you might have a glossary of addresses of people to whom you regularly write and a different glossary of manufacturing phrases. However, most people keep only one glossary with many entries since you must load the glossaries separately.

Creating glossary entries is easy. Simply type into your document the text you want to store in the glossary. Select the text and give the Copy command. Word then prompts you to select a name for the glossary. By using the glossary name and pressing F3, you can insert the text from that entry anywhere else in any document.

Glossary entry names have a maximum of 31 characters, which can be a combination of letters, numbers, underscores, periods, and hyphens but no spaces. The name must begin with either a letter or number. When you save a glossary entry, the formatting is saved as well. This is very convenient for material that is always formatted in a particular way, such as underlining in a book title. Glossaries are stored in files with .GLY extensions.

Since Word always loads the default glossary, NORMAL.GLY, from the Word directory when you start the program, it is the best place to put all your entries. You can merge additional glossaries with the entries currently in use with the Transfer Glossary Merge command. Use the Print Glossary command to print the contents of the current glossary.

Procedure   To create a glossary entry, you must decide what text you want in the entry, how it should be formatted, and the name you want for that text. Type the text, format it, and select it. If you want to leave the text in your document and also create a glossary entry, give the Copy command. If you are typing the text to create a glossary entry and do not want it in your document, give the Delete command.

Word then prompts *Copy to:* or *Delete to:*. Word suggests the name { }, which indicates copying or cutting to the scrap. This is not what you want; instead, type the name under which you want to store the text. If you enter a name that already exists in the glossary, Word prompts *Enter Y to overwrite glossary, N to retype name, or Esc to cancel.* Press Y if you want to delete the previous text stored under that name, or press N to give a different name.

When you want to use a glossary entry in your document, simply type in the name of the glossary entry and press F3. Alternately, you can give the Insert command and enter the glossary name in the *from* field, and Word will insert the text at the cursor. If you type a name that is not in the glossary, Word will beep; Word can help you if you do not remember the name of the entry you want. Simply give the **I**nsert command and press F1, and Word will display a list of all the glossary entries. Select the one you want and press Enter.

If you want to change text in a glossary entry, you must overwrite the entry. Type the entry's name and press F3, and edit the entry (including formatting). Select the text, give the **D**elete command, and type the entry's name at the prompt. When Word prompts *Enter Y to overwrite glossary, N to retype name, or Esc to cancel*, press Y. There is no direct method of editing the glossary text in the glossary itself.

Special Glossary Entries   Word has seven entries that are automatically included in any glossary. These entries are used for printing and including special text. The entries and their uses are listed below.

NAME	INSERTS INTO THE DOCUMENT
date	The current date (at the time you insert this in your document)
time	The current time (at the time you insert this in your document)
page	When printed, this becomes the current page number in the document. On the screen, it is displayed as (*page*).
dateprint	When printed, this becomes the date that the document is printed (not the date this entry is included in the document). On the screen, it is displayed as (*dateprint*).
timeprint	When printed, this becomes the time that the document is printed (not the time this entry is included in the document). On the screen, it is displayed as (*timeprint*).
clipboard	This is available only when you are running Word under Microsoft Windows version 2 or later. When you insert from this entry, the contents of the Windows Clipboard are inserted in your document; when you save text in this glossary entry, the text is saved in the Windows Clipboard. In version 5, you can retrieve graphics from the Clipboard, but you cannot store graphics to it. (See Graphics.)
footnote	The current footnote reference number. (See Footnotes.) This is rarely used.

Glossary Management   After adding entries to a glossary, you can save them on disk so they will be available the next time you run Word. If you give the **Q**uit command after you have added entries to the glossary but have not saved them, Word prompts *Enter Y to save glossary, N to lose edits, or Esc to cancel.* Press Y to save the new entries in the NORMAL.GLY glossary.

You can save the current glossary on disk at any time by giving the **T**ransfer **G**lossary **S**ave command and typing the name of the file you want to save the glossary to. If you give the name of an existing glossary, Word prompts you, then replaces it with the current glossary. This is the easiest way to update glossaries other than NORMAL.GLY.

You can get a printout of the current glossary with the **P**rint **G**lossary command. Printing your glossary entries is useful if your glossary is long. Word does not include the special text entries in the printout.

If you keep more than one glossary on disk, you will want to have access to entries in the other glossaries. To do so, use the **T**ransfer **G**lossary **M**erge command and enter the name of the desired glossary. This brings in the entries from the glossary on disk. The old entries are replaced by the new ones if the glossary you are merging has entries with the same names as the current glossary.

Additional Glossary Management (Version 5 Only)   If you want the new glossary you are loading to replace completely the current glossary (that is, remove all entries from the current glossary before loading the new one), use the **T**ransfer **G**lossary **L**oad command.

To delete some of the entries in the current glossary, use the **T**ransfer **G**lossary **C**lear command. At the prompt, enter the names of the entries you wish to delete; separate names with commas. If you want to delete just one entry, press F1 and select the entry to be deleted.

To save the current glossary in a file other than NORMAL.GLY, use the **T**ransfer **G**lossary **S**ave command. Since the **T**ransfer **G**lossary **S**ave command saves all the entries from the current glossary, you may want to check what the glossary contains before using it. You can see a list of the names by selecting any text, giving the **C**opy command, and pressing F1. When you are finished looking at the list, press Escape.

Warnings   Using the /L option on the Word command line loads the glossary last loaded, not necessarily NORMAL.GLY. Thus, if you load a glossary called TERMS.GLY with the **T**ransfer **G**lossary **L**oad command, quit from Word,

G

and give the WORD/L command at the MS-DOS command line, Word will automatically load TERMS.GLY.

If you load a glossary, remove some of the entries, and save the new glossary under the old name, those entries are permanently lost. Also, if you load a glossary then merge in another glossary with some entries having the same names, then save the glossary under the first name, the previous definitions will be lost. For example, assume that you have two glossaries called NAMES1.GLY and NAMES2.GLY. NAMES1 has an entry for FRED that is "Fred Meyers"; NAMES2 has an entry for FRED that is "Fred Kobayashi." You load NAMES1.GLY with the **T**ransfer **G**lossary **L**oad command, then merge in the entries in NAMES2.GLY with the **T**ransfer **G**lossary **M**erge command. You then give the **T**ransfer **G**lossary **S**ave command, and give NAMES1.GLY as the name. Since the current glossary has "Fred Kobayashi" as the entry for FRED, that name is stored in NAMES1, overwriting the previous value for that entry.

Tips

Glossary entries retain their formatting characteristics. Thus, if you always print a particular paragraph in small type, format it before saving it in the glossary. When you retrieve the paragraph, it will have the proper formatting.

There are many uses for glossaries. Even if you do not type the same text over and over, you may find it useful to keep particular text in a glossary to reduce typing mistakes and search time. Some ideas for glossary uses are listed below.

- Foreign characters (so that you do not have to type in the Alt codes)
- Copyright and trademark notices
- Chemical names
- Names that are difficult to spell
- Names of files that are used by many people
- Building names and locations
- Tables (such as sales figures)
- Names in the "To:" or "cc:" field of a memo
- Legal case names
- Model names for machinery
- Actions (such as "Press Alt F8, enter a font name, and press Enter")

Graphics

[Version 5 Only]

Overview Most of Word's graphics capabilities are new to version 5, although version 4 allows you to indirectly include some graphics. Using graphics in your documents has many benefits: in particular, reports and newsletters will look much more interesting and will be more informative. You will certainly discover that a business graphic such as a pie graph or bar chart can communicate your data much more effectively than a table of numbers can.

In Word, a graphic is stored as a paragraph and can be manipulated with the standard paragraph formatting features. The graphics you use in Word can come from a wide variety of sources. If you are artistically inclined, most drawing programs let you easily create pictures using a mouse. More advanced drawing pictures let you include text in a variety of fonts, special shading, or even retouch photographs scanned in with an image scanner. Business graphics programs or spreadsheets with business graphics features let you convert tables of numbers into a variety of charts. More and more graphics-based packages are being released for the PC, and the output from most of them can be used in any Word document.

The **Library Link Graphics** command prompts you for the name of the graphic file to include in your document. The many formats of graphics files that Word can read are listed below.

- Lotus graphics files (.PIC format)
- PC Paintbrush files (.PCX format)
- HPGL files
- Files of PostScript commands
- Encapsulated PostScript files
- Windows Clipboard format
- Microsoft Pageview documents (unfortunately, the size and clipping information is lost)
- Some TIFF documents (there are many variants on the TIFF standard)
- Files already formatted with the printer codes for the printer on which you are printing
- Files created with Word's Capture program (.SCR files)

Depending on the mode of the display you are using, a graphic may appear in one of the following three ways listed. (See Layout.)

- In galley mode, only the *tag*, which is Word's identifier of the graphic, is shown. The tag consists of the characters ".G." in hidden text, followed by the name of the graphic's file, followed by a paragraph mark.
- In layout mode, the tag is shown and an empty frame surrounds the area in which the graphic will appear. This lets you see how large the graphic will be relative to the text on a page.
- In preview mode, you will see the actual picture in some cases. Some formats, such as PostScript files, are not displayed, but an empty frame surrounds the area in which the graphic will appear. If you have set *draft* to *Yes* in the **Print O**ptions command, the graphic will not be displayed, but its frame will be.

Most, but not all, printers can print graphics. See the *Printer Information* manual for information on your specific printer.

Procedure   When you give the **Library Link G**raphics command, you see the prompts shown in Figure 29. Enter the name of the graphics file for *filename*. If the file is not in the same directory as the document, Word makes the name an absolute reference from the root directory of the disk. After you enter the file name and select another field in the dialog, Word attempts to determine the graphics format of the file. If it is successful, Word enters that information in the *format* field; otherwise, you must fill in the format yourself.

If you are using Word under Microsoft Windows, you can enter CLIP-BOARD for the file name, and Word will use the graphic on the Clipboard. If you use this to read a graphic, Word will store the graphic into a file.

Note that some complex Windows files cannot be imported. For example, Excel charts cannot be read directly by Word, though you can copy the charts as pixels (instead of objects) to the Windows Clipboard and import

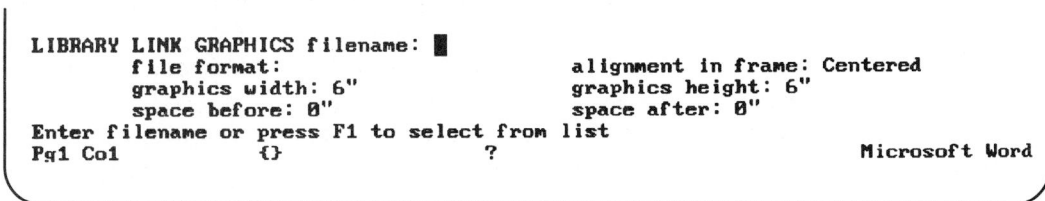

```
LIBRARY LINK GRAPHICS filename: █
        file format:                        alignment in frame: Centered
        graphics width: 6"                  graphics height: 6"
        space before: 0"                    space after: 0"
Enter filename or press F1 to select from list
Pg1 Co1           {}              ?                        Microsoft Word
```

Figure 29

them by typing CLIPBOARD for the file name. To copy an Excel chart to the Clipboard as pixels instead of objects in Excel, select the chart, hold down the Shift key, select the Edit menu, select the **C**opy command, and select OK, holding down the Shift key all the while. Alternately, you can copy the Excel graphic to Windows Paint, save it, and copy it into Word.

When you execute the **Library Link G**raphics command, Word creates the paragraph tags. The paragraph can be treated like any other paragraph in your document and can move in the scrap.

Size and Position   The other choices in the dialog let you describe the size of the frame for the graphic, how it should align within its frame, and the space above and below the graphic. Select *graphics width* and *graphics height* for picture size. Word fills in these fields if the file has information that it can use to determine the dimensions. You can also select *Same as column* for the *graphics width* to make the graphic as wide as the column or the page (if there is only one column). If Word cannot determine the suggested height of the graphic but knows the preferred ratio of the height to the width, it will attempt to keep the ratio when you enter a size for *graphics width*. You can enter any value you want for either field.

The choices for *alignment* are *Centered, Left, Right,* or a measurement from the left side of the frame. The *space before* and *space after* fields are also similar to their functions in the **Format P**aragraph command. If you do not specify any amounts for *space before* and *space after*, Word inserts space to prevent objects from touching surrounding text.

To resize or reposition a graphic, select the tag and give the **Library Link G**raphics command. Word displays the current settings for that paragraph. You can change those settings as desired.

Captions   You can include a caption with a graphic and ensure that the caption always appears with the graphic. First create your graphic with the **Library Link G**raphics command, then create the caption paragraph and format it as you normally would. Select the graphic paragraph, give the **Format P**aragraph command, and set *keep follow* to *Yes.* If you set the paragraph and caption on the page with the **Format pO**sition command, select both paragraphs before giving the command to change the position.

Printing   When you give the Print Printer command, Word uses the *draft* field in the Print Options command to determine whether to print the graphics in the document. If the *draft* field is set to *Yes*, Word does not print the graphics, but leaves the specified amount of empty space for them. If a graphic goes off the side of the page, Word truncates the graphic when it is printed.

Some printers have different printer drivers for different print resolutions. (See Printer Drivers.) Others allow you to set the resolution in the Print Options command with the *graphics resolution* field. You can find the resolutions available by selecting the value for this field and pressing F1.

Capturing Screens with the Capture Program   Word includes the Capture program, which lets you capture graphics screens from other programs and include them in your Word documents. The program is on the Utilities 3 disk. This is especially useful if you use Word to create manuals about computers and software programs. You can take the files that Capture creates and include them in your Word documents.

Note that there are many other programs that capture graphics screens and often include many other features as well. Hotshot (from Symsoft, PO Box 4477, Mountain View, CA 94040), one of the more popular screen capture programs, includes features that allow you to capture text screens and edit them before saving them in files. You can change many of Hotshot's printing features interactively and experiment with different views.

Because it is a TSR program, Capture takes up memory space in your computer and must be loaded into memory by giving the CAPTURE command at the MS-DOS prompt. A message indicates that the program is loaded. Once Capture is loaded, just run the application you want to get the screen dump from, get the program to show what you want in the screen shot, and press the Shift Print Screen key. Capture prompts you for the name of the file where you will save the screen. Type the file name, press Enter, and the screen is saved.

The screens from Capture can be used in Word just like other graphics screens. When you use the Library Link Graphics command, simply enter the file name that you saved.

Capture has many other features for modifying the saved screen, which are discussed in the Word manual. For example, you can add borders and captions to the saved graphics. Note that if you find a need to use some of these features, you should investigate the other screen capture programs since these other programs have a much wider variety of features and it is often much easier to use these programs than it is to use Capture.

Examples   Figure 30 shows the top of a letter without a graphic, and Figure 31 shows the contents of the file LOGO.PCX. Put the graphic on the blank line in the document.

Give the Library Link Graphics command, type LOGO.PCX at the *filename* prompt, and press Tab. Word determines the size of the graphic from the file and fills in some of the prompts, as shown in Figure 32. Press Enter to include the graphic in the document. If you want the graphic to have other paragraph formatting, give the Format Paragraph command. The printed result looks like Figure 33.

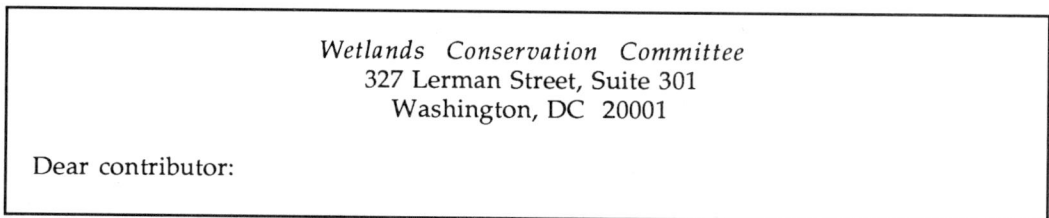

Figure 30

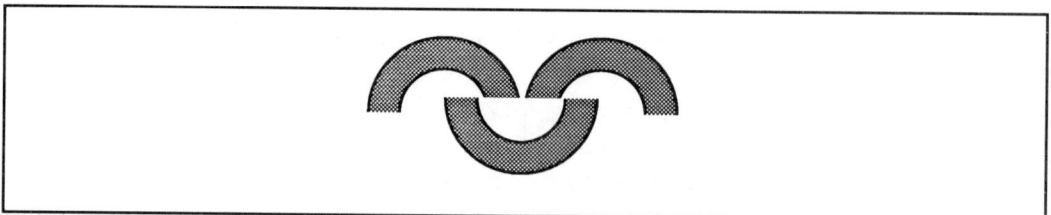

Figure 31

```
LIBRARY LINK GRAPHICS filename: LOGO.PCX
       file format: PCX              alignment in frame: Centered
       graphics width: 6.5"         graphics height: 2.917"
       space before: 0"             space after: 0.167"
Enter graphics file format or press F1 to select from list
Pg1 Col            {}                 ?                  Microsoft Word
```

Figure 32

Wetlands   Conservation   Committee
327 Lerman Street, Suite 301
Washington, DC 20001

Dear contributor:

Figure 33

Warnings   If you are using any of the dynamic graph types, guard against acciden-
                 tally changing or deleting the graphics file after you have specified it
                 in a document. If you delete the file, Word reports an error when you
                 attempt to print your document or view the graphic with the **P**rint pre-
                 View command.

Tips   Using styles for graphics paragraphs makes it much easier to change the
                 formatting throughout the document. This is especially useful if you have
                 captions attached to the graphics. Use two paragraphs (one for the
                 graphic, one for the caption) and two styles. (See Styles.)
                     The graphics in version 4 let you specify only files containing graphics that
                 were formatted for a specific printer. Thus, you can print only on an Epson or
                 Epson-compatible printer if you have imbedded a graphic for an Epson.

Graphics Adapters

Overview
Word works with a wide variety of graphics adapters for the PC. If your adapter supports color and you have a color monitor, you can set the colors that Word uses in the background and menu.

You can change the background and display colors to suit your taste. In version 5, prompts are shown in the menu color, and character attributes are shown in a different color on the screen so that you can more easily differentiate between them. You can change the character attributes in the *colors* field of the **O**ptions command.

Procedure
To switch between graphics and text mode, press Alt F9 or set the *display* field (version 4) or *display mode* field (version 5) in the **O**ptions command. In version 5, Word uses the SCREEN.VID file to determine which mode you will start in. The SCREEN.VID file is created when you install Word and can be changed by running the installation program again or with the MAKEVID program that comes with version 5. The MAKEVID program combines the contents of many files into a new SCREEN.VID file; see the file MAKEVID.DOC for more information on running this program. Rerunning the installation program is usually much easier than using MAKEVID.

In version 4, you can also specify the mode used when you start Word. (Word normally starts in the same mode you were in when you quit from Word before.) You can add the following options to the MS-DOS command line.

OPTION	MEANING
/C	Character (text) mode
/G	Graphics mode
/H	High resolution mode. If your adapter supports this mode, Word displays more characters horizontally and vertically. On a Hercules Graphics adapter, this shows 90 characters across by 43 lines. You can still choose between graphics and text mode in high resolution mode.
/M	EGA high-resolution monochrome mode. You must have 64K of memory on your EGA card and an enhanced color display to use this mode.

To change the menu color in version 4, set the *menu color* field in the **O**ptions command. To change the background color for a window in version 4, set the *background color* field in the **W**indow **O**ptions command. To see a list of the colors available, select the field and press F1.

If you are using a color graphics adapter with version 5, you can specify the color of menus, the background, and each character format with the *color* field in the **O**ptions menu.

Tips

If you are using a terminate and stay resident program (TSR) that does not restore Word's graphics screen after the program pops up on the screen, you can get Word to redraw the screen with Ctrl Shift \.

In version 4, you can make Word work much faster if you are using it with a CGA card that is not made by IBM or Compaq on a PC with a fast processor (such as an 8086, 80286, or 80386). If you are using such a card and processor, set the MS-DOS environment variable NOSNOWCONTROL to TRUE. In your AUTOEXEC.BAT file, add the line

```
SET NOSNOWCONTROL = TRUE
```

This does not always work. Add this line, reboot your PC, and run Word. If you see wavy lines, "snow," or flicker on the screen, re-edit your AUTOEXEC.BAT file and remove the line you added.

Word version 4 attempts to determine the type of graphics card automatically. Due to the way some manufacturers design their cards, however, Word sometimes guesses incorrectly. You can tell Word the type of card you are using with an MS-DOS environment variable. If you are using one of the following cards, you can place the appropriate environment command in your AUTOEXEC.BAT file.

CARD	ENVIRONMENT COMMAND
IBM CGA, 640 × 200	SET CGA = true
IBM EGA, 640 × 350	SET EGA = true
IBM VGA, 640 × 480	SET VGA = true
Hercules GB102 720 × 350	SET HERCGB102 = true
AT&T 6300 640 × 400	SET OLIVETTI = true
Olivetti 640 × 400	SET OLIVETTI = true
Toshiba T3100 640 × 400	SET T3100 = true

Headers and Footers. *See* **Running Heads**

Help

Overview   Word's advanced help facility makes it unnecessary for you to refer back to the documentation each time you have a question. The on-line help in version 5 is significantly improved over earlier versions and contains more information and more references to the documentation.

Procedure   If you have a mouse and need help with a particular command, give that command, point at the question mark in the middle of the bottom of the screen, and click the left button of the mouse. If you are using the keyboard and need help with a command, select the command and press Alt H. (If any styles attached to your document begin with the letter H, you must instead press Alt XH instead of Alt H.) For example, to get help for the Format Character command, give the Format command, select Character, and click on the question mark or press Alt H. If you want help on a particular field in a dialog, simply select that field and ask for help. If Word has specific help it gives it; otherwise, it shows the help screen for the dialog.

When you are in the Help command, your screen looks similar to Figure 34. Most help screens indicate the tutorial in the Learning Word program and the chapter in the Word manual that has additional information on the subject. (If you do not have the Learning Word program, you will be unable to use the tutorials.) Select Exit to get out of the Help system.

Your choices for navigating through the Help command are listed below.

COMMAND	ACTION
Exit	Returns you to where you were in Word. If you started Help while giving a command, you will be able to complete that command.
Next	Shows the next screen
Previous	Shows the previous screen
Basics	Shows basic information about using Word
Index	Shows an index of the Help command. This index contains the same information as Word's Quick Reference Card.

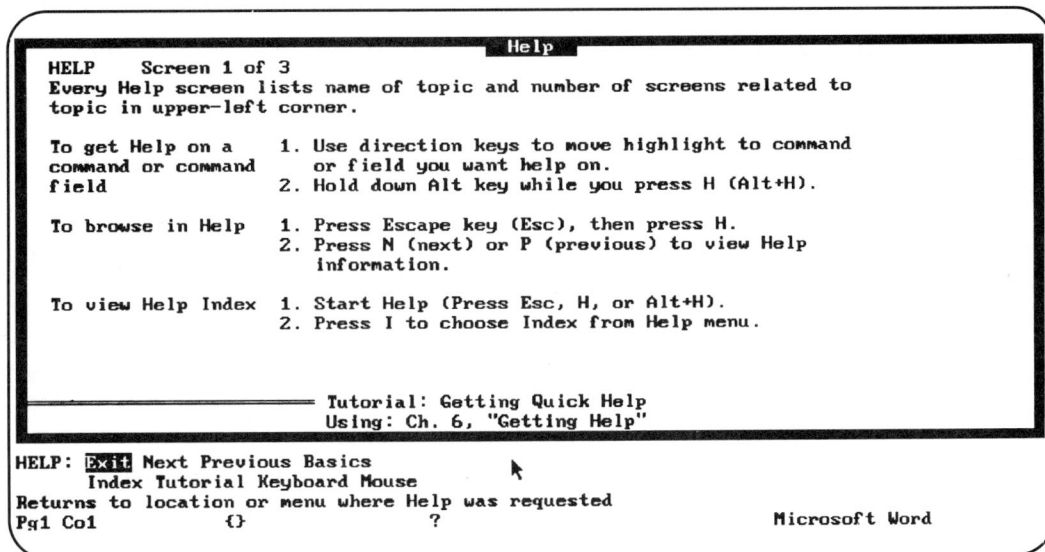

```
┌────────────────────────────────── Help ──────────────────────────────────┐
│ HELP     Screen 1 of 3                                                    │
│ Every Help screen lists name of topic and number of screens related to    │
│ topic in upper-left corner.                                               │
│                                                                           │
│ To get Help on a     1. Use direction keys to move highlight to command   │
│ command or command      or field you want help on.                        │
│ field                2. Hold down Alt key while you press H (Alt+H).       │
│                                                                           │
│ To browse in Help    1. Press Escape key (Esc), then press H.             │
│                      2. Press N (next) or P (previous) to view Help        │
│                         information.                                       │
│                                                                           │
│ To view Help Index   1. Start Help (Press Esc, H, or Alt+H).              │
│                      2. Press I to choose Index from Help menu.            │
│                                                                           │
│                                                                           │
│                 ═══════ Tutorial: Getting Quick Help                       │
│                         Using: Ch. 6, "Getting Help"                       │
└───────────────────────────────────────────────────────────────────────────┘
HELP: Exit Next Previous Basics
      Index Tutorial Keyboard Mouse          ▶
Returns to location or menu where Help was requested
Pg1 Co1              {}              ?                    Microsoft Word
```

Figure 34

COMMAND	ACTION
Tutorial	Runs the Learning Microsoft Word application and starts at the section that relates to this topic.
Keyboard	Lists Word's keyboard actions
Mouse	Lists Word's mouse actions

Tips　　　　Word also comes with the "Learning Microsoft Word" program. This application can be installed when you initially set up Word and can be run separately from Word or as part of the **Help** command. (See Installing Word.) It is unlikely that anyone reading this book will benefit greatly from "Learning Microsoft Word" since it is primarily intended for beginning users. The program covers a wide variety of subjects in a simple and easy-to-follow manner, and the introductory material in the program is much better than the introductory material in the Word manuals. If you are responsible for teaching beginners about Word, you might want them to use "Learning Microsoft Word" before you give them other lessons.

Hidden Text. *See* **Character Formatting, Annotations, Indexes,** *and* **Tables of Contents**

Hyphenation

Overview   When you write documents, Word automatically breaks lines to make them as long as possible. If Word breaks a line just before a long word, it might leave many spaces at the end of the line; if the paragraph is justified, there may be many inter-word spaces on the line. With hyphenation added to your documents, Word breaks words at hyphens within words, making it less likely that there will be large gaps.

The example in Figure 35 shows an example of a paragraph that has many odd visual breaks due to word wrap. The second paragraph is the same as the first, except that the addition of hyphens has improved its appearance.

Adding hyphens to words is easy. Word has three types of hyphens: normal, optional, and nonbreaking. You enter each type with different keys; each type of hyphen has a different effect both on what Word shows on the screen and printout and how Word breaks lines.

Normal hyphens are entered by pressing the hyphen key on the main keyboard (or the grey minus key on the numeric keypad). Use normal hyphens in words that are hyphenated (such as "all-around" and

```
Finding the result may not be easy. First you must not calculate
based only on the net sales; you must also add all the
extraordinary transfer rates to the net sale price. Then you
multiply the costs of goods by the final arbitrated price at the
time of transaction.

Finding the result may not be easy. First you must not calculate
based only on the net sales; you must also add all the extraordi-
nary transfer rates to the net sale price. Then you multiply the
costs of goods by the final arbitrated price at the time of
transaction.
```

Figure 35

"small-time"). Normal hyphens are always shown and printed. Word breaks a line at a normal hyphen when wrapping words.

Optional hyphens are entered by pressing Ctrl Hyphen. Word breaks a line at an optional hyphen when wrapping words. Since optional hyphens are only shown and printed when Word breaks a line, it is safe to put optional hyphens in words because they will not be seen unless Word breaks a word at the optional hyphen. You can add optional hyphens by hand or with the **Library Hyphenate** command.

Nonbreaking hyphens are entered by pressing Ctrl Shift Hyphen. Word never breaks a line at a nonbreaking hyphen; nonbreaking hyphens are always shown on the screen and in printing. Use nonbreaking hyphens when you want to be sure that Word does not break the word at the hyphen, such as in mathematical equations ("27-3") and hyphenated names ("Sir William Dean-Ansell").

The list below summarizes the ways in which the three types of hyphens function.

TYPE	ENTER WITH	SHOWS ON SCREEN/PRINTOUT	WORD WILL BREAK
Normal	Hyphen	Yes	Yes
Optional	Ctrl Hyphen	Not unless broken	Yes
Nonbreaking	Ctrl Shift Hyphen	Yes	No

Procedure

To add optional hyphens to your document, select the region you want to hyphenate and give the **Library Hyphenate** command. If you want to hyphenate from a particular part of the document to the end, put the cursor at the beginning of where you want to hyphenate. You can stop hyphenating at any time by pressing Escape.

Word adds hyphens only to words that are at the ends of lines as it hyphenates. Hence, you should rehyphenate if you edit the lines, change the margins, or change fonts in such a way that the lines change.

Note that the **Library Hyphenate** command does not remove unneeded optional hyphens; it simply adds new ones where needed at the time that the command is given. Also, the **Library Hyphenate** command will not add optional hyphens to a word that already has any hyphens in it. Thus, if you have added normal or nonbreaking hyphens or have added optional hyphens by hand, the command will not add optional hyphens to the word.

In the *confirm* field, select *No* if you want Word to hyphenate without prompting you for each word; select *Yes* if you want to check each hyphenation. Unless your document is very long, it is probably a good idea to select *Yes* and follow along as Word hyphenates. The *hyphenate caps* option lets you tell Word whether to hyphenate words that start with a capital letter. Words that begin with a capital letter are usually proper names or the first letter in a sentence. Since some people prefer not to hyphenate such words, you might want to set this to *No* to prevent Word from hyphenating them. Most people, however, leave this set to *Yes*.

Word switches to printer display and scrolls the screen horizontally if necessary. As the command is running, Word selects any word at the end of a line that can be hyphenated to make the line break closer to the end. Word prompts *Enter Y to insert hyphen, N to skip, or use direction keys.* Press Y to accept the hyphenation or N if you do not want to hyphenate the word. If you want to hyphenate the word at a different syllable, press the Down Arrow or Up Arrow keys to move back and forth. If you do not agree with Word's choice of where to break the syllables, use the Left Arrow or Right Arrow keys to move the hyphenation point back and forth character-by-character. Press Y when the hyphen is in the correct place. Word will not allow you to add a hyphen to the left of the second character or further to the right than where a hyphen must appear for the word to stay on the same line.

Warnings

Hyphenation rules are not universal. The hyphenation dictionary used for the Library Hyphenate command is very good, but some people might not agree with all of its choices. It is a good idea to scan the right margin of a document before printing the final draft to make sure you agree with all of Word's choices for automatic hyphenation.

Tips

Your document becomes harder to read when many adjacent lines end in hyphens. A general rule in book publishing is that no more than two adjacent lines can end in hyphens (some publications are stricter and say that no two adjacent lines can be hyphenated). As you scan your document before final production, look for adjacent lines that end in hyphens and remove optional hyphens from words to make the lines easier to read.

If you use two dashes to make an "em dash" in text, the first dash should be a nonbreaking hyphen and the second one a normal hyphen. It is better to enter an em dash by pressing Alt Ctrl Hyphen. This causes Word to enter a special character in your text that the printer driver will translate to an em dash when printed. Note that most laser printers have special characters for em dashes that can be entered as a single character. For example, the em dash on PostScript printers can be inserted in documents with Alt 234 (version 5) or Alt 208 (version 4).

There are many rules for hyphenation, and you may want to consult one or more of the standard references on them. One of the most concise and clear sources is *Webster's Standard American Style Manual* (1985, Merriam-Webster).

Importing and Exporting Files

Overview   People typically use Word in conjunction with other programs. For example, you might use Word to put text around the output of a data base management system or spreadsheet, to take material transmitted from other word processing programs (possibly from other computers) and for inclusion in your own documents, or to enter material that will be processed by other programs.

Word can read (*import*) files that are produced by other programs. Almost every PC program that works with words or numbers can write files that are plain text. These files, also called *ASCII files* and *text files*, contain characters but almost no formatting information; the only formatting they might contain are tab characters and paragraph marks. Only a very few programs can write out files with Word's formatting.

Word can also write (*export*) files to be read by other programs. Since Word is one of the best-selling programs for the PC, many software manufacturers have adapted their programs to read Word document files; Ventura Publisher from Xerox is one such program.

Word exports plain text files to programs that cannot read document files. The two primary commands for exporting plain text files are the **T**ransfer **S**ave command and the **P**rint **F**ile command. With the proper options set, these commands can write plain text files. You can also use the

Print File command to create documents that can be used by other programs that require a paragraph mark (usually called a *carriage return*) at the end of each line.

If you use Word on both the PC and the Apple Macintosh, you can convert documents between the two fairly easily. However, some information (such as styles and some formatting) is lost when you convert. When exporting files created by Word for the PC (Word/PC) to Word for the Macintosh (Word/Macintosh), character and division styles are lost since those features do not exist on the Macintosh. When importing from Word/Macintosh, style sheets are converted to formatting. Documents will look the same, but you will lose the advantages of using style sheets. (See Microsoft Word on the Apple Macintosh.)

If you want to read files from or write files to IBM's DisplayWrite, you can convert documents between the programs with Word's WORD _ DCA program. DisplayWrite and other IBM programs can often store and read files in a format known as DCA-RFT (Document Content Architecture - Revisable Form Text). Note, however, that the WORD_DCA program does not do a very complete job of converting the files back and forth due to limitations in DCA-RFT. The WORD _ DCA.DOC file on the Utilities disk explains the limitations of the program.

Word can also produce files in Microsoft's RTF format. A few programs from vendors other than Microsoft can read RTF files. In version 4, you must run the WORD _ RTF program to convert documents to RTF format. In version 5, you use the **T**ransfer **S**ave command and select *RTF* in the *format* field. Like the DCA conversion program, the WORD _ RTF program does not do a very complete job of converting the files back and forth due to limitations in RTF that Microsoft has not fixed. There is a file called WORD _ RTF.DOC on the Utilities disk that explains the limitations of the program.

Procedure **Importing and Exporting Text Files** To read a text file created by another program, simply give the **T**ransfer **L**oad command and enter the file's name. If the lines in the file are longer than Word's default line lengths, Word will wrap the lines; however, this might result in files that are hard to read. A better method is to start a new file, use the **F**ormat **D**ivision **M**argins command to set long lines, then use the **T**ransfer **M**erge command to read the file into the new file. You can then save this file formatted or unformatted.

To create a text file, use the **T**ransfer **S**ave command. In the **T**ransfer **S**ave command, you must set the *formatting* field to *No* (for version 4) or the *format* field to *Text-only* or *Text-only-with-line-breaks* (for version 5). Word will create a file with all characters, including Tab characters and paragraph marks. The paragraph marks will appear only at the end of paragraphs rather than at the end of each line, unless you select *Text-only-with-line-breaks* (for version 5).

Use the **P**rint **F**ile command if you need paragraph marks at the end of each line in version 4. First, use the **P**rint **O**ptions command to set the *printer* to either *PLAIN* or *TTY*. Next, give the **F**ormat **D**ivision **M**argins command, set *top, bottom, left*, and *right* to 0 in, and set *width* to 7.9 in; this makes the lines 79 characters long. The **P**rint **F**ile command will now create a file with no extra lines at the top and bottom of the page and no space at the beginning of lines.

Importing and Exporting Documents for Word/Macintosh　　In order to have Word/PC read a document created by Word/Macintosh, the Word/Macintosh file must be saved in Word/PC format. When running Word/Macintosh, give the **S**ave **A**s command, and click the *File Format* button. Choose *Microsoft Word (MS-DOS)* in the dialog box, click *OK*, and save the file, then transfer the file to the PC using your standard method (such as telecommunications or over a network). Word/PC will be able to open the file.

Note that you might have to reformat some paragraphs or characters. Also, since Word/Macintosh has some capabilities not available in Word/PC, some items may be lost or improperly formatted.

Word/Macintosh can read Word/PC documents directly. If your documents have style sheets, be sure to copy them when you copy the documents to the Macintosh. Since Word/PC has some capabilities not available in Word/Macintosh, some items may be lost or improperly formatted.

Importing and Exporting Documents Formatted for DCA　　Use the WORD_DCA program to convert between Word and DCA formats. You can run the program outside of Word or by using the "dca_load.mac" and "dca_save.mac" macros that are part of the MACRO.GLY file. (See Macros.) The program prompts you for the name of the input file (the one you want to convert from) and output file (the file you want to create).

You can also specify the name of the input and output files at the command line of the WORD _ DCA program. The syntax for the command is

```
WORD_DCA -i= input1, input2, ... -c=type-o= output1, output2, ...
```

The type is "dca" to convert from DCA to Word and "msw" to convert from Word to DCA.

Remember that many of Word's formatting features are lost in documents converted to DCA format. If you use styles in your document, you should freeze the formats before you convert to DCA. (See Styles.) If you are transferring files between computer systems or between PC applications, try to find a conversion utility or other format which loses as little of Word's formatting as possible.

Importing and Exporting Documents Formatted for RTF   Version 5 reads RTF files automatically. In version 5, you can save a file in RTF format by selecting *RTF* in the **T**ransfer **S**ave command. You can import or export an RTF file in version 4 with the RTF _ DOS program (if you are using OS/2, the program is called RTF _ OS2). The program prompts you for the name of the input file (the one you want to convert from) and output file (the file you want to create). To export a Word file in RTF format, you can simply use the **T**ransfer **S**ave command and select *RTF* in the *format* field.

You can also specify the name of the input and output files at the command line of the RTF _ DOS program. The syntax for the command is

```
RTF_DOS input output [/S] [/G]
```

Use the /S argument to prevent the program from prompting you for a style sheet if it cannot find one, and use the /G argument to prevent all prompts (such as in batch files).

Warnings   Converting documents usually results in a loss of formatting information. Depending on the conversion you are doing, the process may lose or garble much of the formatting. Before assuming that Word can import or export to another program, be sure to test the conversion. Since some of the conversion routines fail with long files, test the conversion with a long file if you will be importing or exporting a long file.

Tips   Some telecommunications programs require that the files you send have a paragraph mark at the end of each line when you transmit files; others require that you only have a paragraph mark at the end of a paragraph. Check the program's documentation carefully before saving a text file from Word so that you will use the correct procedure.

You can buy programs that convert documents between word processors. These programs often do a more complete job of converting formatting than Word does. Note, however, that you cannot tell how well a program will convert between two formats until you try it. Microsoft has endorsed a full-featured package called Word Exchange (Systems Compatibility Corporation, 401 N. Wabash, Suite 600, Chicago, IL 60611; 312/329-0700) that allows exchange between many PC word processing programs including Word, MultiMate, DisplayWrite, WordStar, and Volkswriter. Another conversion package is R-Doc/X (Advanced Computer Innovations, 30 Burncoat Way, Rochester, NY 14534; 716/454-3188). If you use DCA and RTF conversion, you may find TexDCA useful for converting between word processors (CrossCourt Systems, 1521 Greenview Avenue, East Lansing, MI 48823; 517/332-4353).

Indentation

Overview   Each paragraph in a document has three types of indentation: left, first line, and right. The left and right indentation of a paragraph is always measured from the margins rather than from the edge of the page; the first line indentation is always measured from the left indentation. (See Margins.) If you change the margins in a division, the indentations will move with them. With creative use of indentation, you can format your documents in many attractive fashions. To indent paragraphs, use the Format Paragraph command.

Paragraphs are usually formatted one of two ways: with the first line indented or with no indentation in the first line. Alternatively, some people use *hanging indent* or *outdented* paragraphs where the first line begins to the left of the rest of the paragraph, although this is rare. You might use an outdent, however, in a list of items with bullets or numbers in the left column. (See Lists.)

In most documents, the right indentation remains in the same place unless the left indentation moves. For example, long quotations usually have additional indentations, both left and right, of .5 inch or 1 inch. It is unlikely that you will move the right indentation without moving the left one unless you are formatting paragraphs to be side by side. (See Paragraph Placement.)

Procedure   Select the paragraph or style you want to change and give the **Format Paragraph** command. The *left indent, first line*, and *right indent* fields can be filled in using any form of measurement recognized by Word (inches, centimeters, etc.). The *left indent* and *right indent* fields are relative to the margins (or to the edge of the column if you have more than one column on the page) and the *first line* field is relative to the *left indent*.

You cannot enter a negative number for the *left indent* field. You can enter a negative number for the *first line* field, but this will not cause the first line to go further to the left than the margin. For example, you can enter 1 in for the *left indent* and -.5 in for the *first line*. You can use a positive or negative number for the *right indent* field; a negative number will move the right indentation into the right margin. The following list describes the effect of using positive and negative measurements in the fields.

FIELD	MEASUREMENT	EFFECT
Left indent	Positive	Moves the left side of the entire paragraph to the right of the left margin
Left indent	Negative	Not allowed
First line	Positive	Moves the first line of the paragraph to the right, relative to the left indentation
First line	Negative	Moves the first line of the paragraph to the left, relative to the left indentation
Right indent	Positive	Moves the right side of the entire paragraph to the left of the right margin
Right indent	Negative	Moves the right side of the entire paragraph to the right of the right margin

 I

Word has a few keyboard equivalents to make direct formatting easier.

KEY	ACTION
Alt P	Set *left indent* to 0, *first line* to 0, *right indent* to 0
Alt F	Increase *first line* by one tab stop
Alt N	Increase *left indent* by one tab stop
Alt M	Decrease *left indent* by one tab stop
Alt T	Increase *left indent* by one tab stop and decrease *first line* by one tab stop (hanging indent)

If any styles attached to your document begin with these characters, you must instead press Alt X and the letter for the keyboard equivalents. For example, if you have a style with the name FG, to increase the first line indent you must type Alt XF.

Examples   To indent the first line of a paragraph .5 inches, set *left indent* to 0, *first line* to .5 inch, and *right indent* to 0. Or, if the first paragraph has the three fields set to 0, press Alt F (or Alt XF if you have a style sheet attached). This is shown in Figure 36.

To make a paragraph with a .5 inch hanging outdent, set *left indent* to .5 inch, *first line* to -.5 inch, and *right indent* to 0. Or, if the first paragraph has the three fields set to 0, press Alt T (or Alt XT if you have a style sheet attached). This is shown in Figure 37.

To indent a paragraph .5 inches from each margin, set *left indent* to .5 inch, *first line* to 0, and *right indent* to .5 inch. This is shown in Figure 38.

Tips   Use Word's style sheets for most of your paragraph formatting. (See Styles.) Changing the indentation used in your document is much easier if you use styles rather than direct formatting.

The ships in the painting add depth to the bay, but not as much depth as distant trees. The jade green in the boats' sails adds vibrant contrast to the fog-shaded trees in the background. The dragon, then, is not the only action in the painting; in fact, it is not the primary focus due to the busy background.

Figure 36

The ships in the painting add depth to the bay, but not as much depth as distant trees. The jade green in the boats' sails adds vibrant contrast to the fog-shaded trees in the background. The dragon, then, is not the only action in the painting; in fact, it is not the primary focus due to the busy background.

Figure 37

The ships in the painting add depth to the bay, but not as much depth as distant trees. The jade green in the boats' sails adds vibrant contrast to the fog-shaded trees in the background. The dragon, then, is not the only action in the painting; in fact, it is not the primary focus due to the busy background.

Figure 38

Paragraphs are usually indented when there is no space between paragraphs and unindented when there is a full line space between paragraphs. If you indent the first line of each paragraph, you may want to experiment with how much to indent. People usually indent five spaces, though modern style has moved towards a smaller indent (for example, this book uses only a few spaces).

Indexes

Overview

An index is an invaluable part of most books and long documents. An index will help readers locate specific topics in your document even if you are inexperienced in choosing the contents of an index. Although creating an index requires careful marking of index entries, Word's Library Index command lets you create an index without a great deal of effort.

When you mark a document, you tell Word which words you want in the index. You do not add these words to your document: you simply flag the ones you want included. For example, if the word "violin" appears in your document and you want it in the index, simply put index marks around it. This means that if you want something to appear in the index and it does not appear on the page for which you want it indexed, you must add it to the page in hidden text (so that it won't appear when you print the document) and mark the hidden text. For many subentries (that is, index entries that have a main heading and a list of entries that pertain to that heading) you will have to add the first-level entry in hidden text before the subentry.

Creating an index in Word is similar to creating a table of contents. (See Tables of Contents.) As you edit your document, simply flag words that you want in the index with special codes that are in hidden character format. When you are finished marking index entries, give the Library Index command and Word compiles the index and places it at the end of your document in its own division. Word also adds hidden text at the beginning and end of the index so that it can replace the current index if you give the Library Index command a second time.

After Word creates the index, you can format it as you want. You can use direct formatting or change the formatting in the gallery if you have told Word that you want your index entries to be in predefined styles. You can also add a chapter heading to an index, although Word will delete that heading if you recreate the index unless you are careful where you put it. Since Word wipes out all lines in the index when you recreate it, you should probably only add direct formatting after the last time you create the index.

Procedure **Marking Index Entries** Each word you want in your index must be marked. Note that you must mark each occurrence you want in the index, not just the first occurrence. All marks are entered in hidden text, so it is likely that you will want to make hidden text visible when you are adding your index entries with the *show hidden text* field in the **Window Options** command (version 4) or the **Options** command (version 5).

To mark an entry, add the *index code* before the entry and the *endmark* after the entry. For most entries, the index code is ".i." and the endmark is ";", both of which are in hidden text. For example, to mark the words "drum set," you would use the following procedure.

1. Place the cursor on the "d" of "drum."
2. Press Alt E or give the **Format Character** command and set the *hidden* field to *Yes*.
3. Type .i., which will display with a dotted underline (indicating that it is hidden) if you have hidden text displayed using the **Options** command.
4. Move the cursor to after the "t" in "set."

5. Press Alt E or give the **F**ormat **C**haracter command and set the *hidden* field to *Yes*.
6. Type ;, which will display with dotted underline (indicating that it is hidden).

Clearly, using a macro is a better solution. (See Macros.) A common practice is to define one macro to insert a hidden ".i." at the current location and another to add a hidden ";" at the current location. You can assign these macros to keys that are easy to remember (such as Ctrl I and Ctrl ;). You can also use the glossary to hold the hidden ".i." and ";." (See Glossaries.)

So far, you have seen only how to mark entries for a one-level index. Most indexes in longer works are generally two levels. For example, a book about home building might have a main entry "windows" with subentries "sliding," "picture," "attic," and so on. The index would have the heading on a line by itself, with the subentries on separate lines indented from the margin.

To mark a subentry, enter .i. followed by the name of the main entry and a colon, all hidden. The endmark is the same (a hidden semicolon). For example, Figure 39 shows how to mark "sliding" as a subentry under "windows." Since this entry marks only "windows," there will be no page number after "windows" in the index.

Figure 40 shows an example of an entry for text that does not appear in the document. The word "adjusting" does not appear in the text, but makes a sensible index entry, especially if it is used in other places in the document. Figure 40 also shows an example of how one word can have more than one index entry. The first entry is for a phrase that is shown, but the second one is completely hidden.

```
Remember that .i.windows:sliding; windows must be
checked for leaks each year.
```

Figure 39

```
If the .i.door frame; needs to be altered,
.i.adjusting;you should do it before the first rains.
```

Figure 40

Special Characters   You can index a single word, a short phrase, or a long string of text; most indexes usually have only short entries. You must be careful if the entry you want has a colon, a semicolon, or a quotation mark. Since Word uses these as special characters, extra steps are required when marking the entry. If the entry contains a colon or semicolon, enclose the entire entry in hidden quotation marks. If the entry contains a quotation mark, enclose the entire entry in hidden quotation marks. For example, the phrases

```
3:1 split
"short" selling
```

would be marked as shown in Figure 41.

Creating the Index   You can compile the index once your document is completely marked. However, first be sure hidden text is not shown. If hidden text is shown, Word will include it when paginating, thereby creating page number errors in the index. You should also be sure that you have specified a printer driver in the **Print Options** command so that Word can determine the page sizes.

Give the Library Index command, and you will see the dialog in Figure 42. After selecting the options, press Enter. If the document already has an index, Word asks if you want to replace the existing index; press Y to create the new index. The choices and actions for the Library Index command are as follows.

```
     .i."3:1 split";
     .i.""short" selling";
```

Figure 41

```
LIBRARY INDEX entry/page # separated by: ███    cap main entries:(Yes)No
            indent each level: 0.2"              use style sheet: Yes(No)
Enter text
Pg1 Co1              {}                    ?                      Microsoft Word
```

Figure 42

FIELD	ACTION
entry/page # separated by	This character separates the entry and the page number. Word's default is two spaces; other common choices are a comma and one space, or a Tab character (enter ^t to get a tab).
cap main entries	Word normally capitalizes the first letter of an entry in the index. If you want it to leave the entries in the cases in which they appear in the text, select *No*. Note that if two entries differ only in capitalization, Word treats them as the same and includes both page numbers in one entry, regardless of how this field is set. If you specify *No* and both capitalized and uncapitalized entries exist, Word will use the first entry for the index.
indent each level	For direct formatting, this field tells Word how much to indent subentries from the preceding level.
use style sheet	It is often convenient to use a style sheet for the index entries. If you select *Yes* for this field, Word formats each entry as "Index level 1," "Index level 2," and so on instead of using direct formatting. You can then change the appearance of the lines in the index in the gallery.

When you execute the command, Word compiles, sorts, and enters the entries at the end of the document. This can take quite a while, depending on the size of your document and the number of index entries you have specified. Word also puts a division mark before the index and inserts hidden text *.Begin Index.* before the index and hidden text *.End Index.* after the index.

Formatting the Index   To add a heading to the index, you must first create an index and show the hidden text. Place your heading after the division mark but before the hidden text *.Begin Index.* When Word recreates the index, it will only delete the text between (and including) the hidden text. If you want running heads in that division, you should put them before your heading.

If you want to change the styles of some of the entries, you can use either direct character formatting or character styles. For example, you might want to put all main entries that have subentries in boldface.

Warnings   You can accidentally alter the index marks if you add hidden text for the index entries, hide the hidden text, then continue to edit your document. If you hide the hidden text then insert text at the location of the hidden text, you will not know if you are adding before, after, or in the middle of the hidden text. Thus, once you add index entries, you should either edit with the hidden text shown or review the contents of your document with hidden text showing before you generate your index. The location of the hidden text is marked with a two-headed arrow if the *show nonprinting symbols* option is set to *Partial* or *All* when *show hidden text* is set to *No*. Thus you can see whether you are inside an index entry without revealing the hidden text.

Note that Word adds a division mark before the index, and running heads only are active in the division in which they are defined. Consequently, if you want running heads in your index, you must add them yourself after giving the Library Index command.

Tips   Add index marks to entries after you have finished editing your text rather than during the writing process. There are two reasons for waiting until the end: First, unless you make the hidden text visible, it is difficult to edit text after adding a great deal of hidden text. However, if the hidden text is visible, the screen can get very cluttered. Second, you can usually better determine which words should be included in the index after you have completed writing since the concepts and discussions in the paper are clearer in your mind.

Some indexes include *see references* (such as "Office buildings: see Commercial property"). You can create these references by adding the entire phrase in hidden text with index marks (`.i."Office buildings: see Commercial property":;`). Having too many see references can make an index hard to use, but extra entries often help people who are unfamiliar with the material in your document.

Using style sheets with indexes makes reformatting each level of the index much easier. This is especially true with single-column indexes in which you specify a Tab character as the separator in the Library Index command. You can quickly change the way each level uses the Tab characters and include such things as leader characters in the entries. (See Tables and Tab Stops.)

There are many books about how to index. If you index only once in a while, these books are not necessary. However, if you must index long books or index often, you may find the material in these books valuable. Most style guides also give good advice on choosing material for indexes.

Insert Command

Overview   The Insert command has two distinct capabilities: it inserts a copy of the scrap or a glossary entry into your document, and it runs macros by name. When inserting, you use the **Delete** command to cut some text to the scrap, move the cursor to where you want the text to be, and give the Insert command.

Procedure   To insert the text in the scrap into your document at the current cursor location, give the Insert command and press Enter or press the Insert key. If you are using a mouse, click on the Insert command with the right button.

To insert text from a glossary into your document at the current cursor location, give the Insert command, type the name of the glossary at the prompt, and press Enter. If you are running Word under Microsoft Windows, you can include the contents of the Windows Clipboard by entering CLIPBOARD for the glossary name.

To run a macro, give the Insert command, enter the name of the macro at the prompt, and press Enter.

Tips   You can get a list of available glossary names and macros names by pressing F1 at the Insert command's prompt.

Word shows part of the contents of the scrap at the bottom of the screen between the curly braces. Give the Insert command if you want to see everything in the scrap. Once you see the contents of the scrap, you can easily remove the new material with the **Undo** command.

Inserting Text

Overview   Most of the work in typing in a document is inserting text. Word makes entering text easy, since you are always either inserting text or giving a command, and it is clear which you are doing if you look at your screen. You can quickly correct mistakes by pressing the Backspace key.

Procedure   As you type, characters appear at the position before the cursor. All characters to the right of the cursor move to the right as you type. If you want to overtype the characters on the screen, press F5 to put Word in *overtype* mode. In this mode, each letter you type replaces the character under the cursor. To return to normal inserting, press F5 again. Word displays *OT* at the bottom of the screen when you are in overtype mode. Note that you can not use overtype mode when you are using revision marks. (See Revision Marks.)

Word has many special characters you can enter as you type. There are three types of hyphens: normal, optional, and nonbreaking. (See Hyphenation.) You can also enter *nonbreaking spaces* in your document. (Word will never break a line at a nonbreaking space.) You might use nonbreaking spaces between a formal address and a name (such as "Mr. Chu"). Press Ctrl Space Bar to enter a nonbreaking space.

You can also enter foreign characters and special symbols in Word if you know the character's ASCII code. To enter a special character, hold down the Alt key and type the three-digit ASCII code on the keypad (not on the numbers at the top of the main part of the keyboard). Be sure to hold down the Alt key while you type all three digits.

For example, you may want to include an "o" with an umlaut over it. The ASCII code for the "o" with umlaut is 148. To enter the character, hold down the Alt key and type 148 on the keypad. Figure 43 shows the ASCII codes of all the graphics characters for the IBM PC.

The following list shows how to create Word's special characters.

CHARACTER	TYPE	COMMENTS
Space	Space Bar	
Nonbreaking space	Ctrl Space Bar	Word will not break a line here.
Normal hyphen	Hyphen	
Optional hyphen	Ctrl Hyphen	Not shown on screen unless Word breaks a line.
Nonbreaking hyphen	Ctrl Shift Hyphen	Word will not break a line here.
Em dash	Alt Ctrl Hyphen	Long hyphen
Paragraph mark	Enter	
New line mark	Shift Enter	
Page mark	Ctrl Shift Enter	
Division mark	Ctrl Enter	

You can repeat the last text insertion with the F4 key. Pressing F4 causes Word to repeat all typing you did since your last cursor movement or command.

128	Ç	171	½	214	╥
129	ü	172	¼	215	╫
130	é	173	┴	216	╪
131	â	174	«	217	┘
132	ä	175	┐	218	┌
133	à	176	▒	219	█
134	å	177	▓	220	▄
135	ç	178	█	221	>
136	ê	179	│	222	<
137	ë	180	┤	223	▀
138	è	181	╡	224	α
139	ï	182	╢	225	ß
140	î	183	╖	226	Γ
141	ì	184	╕	227	π
142	Ä	185	╣	228	Σ
143	Å	186	║	229	σ
144	É	187	╗	230	µ
145	æ	188	╝	231	τ
146	Æ	189	╜	232	Φ
147	ô	190	╛	233	Θ
148	ö	191	┐	234	Ω
149	ò	192	└	235	δ
150	û	193	┴	236	∞
151	ù	194	┬	237	φ
152	ÿ	195	├	238	ε
153	Ö	196	─	239	∩
154	Ü	197	┼	240	≡
155	¢	198	╞	241	±
156	£	199	╟	242	≥
157	¥	200	╚	243	≤
158	₧	201	╔	244	⌠
159	ƒ	202	╩	245	⌡
160	á	203	╦	246	π
161	í	204	╠	247	±
162	ó	205	═	248	°
163	ú	206	╬	249	˜Ñ
164	⌐	207	╧	250	˜Ñ
165	ñ	208	╨	251	├
166	►	209	─	252	ⁿ
167	º	210	"	253	²
168	L	211	"	254	■
169	⌐	212	'	255	╨
170	¬	213	'		

Figure 43

Warnings Most printers cannot print the IBM foreign and graphics characters (those characters with ASCII codes below 31 or above 127). If you enter these characters in your text and print them, the results can be unpredictable. Check whether your printer can print these characters before you enter them in your document. Note that you cannot easily convert documents for Word/Macintosh if you use these characters since they are not the same on the Apple Macintosh.

Installing Word

Overview Word's SETUP program makes installing Word fairly easy. However, SETUP has many limitations and is not particularly suited to revising the setup once you have installed Word.

Clearly, it is much easier to run Word on a hard disk system than on a floppy-based system. With a hard disk system, you can put all the files needed by Word on a single part of your hard disk and access those files without changing floppy disks.

If you have the network version of Word, installation is very similar to the regular version, but you must be sure that users understand how network Word differs from regular Word. Since the program is stored on a network file server, the user will have some of Word's special files (such as MW.INI) stored on their local disks. To use Word effectively, each user must start Word from the directory that contains these special files. (See Networks.)

Procedure If you are on a 5.25-inch floppy-based system with low-density (360 kilobytes per floppy) drives, format at least five diskettes before installing Word. If you are on a 3.5-inch floppy-based system, format at least three diskettes. If you intend to use the Learning Microsoft Word program, format two additional disks. (See Help.) Put blank labels on these disks in preparation for the SETUP program. If you are on a floppy-based system with high-density (1.2 or 1.44 megabytes per floppy) drives, format at least two diskettes before installing Word.

To copy Word either to diskettes or your hard disk, put the Utilities #1 disk in drive A (the names of the disks are in the upper-right corner of the disk labels). At the DOS prompt, type A:, press Enter, type SETUP, and

87

press Enter. Word's SETUP program prompts you for many things, including which programs you want to copy, the type of printer you are using, and so on.

After the initial screen, Word presents a set of installation steps that you should follow in order. You will probably want to perform each step in the list unless you are not using a mouse; in that case, you can skip the step about installing the mouse driver. When installing the printer driver, Word prompts you for just one printer. However, after SETUP has copied the necessary files for that printer, you can list additional printers you want to install. Find out the port (such as COM1: or LPT1:) to which your printer is attached before running SETUP.

Installing on a Hard Disk   Word asks onto which directory you want to install the files. It is a good idea to put all of Word's files on a directory that you use only for Word so that you can update the directory without worrying about other programs. A common name for the directory is simply "\WORD." SETUP creates the directory for you if it does not already exist.

If you use Word frequently, you will want to put Word's directory in your MS-DOS path list, which tells MS-DOS where to look for programs when you enter a program name. Your AUTOEXEC.BAT file may already have a path list in it; if not, you can create one easily. Run Word, give the **T**ransfer **L**oad command, enter \AUTOEXEC.BAT, and press Enter. If the file exists (most people have an AUTOEXEC.BAT file), look for a line that begins "SET PATH=" followed by one or more directory names. If such a line exists, add the directory name of the directory SETUP used to load Word to the list. Each path in the list must be separated from the other paths by a semicolon. Your path list might look like this:

```
SET PATH=C:\DOS;C:\WORD
```

Installing on Floppies   Most of the installation prompts are the same for floppy-based systems as they are for hard disks. Instead of asking for a subdirectory, you are prompted to insert new floppies. Of course, using high-density floppies is better than using low-density floppies. To reduce the number of floppies that you use, you can probably skip the step that adds the Learning Word files.

Installing on a Network   You use the SETUP command to install Word on the network file server just like you use it for installing on a hard disk. In version 5 a prompt will ask whether you are installing for a network. Note that Word automatically sets up the system for a network if you use the "/N" option on the SETUP command line.

The directory in which Word is installed is called the *program directory*. All users must have the program directory listed in their path in order to use Word. If you are responsible for the contents of the users' AUTOEXEC.BAT files, be sure to update their "SET PATH = " commands to include Word's program directory. You must also copy the MW.INI file from the program directory to each user's disk since Word needs to find that file on the directory from which they start Word. Use the MS-DOS COPY command to copy the file to each user's disk, and be sure that all users understand that they must always start Word from that directory. (If they start Word from other directories, they will end up with many copies of MW.INI on their disk, and the files will contain different information). If the user runs Word's spelling checker, that startup directory will also contain a file, UPDAT-AM.CMP, which contains the user's changes to the main dictionary. Word also stores its temporary files on the user's system.

Warnings   If you give the SETUP program the name of a directory to use and that directory already exists and has a copy of Word on it, SETUP will copy over the files in that directory. While this is often useful (for example, to update to a newer version of Word), you risk losing settings in your Word initialization file (MW.INI).

Tips   If you start using a different printer after you have installed Word, use the SETUP program to install the driver files for that printer. Although you can simply copy the files yourself from the printers' diskettes, some printers require you to copy more than one file and you may not remember to copy all the necessary files. The SETUP program always copies all the correct files for you.

You should definitely read the material in the README.DOC file which SETUP copies when it installs Word. This file contains numerous changes to the documentation and some tips from Microsoft that are not in the manual.

Jump Command

Overview
The Jump command lets you move directly to a particular page, footnote, annotation, or bookmark in your document. Obviously, jumping to a known page is easier than guessing where an item appears in the file. It is also an easy way to jump to particular text in a footnote or to a specific footnote. (See Footnotes.)

The Jump command in version 5 also lets you find annotations in a fashion similar to jumping to footnotes. (See Annotations.) You can also jump to bookmarks by name. (See Bookmarks.) Jump Footnote will find the next footnote or annotation while Jump Annotation will only find annotations.

Procedure
To jump to a specific page, give the Jump Page command and enter the desired page number. If your document has more than one division and the divisions have repeating page numbers (for example, if each chapter starts the page numbering at 1), type the desired page number, the letter D, and the division number. For example, to find page 7 in the fourth division, enter 7D4.

If you are looking in your document and you want to find the next footnote reference, give the Jump Footnote command. After finding the reference mark, you can select the text associated with the reference mark by giving the Jump Footnote command again. To jump back to the mark from the footnote, give the Jump Footnote command one more time.

The Jump Annotation command acts just like the Jump Footnote command except that it jumps to annotation marks and annotation text. The rules for the Jump Footnote and Jump Annotation commands follow:

SELECTION	JUMPS TO
Text in document	Next reference mark
Reference mark	Text associated with reference
Text in footnote window	Reference associated with the text

The Jump bookmarK command prompts you for the name of the bookmark you want to find. Type in the name and press Enter; Word will select the entire bookmark.

Warnings If Word is automatically repaginating your document (by setting *repaginate* or *paginate* to *Auto* in the **O**ptions command in version 5), the page numbers you jump to with the **J**ump **P**age command may change. Do not assume that the page numbers from the last printout are accurate if you are automatically repaginating your document, or if you manually repaginate it with the **P**rint **R**epaginate command after editing.

Keeps

Overview You can specify that particular text in your document be kept on the same page with other text in the paragraph or in a following paragraph; making sure that text is kept together is called a *keep*. You can keep two words on the same line by inserting a nonbreaking space or nonbreaking hyphen between the words. (See Inserting Text.) However, most keeps prevent text from spilling across page boundaries. Note that these commands also affect multi-column divisions; any keep will also prevent splitting paragraphs across columns.

    Word normally does not break a paragraph at a page boundary after its first line or before its last (unless you specify that this is acceptable in the **P**rint **O**ptions command). Word does not allow these breaks because standard style forbids having the first line of a paragraph at the bottom of a page (called a *widow*) or the last line of a paragraph at the top of a page (called an *orphan*). Word keeps at least two lines together at the top or bottom of the page.

    You can also prevent Word from splitting a paragraph at any point, or from separating a paragraph from the paragraph following. The **F**ormat **P**aragraph command has two fields that affect keeps: *keep together* and *keep follow*. "Keep together" guarantees that Word will prevent the paragraph from being split at the bottom of the page. Instead, it will leave blank space at the bottom of the page and move the entire paragraph to the next page. "Keep follow" guarantees that a particular paragraph will always be on the same page as the following one. This command is most often used to keep headings and following text on the same page.

Procedure   Use the **Print O**ptions command to control how Word handles widows and orphans. If you do not object to widows and orphans, choose *No* for the *widow/orphan control* field.

Use the **Format P**aragraph command to keep a paragraph together or with the following paragraph. Set the *together* field to *Yes* to ensure that the paragraph will never be split. Set the *keep follow* field to *Yes* to ensure that at least the last two lines of the selected paragraph and the first two lines of the following paragraph will appear on the same page (assuming that the widow and orphan control is on).

Warnings   Avoid having too many contiguous paragraphs formatted with *keep follow* set to *Yes*. If the aggregate length of the paragraphs becomes long, Word might leave large blank spaces at the bottom of the pages as it determines pagination. For example, if the headings and lines in a table are formatted with *keep follow* set to *Yes*, and you have a table heading and a table followed by another table heading and table, Word will try to keep the two tables on the same page.

If your document has many short pages, look at the paragraphs after the gaps to be sure that you do not have more keeps than you intended.

Tips   If you use style sheets and your document has headings, every heading should be formatted with the *keep follow* field set to *Yes* in the **Format P**aragraph command. You should also set the *keep together* field to *Yes* since you may have headings that are longer than one line. For example, when you enter your document, every heading may be only one line long; however, if you change the format to two columns, some headings may become longer than one line and you would not want them to split across column boundaries.

If your graphics always have captions under them, you should format the style for the graphics paragraphs to keep the caption together with the graphic; you will probably also want to be sure that all the text in the caption paragraph is kept together.

Keyboard

Overview   Since many PC users prefer not to use the mouse, Word allows you to perform almost every word processing task from the keyboard. Giving commands and selecting text with the keyboard is usually about as fast as using the mouse, although selecting options in dialogs and skipping around the screen is often faster with a mouse. Still, since people work better if they can use a technique they like, Word gives you many easy methods for working with the keyboard.

Procedure   **Moving in the Document**   The following keys move the cursor.

KEY	MOVEMENT
Up Arrow	Up
Down Arrow	Down
Left Arrow	Left
Right Arrow	Right
Home	Beginning of line
End	End of line
Pg Up	Up a windowful
Pg Down	Down a windowful
Ctrl Up Arrow	Beginning of previous paragraph
Ctrl Down Arrow	Beginning of next paragraph
Ctrl Left Arrow	Beginning of previous word
Ctrl Right Arrow	Beginning of next word
Ctrl Home	Top of window
Ctrl End	Bottom of window
Ctrl Pg Up	Top of document
Ctrl Pg Down	Bottom of document
Ctrl Tab	Next object (in layout mode)
Ctrl Shift Tab	Previous object (in layout mode)

Selecting Text   To select a group of characters, move the cursor to one end of the group, hold down the Shift key, and press one of the keys for moving shown above. The Shift key is used here to extend a selection. As long as you hold down the Shift key, Word makes the selection grow or shrink in the direction you are moving.

You can also extend the selection by pressing F6. Upon pressing F6, *EX* appears at the bottom of the screen to indicate that any cursor movement will extend the selection. To select a column, put the cursor at one corner of the desired selection, press Shift F6 (you will see CS at the bottom of the screen), and move the cursor to the opposite desired corner. (See Tables and Tab Stops.)

You can directly select groups of characters with the following keys. Note that if you have already selected less than the amount that the selection will move, Word will first select the current text. For example, if you have three words in a sentence selected and you press Shift F7, Word will select the current sentence; if you press Shift F7 again, Word will select the preceding sentence.

KEY	SELECTION
F7	Previous word
F8	Next word
F9	Previous paragraph
F10	Next paragraph
Shift F7	Previous sentence
Shift F8	Next sentence
Shift F9	Current line
Shift F10	Entire document

Formatting Text   You can use the Alt key in combination with letters, numbers, and characters to add character and paragraph formatting to your document. If you have a style sheet attached to your document, you must press Alt X before using the keyboard commands below.

The following keys are used to format characters.

KEY	FORMAT
Alt B	Boldface
Alt D	Double underline
Alt E	Hidden
Alt I	Italic
Alt K	Small caps
Alt S	Strikethrough
Alt U	Underline
Alt +	Superscript
Alt -	Subscript
Alt Space Bar	Normal character

The following keys are used to format paragraphs.

KEY	FORMAT
Alt C	Centered
Alt F	Increase first line indentation by one tab stop
Alt J	Justified
Alt L	Left flush
Alt M	Reduce left indentation by one tab stop
Alt N	Increase left indentation by one tab stop
Alt O	One line before
Alt P	Normal paragraph
Alt Q	Increase left and right indent by one tab stop
Alt R	Right flush
Alt T	Increase hanging indentation by one tab stop
Alt 2	Double space

Other Keyboard Commands   The following keys perform a variety of tasks.

KEY	COMMAND
F1	Next window
F2	Calculate
F3	Expand from glossary
F4	Repeat last editing or inserting command
F5	Overtype on/off
F6	Extend selection on/off
F11	Collapse heading
F12	Expand heading
Shift F1	**Undo**
Shift F2	Outline view on/off
Shift F3	Record macro on/off
Shift F4	Repeat last search
Shift F5	Outline edit on/off
Shift F6	Column selection on/off
Shift F11	Collapse body text
Shift F12	Expand body text
Ctrl F1	Zoom window
Ctrl F2	**F**ormat **R**unning-head *position Top*
Ctrl F3	Step macro
Ctrl F4	Change case
Ctrl F5	Line drawing on/off

KEY	COMMAND
Ctrl F6	**L**ibrary th**E**saurus
Ctrl F7	**T**ransfer **L**oad
Ctrl F8	**P**rint **P**rinter
Ctrl F9	**P**rint pre**V**iew
Ctrl F10	**T**ransfer **S**ave
Ctrl F12	Expand all
Ctrl Shift \	Redraw the screen (graphics mode only)
Alt F1	**F**ormat **T**ab **S**et
Alt F2	**F**ormat **R**unning-head *position Bottom*
Alt F3	**C**opy to scrap
Alt F4	Show layout
Alt F5	**J**ump **P**age
Alt F6	**L**ibrary **S**pell
Alt F7	**O**ptions *printer display Yes/No*
Alt F8	**F**ormat **C**haracter *font name*
Alt F9	**O**ptions *display Text/Graphics*
Alt F10	**F**ormat **S**tylesheet **R**ecord

Using the Keyboard in Dialogs Use the keyboard in a dialog or prompt to enter and change choices quickly, and to use the Up Arrow, Down Arrow, Left Arrow, and Right Arrow keys to move among the fields. You can also use the Home and End keys to go to the first or last field, respectively. Press Enter to give the command; press the Escape key to get out of the dialog without executing the command.

If a field allows you many choices that are not shown, press F1 to get a list. (See F1 Enumeration.) In a dialog field where you type in text, you can move through the text with the following keys:

KEY	MOVE TO
F7	Previous word
F8	Next word
F9	Previous character
F10	Next character

Tips

If you have assigned a macro to a function key and want to get the normal action of the function key, press Ctrl X before pressing the function key. For example, if you have a macro assigned to Ctrl F5 and you want to begin line drawing, press Ctrl X then Ctrl F5.

The F1 key in dialogs has many uses. If you cannot figure out what you are supposed to type in a field, try pressing F1 to see if there is a list of choices from which you can select.

If you are in a dialog and want to cancel the current command but give another one immediately, press Ctrl Escape. Unlike pressing the Escape key, which puts you back in insert mode, Ctrl Escape lets you enter another command directly.

Layout   [Version 5 Only]

Overview   There are three ways to view your Word document: in galley mode, in layout mode, and in preview mode. You use galley and layout modes while entering and editing text. Preview mode is only available if you have a graphics adapter. Versions of Word prior to version 5 always use galley mode, although you can purchase Microsoft Pageview to see documents in preview mode for version 4. The modes and their uses are described below.

MODE	USE
Galley mode	This is the simplest and fastest mode to use when editing. Because it uses relatively few computing resources of your PC, all commands and operations happen almost instantaneously. The disadvantage of using galley mode is that you cannot tell what your page will look like when you print it. For many people, seeing the layout as they enter or edit is not important, although you may want to see the layout before printing your document. You can use galley mode with automatic repagination if you want to always see where your pages will break but do not care about seeing other formatting. (See Repagination.)
Layout mode	Seeing the layout lets you view many formatting features of Word on the screen as you edit. For example, if you have side-by-side paragraphs, newspaper columns, and absolutely positioned paragraphs and graphics, you may want to see how the page looks as you enter and edit your text. Since layout mode gives Word many of the capabilities of desktop publishing programs, you can see how each element of your page looks relative to the other elements. Graphics are not displayed, but their tag and the space they take up is shown. (See Graphics and Columns and Paragraph Placement.)

MODE	USE
Preview mode	This is a view-only mode; you cannot edit your document. However, you can see the document exactly as it will look when you print it. In preview mode, you can scroll back and forth in your document page by page. If you have used Pageview under Microsoft Windows or the Page Preview command in Word/Macintosh, you will recognize that preview mode is almost identical to these. Even though you cannot edit in preview mode, you can jump to pages and bookmarks, set the printer options to see how different options affect the look of the page, and print the document.

Procedure   Use the **O**ptions command to select between galley and layout modes. From either mode, you can select preview mode by pressing Ctrl F9 or giving the **P**rint pre**V**iew command. In the **O**ptions command, setting the *show layout* field to *Yes* selects layout mode; setting it to *No* selects galley mode. You can also use the Alt F4 key to switch to and from layout mode.

Using Layout Mode   In layout mode, you will see line breaks as they will be printed if you have set *printer display* (version 4) or *show line breaks* (version 5) to *Yes* in the **O**ptions command. Note that this can slow down Word's performance significantly, especially on pages that have many formatting elements (such as many fonts and/or many font sizes). Thus, if you use layout mode for editing, you should turn off printer-specific line breaks for most of your work.

If you use small font sizes and have printer display on, Word will compensate as it does in galley mode by making the lines on the screen longer. If you have more than one column or one or more absolutely positioned paragraphs, Word will still display the columns correctly; however, it will scale the ruler in order to fit all that is necessary to make the columns line up correctly. Word slides the ruler as you move from object to object. (See Rulers.)

Moving the cursor and selection in layout mode is similar to galley mode, although some of the rules are different because there may be more than one column on the screen or one or more absolutely positioned paragraphs on the page. The cursor movement rules are slightly different than in galley mode, but they are easy to understand.

Word considers each column or absolutely positioned paragraph to be an *object*, and its rules for moving around in layout mode are based on movement within and between objects. The cursor movement keys always move within an object before jumping to the next object; for example, if you have two columns and you press the Right Arrow many times, Word will move within the column rather than back and forth between the two columns.

The cursor control keys act differently when you get to the beginning or end of an object. The horizontal motion keys (Left Arrow, Right Arrow, Home, End, F7, F8, F9, and F10) move the cursor to the previous or next object as defined by the way the objects appear on the page in galley mode, and the vertical motion keys (Up Arrow, Down Arrow, Pg Up, and Pg Dn) move the cursor to the previous or next objects as they appear in layout mode. Thus, to move between objects as they appear on the screen, use the vertical motion keys; to move as if you were in galley mode, use the horizontal motion keys. There are two additional keys you can use in layout mode: Ctrl Tab moves directly to the next object, and Ctrl Shift Tab moves to the previous object.

Using Preview Mode   You cannot edit in preview mode, but you can page through your document quickly to check for page breaks and paragraph positions. When you enter preview mode, Word displays the page where the cursor was when you gave the command. Note that the font you see on the screen will not match the font or fonts you have specified; instead, it will be a single preview font scaled to different sizes.

There are a limited number of commands you can use in preview mode. Exit takes you out of preview mode and back to the mode in which you were previously; Jump allows you to jump to a specific page or bookmark; and Options lets you set whether you want to see one or two pages in preview mode. The Print command works similarly to the Print command in the other modes, although the only two options are Printer and Options. Word will repaginate the document if you change a print option that affects pagination (such as *hidden text* and *widow/orphan control*).

If you are using a mouse, you can scroll and thumb like you do in galley mode, although there is no scroll bar. To scroll with the keyboard, press

Pg Up and Pg Dn. Ctrl Pg Up and Ctrl Pg Dn will move you to the first and last pages of the document. The only other keys you can use are those that select preview commands, Alt H to get help, and any macros you have assigned to Ctrl key combinations.

To speed up scrolling and viewing in preview mode, give the **P**rint **O**ptions command and set *draft* to *Yes*. The graphics will not be displayed, although the borders for each graphic will still be shown. This can give you much faster performance, depending on the speed of your computer and the complexity of the graphics in your document.

Examples   Figure 44 shows a document in galley mode; the same document in layout mode is shown in Figure 45. Figure 46 shows the same part of the document in preview mode.

Tips   Don't be too concerned about the look of your document as you type it in. Use galley mode for entering text, and switch to layout mode when you start looking at the formatting. Using layout mode for entering text in

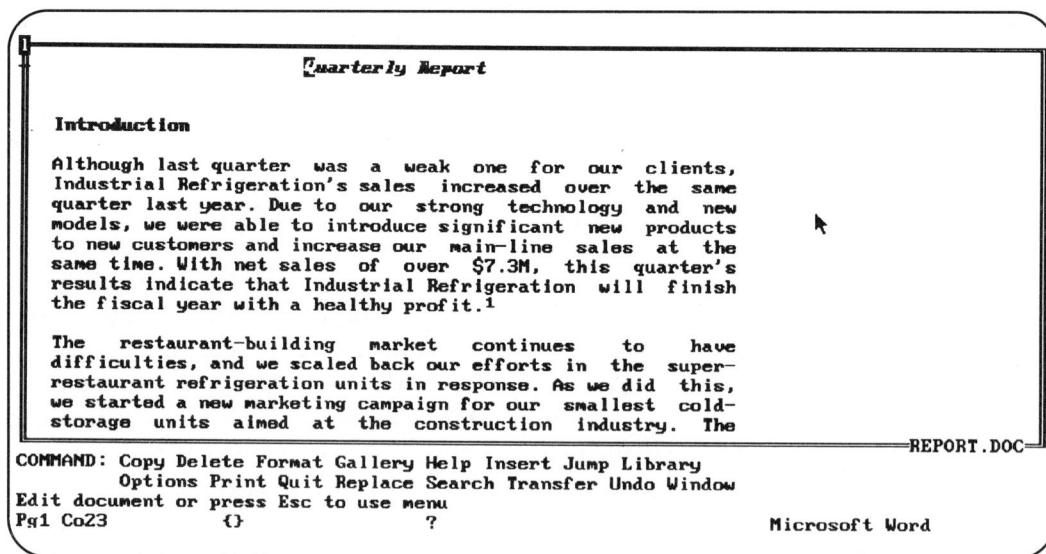

```
┌──────────────────────────────────────────────────────────────┐
│ ▌                                                              │
│ ▌               Quarterly Report                              │
│ ▌                                                              │
│ ▌  Introduction                                               │
│ ▌                                                              │
│ ▌  Although last quarter  was  a  weak  one  for  our  clients,│
│ ▌  Industrial Refrigeration's sales  increased  over  the  same│
│ ▌  quarter last year. Due to  our  strong  technology  and  new│
│ ▌  models, we were able to introduce significant  new  products│
│ ▌  to new customers and increase our  main-line  sales  at  the │
│ ▌  same time. With net sales  of  over  $7.3M,  this  quarter's │
│ ▌  results indicate that Industrial Refrigeration  will  finish │
│ ▌  the fiscal year with a healthy profit.1                     │
│ ▌                                                              │
│ ▌  The   restaurant-building   market   continues   to   have  │
│ ▌  difficulties, and we scaled back our efforts in  the  super-│
│ ▌  restaurant refrigeration units in response. As we did  this,│
│ ▌  we started a new marketing campaign for our  smallest  cold-│
│ ▌  storage  units  aimed  at  the  construction  industry.  The │
│                                                    ═REPORT.DOC═ │
│ COMMAND: Copy Delete Format Gallery Help Insert Jump Library    │
│          Options Print Quit Replace Search Transfer Undo Window │
│ Edit document or press Esc to use menu                         │
│ Pg1 Co23          {}                 ?          Microsoft Word  │
└──────────────────────────────────────────────────────────────┘
```

Figure 44

Figure 45

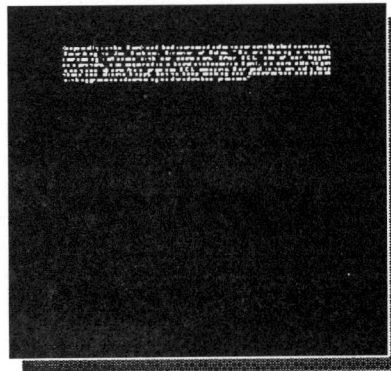

Figure 46

complex documents can slow down even the most powerful PC. Layout and preview modes are most appropriate for adding the finishing touches.

Layout mode works well with side-by-side paragraph styles. As you change the styles in the gallery, you can quickly switch back and see the effects in layout mode.

Word does not show running heads in layout mode. To see these, you must switch to preview mode.

Library Commands

Overview   The Library commands do not generally fit into the categories of editing or formatting. Originally, Microsoft put them under this category so that other manufacturers could add their own commands to the Library commands' menu. However, no one did that, so this menu is used for miscellaneous commands. Each command in the Library commands' menu is described in its own section in this book.

The Library commands and their locations in this book follow.

COMMAND	LOCATION
Autosort	See Sorting.
Document-retrieval	See Retrieving Documents.
Hyphenate	See Hyphenation.
Index	See Indexes.
Link	See Graphics and Spreadsheets.
Number	See Numbering.
Run	See MS-DOS Commands.
Spell	See Spelling.
Table	See Tables of Contents.
thEsaurus	See Thesaurus.

Line Drawing

Overview   Word uses the line drawing mode to create simple box drawings. Note that the printed output from this mode varies widely between different printers. When you use line drawing mode, Word draws lines on your screen using the PC's line drawing characters. Some printers can duplicate these characters fairly well, but others cannot. If you are simply drawing boxes or lines, you will usually be more successful if you use Word's border feature. (See Borders and Boxes.)

When in line drawing mode, pressing Up Arrow, Down Arrow, Left Arrow, Right Arrow, Home, and End directs Word to draw a line in that direction. If you change directions, Word draws a corner. When you exit line drawing mode, the line drawing characters in your document are just like characters you might have entered with the Alt key combinations. You can edit the characters in the usual way, but you should not format them since formatted line drawing characters might not line up correctly when printed. Line drawing characters should always be in a monospace font. (See Fonts.)

You have three choices for setting line drawing characters: single, double, and hyphen/bar. Figure 47 shows examples of each. You can also specify other characters for Word to use in line drawing mode, but Word will then use those for every direction and there will be no difference between vertical, horizontal, or corner characters. You can use the single-character mode for making very dark borders if your printer is capable of printing those characters.

After drawing the lines or boxes in line drawing mode, you can enter text in the usual way. If you want to put text in a box, draw the box, then type in the text in overtype mode. (See Inserting Text.) Since line drawing mode simply puts characters into your document, they will move around if you insert text before them.

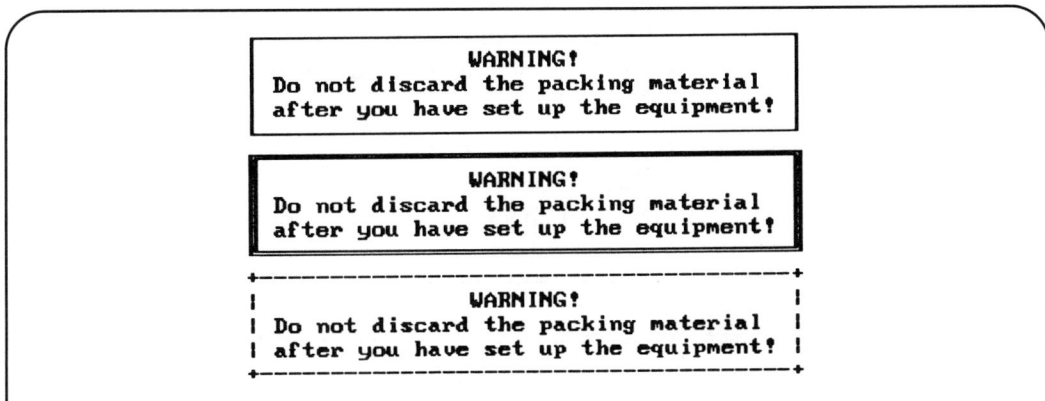

Figure 47

Procedure   Before entering line drawing mode, select the characters you want Word to use. Give the **O**ptions command, select the *linedraw character* field, and press F1. You will see the menu shown in Figure 48. The first three choices select sets of characters to use; the other choices specify individual characters. If you want to use some other character, type that character in the *linedraw character* field instead of pressing F1 in the **O**ptions command.

Press Ctrl F5 to enter or exit line drawing mode. Pressing the Escape key also causes Word to leave line drawing mode. When you are in line drawing mode, Word displays *LD* at the bottom of the screen. Pressing the Up Arrow or Down Arrow keys will draw vertical lines, and pressing the Left Arrow or Right Arrow keys will draw horizontal lines. You can use the Home and End keys to draw lines to the margins.

When you are finished, you can remove any of the characters you placed with the **D**elete command or by backspacing over the characters. You can also cut or copy the characters to the scrap.

You can change the character formatting (such as the font or size) of the line drawing characters in the gallery. (See Styles.) Give the **I**nsert command, in the *usage* field choose *Character*, in the variant field press F1 and choose *Line draw*, and then press Enter. Give the **F**ormat **C**haracter command and choose the character formatting you want. This changes the default character style for the line drawing characters.

Warnings   Printers vary widely in their ability to print line drawing characters. Some printers can print all of these characters; others print some or none. Thus, if you use the single- or double-line characters, you may not be able to print them on your printer. Note, however, that these characters form much better looking boxes than do the plain characters.

Tips   For best results, set the *visible* (version 4) or *show non-printing symbols* (version 5) field of the **O**ptions command to *None* and the *show hidden text* field to *No*. This will help you check the alignment of the lines. Be sure the

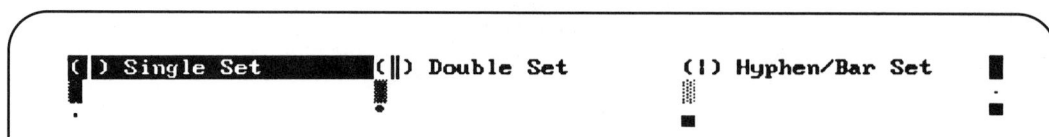

Figure 48

paragraph in which you start line drawing is left-aligned with no indentation. Select a monospace font such as Courier.

If you plan to produce corporate charts and graphs, consider purchasing a graphics package that performs these tasks. Such packages often produce superior quality pictures, and the output can often be used directly in Word. (See Graphics.)

Line Numbering

Overview   Lawyers preparing pleadings and motions often need to number the lines of their documents. This is often called *pleading numbering* since it is rarely used for any other purpose. The Format Division line-Numbers command lets you print out divisions with pleading numbering.

Word gives you a great deal of flexibility in determining the look of divisions that have numbered lines. You can choose to number each line or only some increment, such as every fifth line. You can place the numbers close to or far away from your text, and you can even change the formatting for the line numbers.

Procedure   Select the division you want to number and give the Format Division line-Numbers command. Change the first field to *Yes* to turn line numbering on for this division. Set *from text* to the amount of space you want between the left margin and the right side of the numbers; avoid setting this too high or the numbers will run off the left side of the page.

Set the *increments* field to the frequency you want the line numbers. For example, if you set *increments* to 10, Word will only display line numbers for lines 10, 20, 30, and so on. For most pleadings, the increment should be set to 1. Set *restart at* to either *Division* or *Continuous* if you do not want the line numbers to be reset to 1 at the top of each page.

Since Word numbers all the lines in the selected division, you should put the section of your document that will be numbered in its own division. Enter a division mark by pressing Ctrl Enter before and after the part that will be numbered. Note that most lawyers prefer that the cover page and the signature page be unnumbered.

You can set the style for the line numbers separate from the style of the text in your document; you will probably want to use Courier or some other monospace font for the line numbers. You can also use the gallery's predefined character style called Line Number for the line numbers that are applied by the **F**ormat **D**ivision line-**N**umbers command. Specify the character formatting you want for the line numbers in this style.

Examples   Figure 49 shows the printout of a page with pleading numbering. The settings in the **F**ormat **D**ivision line-**N**umbers command were the default (.4 inches from the text, restart at every page).

Warnings   Most courts have specific rules about pleading numbering. It is very rare for a court to allow only every fifth or tenth line to be numbered. Generally, each line is numbered to provide easy reference during oral arguments. It is also rare for courts to allow line numbering to continue from page to page. Thus, you should probably leave the defaults for *restart at* and *increments* set to *Page* and *1*.

Do not set the value of *from text* too high since the numbers might not fit on the page. Word will truncate the numbers on the left, which can cause incorrect numbering. Be sure to leave enough space for the largest number you might have.

Tips   Empty lines caused by paragraph formatting are not counted when Word numbers lines. If you want white space in your document to have its own line numbers, add extra blank paragraphs to your document instead of using the *space after* field in the **F**ormat **P**aragraph command. Note that the blank lines created by paragraph formatting in Figure 49 do not increase the line number count.

```
 1              In Pacific Intermountain Express Co. v. Acme

 2      Carriers, Inc., 30 F.R.D. 525 (S.D.N.Y. 1962), plaintiff

 3      moved for an order requiring defendant's president to answer

 4      deposition question which sought to clarify the allegation

 5      of defendant's counterclaims. Granting this motion, the

 6      court cited Moore's discussion approving the use of

 7      contention interrogatories as a mechanism enabling the

 8      parties "to find out what the case against [them] is about."

 9      Id. at 526, quoting 4 J. Moore, Moore's Federal Practice

10      section 33.17 at 2311-12 (2d ed. 1987). The court explicitly

11      observed that "[t]his discussion of the scope of

12      interrogatories, of course, applies to deposition upon oral

13      examination." Id. fn 3. In Cutler v. Lewiston Daily Sun, 105

14      F.R.D. 137, 142-43 (D. Me. 1985), the court noted that

15      deposition questions seeking the witness's opinion on

16      significant legal issues in the case are proper and should

17      be answered.

18              Cases in the analogous area of patent infringement

19      are particularly informative on this point. In this context,

20      the courts have frequently ruled that a party seeking

21      discovery may require its opponent to state exactly what its

22      claims are. Babcock & Wilcox Co. v. Foster Wheeler Corp., 54

23      F.R.D. 474, 478 (D.N.J. 1971) and cases cited therein.

24      Defendant is entitled to ascertain the exact nature of

25      plaintiff's claim by asking which part of plaintiff's patent

26      plaintiff will claim  defendant incorporated into his
```

Figure 49

Linking Documents

Overview   If many people work together on a single document, you may find that it is difficult to coordinate all the people's writing. If each person is responsible for an individual part of the document, it would be a good idea to have each person work in his or her own file and to link all the documents together. Of course, you would want these links to reflect the latest versions of each person's documents.

Word's **Library Link D**ocument command gives you this capability. The command copies a marked portion of another Word document into the current document and leaves a tracer so that it can update the information in the future. The desired portion is marked with a bookmark. (See Bookmarks.) You use the command to create a master document that contains copies of parts of other documents. Another common use of the **Library Link D**ocument command is to create compilations of other documents, where the entire document that is linked is copied in. It works much like the **Library Link G**raphics and **Library Link S**preadsheet commands.

Procedure   Put the cursor where you want the linked information to appear. The linked information must start at the beginning of a new paragraph. Give the **Library Link D**ocument command, which prompts for the name of the file and the bookmark. If you leave the *bookmark* field blank, Word will use the entire file.

When you press Enter, Word reads the document, finds the bookmark if one is specified, and copies the text to your document. Word surrounds the data with hidden tag text so that it knows that the data is to be updated when you open the file again. The leader tag text consists of a leading hidden paragraph with ".D.*filename,bookmark*," and the trailer tag consists of a hidden paragraph with ".D.". You can see these tags if you set *show hidden text* to *Yes* in the **W**indow **O**ptions command (version 4) or the **O**ptions command (version 5). If you later want to move the spreadsheet data to some other part of your document, be sure to move the two tags with it.

To update the information in a linked document, select the entire range in which the data resides and give the **Library Link D**ocument command again. Don't fill in the fields; simply press Enter. Word prompts *Enter Y to update, N to skip, or Esc to cancel*. Press Y, and Word updates the information. If you select more than one linked document in your document, Word prompts you for each one. Thus, you can bring all the linked documents in a document up to date by selecting the entire document and giving the Library Link Document command.

To unlink a master document from the linked file, simply delete the header and trailer tags. Word then views the data just like data you entered manually. To relink it, delete the data and give the Library Link Document command again, specifying the document name and bookmark.

Lists

Overview

Many documents contain various kinds of lists; Word makes it easy to create attractive lists.

There are three types of lists in standard style: numbered, bulleted, and plain. Each element in a numbered list is preceded by a number, and the numbers are sequentially ordered. The numbers may be in parentheses, followed by a period, or some other delineation. Bulleted lists have a bullet mark (such as •, *, or —) before each element. Plain lists have no mark preceding the elements.

Lists can have lists within them. Figure 50 shows a bulleted list with numbered lists nested beneath some elements.

- Determine who has funding

- Send letters

    1. Call each recipient first

    2. Check nick names

    3. Get sponsor's signature

- Follow up

    1. Call recipient again

    2. Verify all information

- Report to Accounting Department

Figure 50

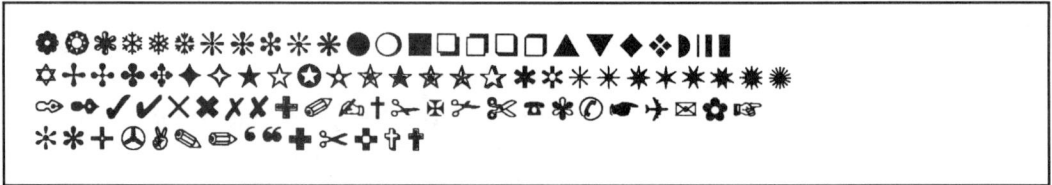

Figure 51

Tips   Lists often have paragraph formatting to differentiate them from regular paragraphs. Numbered and bulleted lists usually have a hanging outdent with a tab stop at the same position as the left indent. In the previous example, the left indent and the first indent for the bulleted list is .25 inches. Alternately, you could have a right tab for the number or bullet and another for the left indent. This causes multi-digit numbers to align on their right sides.

   If you are printing with a laser printer, you might have fonts that contain many different types of bullets. These fonts are often called "Symbol" or "Dingbats." Some of the bullets available in the Zapf Dingbats font are shown in Figure 51.

   You can use Word to sort lists (see Sorting) and to have Word add numbers to list elements (see Numbering).

Loading Documents.   *See* **Transfer Command**

Macros

Overview   If you use Word often, you have probably noticed that you often repeat many steps. For example, you might often indent a paragraph and make the first word in the paragraph bold, or you might print only the first page of a dozen different documents. Whenever you find yourself repeating an action, consider creating a macro that describes the steps you are repeating. Note that you cannot put mouse actions into macros.

   A macro is a glossary entry that contains Word instructions instead of text to be inserted in your document. You can create a macro by having Word record your actions, or you can type your actions in a shorthand and

110

save the text in the macro. Either way, you can later edit your macro to change the action (for example, if you make a mistake when recording) or to add other actions to a macro.

When creating a macro, you give it a name with a maximum of 31 characters. Like glossary names, macro names are limited to letters, numbers, underscores, periods, and hyphens. The name must begin with either a letter or number, and you cannot have a space. You can then execute the macro by name or choose it from a list.

You can also assign a key combination to a macro. After loading the glossary that contains the macro, pressing the assigned key combination (such as Ctrl A or Shift Ctrl C) causes Word to execute the macro. You can even assign a key combination that Word already uses to a macro; this directs Word to execute the macro instead of the action Word would normally take. For example, most people use the **Jump P**age command more often than the overtype mode. You could make a macro to perform the **Jump P**age command and assign it to F5. You can still get to overtype mode with a different key sequence.

Macros can be used for a very wide variety of purposes, the most common of which is combining many keystrokes into one. However, you can also use macros to perform actions requiring many Word commands that are difficult to remember. If you are helping novice Word users, you can set up macros to simplify some of their tasks and to make difficult actions easier. You can even write a macro that automatically executes at the beginning of each Word session.

You can add special commands to macros that will greatly enhance their usefulness. For example, some macro commands allow you to loop in your macro until a certain condition is met. Thus, you can construct a macro that performs an action on each line of a document and execute the macro just once for the entire document.

Word comes packaged with many macros that Microsoft has created both to demonstrate the power of macros and to help you create your own. These macros are stored in the file MACRO.GLY. To use them, use the **Transfer Glossary Load** command to load MACRO.GLY. Note that some of Microsoft's macros do not always work as expected.

Procedure   **Recording a Macro**   The easiest way to create a macro is to have Word record your steps into a new macro. To start recording, press Shift F3. Word displays *RM* at the bottom of the screen. Perform the steps you want

111

in the macro (such as moving around, giving commands, entering text, and so on), and press Shift F3 again to stop recording. Word executes the Copy command and prompts *to:* {}. Type the name that you want to give the macro and press Enter.

You will probably make mistakes the first few times you try to record a macro. If so, simply press Shift F3 and press the Escape key when Word prompts *to:* {}. This cancels the recording and does not save the macro.

Typing in a Macro   The other method for creating a macro is to type it into a document in a special format, select the macro, and give the **Delete** command. When Word prompts *to:* {}, enter the name you want for the macro, and press Enter. Thus, you type characters into whatever document you are working on at the time, select those characters, and delete them to a new macro name.

Since you cannot "type" keyboard actions such as Down Arrow or pressing the Escape key, you need to enter them in a special format. All key actions can be entered by putting them in angle brackets (< and >) and spelling out the key names. For example, to indicate pressing the Down Arrow key, enter <down>. To indicate giving the **Transfer Save** command, enter <esc>TS<enter>.

Word does not distinguish between uppercase and lowercase letters in key names. Thus, you can use <down> or <DOWN>. The key names are mostly identical to what you would expect: <alt>, <backspace>, <capslock>, <ctrl>, <del>, <down>, <end>, <enter>, <esc>, <home>, <ins>, <left>, <numlock>, <pgdn>, <pgup>, <right>, <scrolllock>, <shift>, <tab>, and <up>. Function keys are also indicated as you would expect: <f3>. A combination such as Ctrl F5 is indicated by <ctrl f5>.

Use <keypad*>, <keypad+>, and <keypad-> to get the symbols on the keypad. To indicate pressing the Space Bar when selecting fields in a dialog, enter <space>. For example, to select *Text-only* in the *format* field of the **Transfer Save** command, type <esc>TS<tab><space><enter>.

You can use special shortcuts for some repeated keys when typing in a macro. For <backspace>, <del>, <down>, <enter>, <esc>, <ins>, <left>, <pgdn>, <pgup>, <right>, <tab>, and <up>, you can add a space and a number in the angle brackets to indicate the number of times the key should be pressed. For example, to indicate pressing Right Arrow four times, type <right 4>.

Note that you can add paragraph marks and newline characters to your macro for clarity. If a macro runs longer than one line and you want to make it more readable, simply put a paragraph mark in the middle. Word ignores these characters.

Naming a Macro   When Word prompts for the macro name, enter any name that is not already in the glossary. If you want to assign a key combination to the macro, follow the name with a caret (^) and the key name. You can use any function key or function key combination, a Ctrl key, or a Ctrl key followed by one or two characters. You must enter the key name in angle brackets, as described above. For example, to name a macro "select_5" and make it executable by pressing Ctrl F, type select_5^<ctrl f>.

If you enter a macro name that already exists in the glossary, Word asks if you want to overwrite the current glossary entry, give a different name, or cancel the save. If you enter a key sequence that is already defined, Word prompts *Duplicate macro code* and lets you enter a different key sequence. If you give a macro a key sequence (such as redefining a function key) that is already used by Word, you can no longer access that key directly. Instead, you must press Ctrl X first, then the desired key. Thus, you must press Ctrl X F5 if you define a macro with the key sequence F5 and later want to go into overtype mode.

Running a Macro   To run a macro, type the macro's name and press F3. You can also give the Insert command, press F1, select the macro name from the list, and press Enter. You can interrupt a running macro by pressing the Escape key. If a macro has a key combination in its name, you can run the macro by pressing those keys.

You can test the macro by having Word execute the macro one step at a time. To have Word run macros in step mode, press Ctrl F3. Word displays *ST* at the bottom of the screen. When running a macro, Word only executes one step; press any key to have Word execute the next step. Keep pressing any key to see the steps the macro is taking. To stop execution in step mode, press the Escape key. To get out of step mode, press Ctrl F3; if you do this while Word is executing a macro, the macro will finish in the usual way.

Editing a Macro   To view or edit a macro, you must first insert it into a document. You can start a new document for this, or you can simply insert it into your current document and remove it later. To insert a macro's text, give the Insert command, press F1, select the macro's name, type ^, and press Enter. If you know the macro's name, simply type the name in the document, insert ^ after the name, and press F3.

You can edit the macro just as you would edit normal text. When you are finished, you must put it back in the glossary, replacing the old macro. Select the text and give the **D**elete command. When Word prompts *DELETE to* {}, type in the macro's name and keycode and press Enter. Word asks if you want to overwrite the current entry; press Y.

Macro Instructions   You can use macro instructions to control the way your macro runs. Macro instructions can help make macros more responsive to users by asking questions or checking the contents of the selection or scrap. Macro instructions are similar to Word's merge instructions. (See Form Letters.) To include an instruction in your macro, you must enclose the instruction in chevrons (« and »), which are typed by pressing Ctrl [and Ctrl].

Many macro commands use macro variables, which are described below. The macro commands and their uses follow.

COMMAND	USE
«COMMENT *text*»	Places a comment in the macro but does not have any effect. The comment can help you later recall the macro's purpose. You can also include a comment with «COMMENT»*text*«ENDCOMMENT».
«MESSAGE *text*»	Displays a message (maximum of 80 characters) in the message line near the bottom of the screen. The message remains until another MESSAGE command is given or until Word puts a message of its own in that line. This command will not display anything if you do not have menus showing.
«REPEAT *number*»	Repeats the specified number of times all steps between the REPEAT command and the ENDREPEAT command.
«PAUSE *prompt*»	Suspends the macro so that you can perform actions such as entering text or responses, or selecting text. Word resumes macro execution when you press Enter.

COMMAND	USE
«SET *variable = expression*»	Sets a variable to a value. The expression can be the name of another variable, a number, a date, or text enclosed in quotes. If you want to set a variable to be the contents of two or more variables, simply list them as the expression with spaces between each variable name.
«SET *variable = ?*»	Asks you for a value for the named variable. Word displays *Enter text, press Enter when done* in the message area near the bottom of the screen.
«ASK *variable = ?*»	Same as «SET *variable = ?*».
«SET *variable = ?prompt*»	Prompts you for a value for the named variable and displays the prompt you specify in the message area near the bottom of the screen.
«ASK *variable = ?prompt*»	Same as «SET *variable = ?prompt*».
«IF *condition*»	Checks whether the condition is true; if so, Word executes the following commands up to the «ENDIF» statement. Conditions are described below. If the IF command is followed by an «ELSE» statement, this checks whether the condition is true; if so, Word executes the following commands up to the «ELSE» statement. If the condition is false, Word executes the commands between the «ELSE» statement and «ENDIF» statement.
«QUIT»	Stops a macro. This is generally used as part of an IF command to stop a macro after a condition is no longer true.
«WHILE *condition*»	Repeats all the instructions after the WHILE command up to the «ENDWHILE» statement as long as the condition is true

Macro variables hold values that can be tested later in conditions in the IF or WHILE commands. A variable has a name and a value. The name can be a maximum of 64 characters. You can use letters and numbers, but the first character in the variable name must be a letter. Underscores, hyphens, or periods are not allowed. A variable value can be text, a number, or a date.

The macro below uses variables in the prompts for the macro commands.

```
«SET newfont = "Courier"»
<alt f8>«newfont»<enter>
```

When executed, this macro sets the font of the selected characters to Courier.

Macro conditions are tests on a variable value. A condition is usually given in the form *variable operator variable* or *variable operator value*. An operator is a logical math operator that compares the value of the variable on the left to either the value of the variable or to the direct value on the right. The operators are =, < > (not equal), <, >, < =, and > =. A value on the right side of an operator can be a number, a date, or text in quotation marks.

For example, an IF command might be "«IF answer = "Y"»", meaning that the condition is true if the value of the variable called "answer" is "Y." An example of comparing two numeric variables called "lines" and "wanted" might be "«IF lines > = wanted»"; this condition is true if the number in "lines" is greater than or equal to the number in "wanted."

Word provides many special variables that it uses automatically to enhance macro usefulness. These variables are listed below.

VARIABLE	VALUE
echo	(Version 5 only). Whether or not to display updates to the screen from macro actions. If you want to make your macro run faster, set the echo variable to "off" with the SET command; Word will not update the screen until the end of the macro or until you set the echo variable to "on."
field	The value of the selected field in a dialog. For example, if your macro gave a **F**ormat **C**haracter command followed by a Tab character, this variable would be equal to "Yes" if the selected text was italic or "No" if it was not.
promptmode	(Version 5 only). How Word expects prompts to be answered. You can set this to *"user"* if you want the user to respond to prompts; to *"macro"* if you want the macro to respond to the prompts; or to *"ignore"* to have Word ignore any prompts that appear. Unless you specify, Word assumes that the prompts will be responded to by the macro.
scrap	The contents of the scrap. Special characters such as paragraph marks and tab characters are indicated as they are in the **S**earch command. (See Searching.)
selection	The contents of the selection. Special characters such as paragraph marks and tab characters are indicated as they are in the **S**earch command. (See Searching.) You can test whether you are at the end of the file by seeing if this variable is equal to nothing (that is, " ").

VARIABLE	VALUE
window	(Version 5 only). The number of the window. You can use this in two ways: to move the cursor to a specific window, use the SET command, such as "«SET window = 4»"; to determine which window you are in, use the window variable with the IF command: "«IF window = 2»."
wordversion	The version of Word you are running (version 5 only). You can use this to detect if you are running version 5.
zoomedwindow	Whether or not the current window is zoomed. (See Windows.)

You can determine if the last search operation was successful by using the special "found" and "notfound" key instead of a condition. For example, use the "«IF found»" command to check whether the last search was a success.

In version 5, you can use the "save" key word to detect whether the

```
«IF save»<esc>ts<enter>«ENDIF»
```

A condition can also be in the *variable operator expression* form, where "expression" indicates a mathematical formula. For example, if you have variables called "count" and "total," you might have a command like "«IF count = total*2»". You can combine conditions with the OR, AND, and NOT logical connectors. For example, to find if a date variable you have set is between two dates, you might use "«IF billdate > 6/1/89 AND billdate < 6/8/89»".

An expression can also contain macro functions in version 5. Functions determine characteristics of variables or other expressions and are in parentheses after the function name. The available functions are listed below.

FUNCTION	VALUE
int(*number*)	Truncates the number to the next smallest integer
len(*text*)	Gives the number of characters in the text
mid(*text, startpos, count*)	Extracts characters from a string. This function results in the characters beginning with the "startpos" and will be "count" characters long. For example, if the variable "holder" contains "Jerome Miller", then mid(holder, 3, 6) has the value "rome M".

In version 5, you can use variables in the prompt and message strings. For example, you might have a message that uses the field variable such as "«MESSAGE The value is now «field». Do you want to change it?»".

117

Other Macro Topics Almost every command works in its usual way when executed from a macro. The only exception is the **Library Run** command. (See MS-DOS Commands.) Normally, Word displays *Press any key to resume Word* after executing the MS-DOS command. In a macro, however, the command continues automatically and you need not press a key.

If your macro uses a caret, you must use two carets. For example, a macro that searches for a paragraph mark would be <esc>s^^p<enter>. You must precede the character with a caret if you want to indicate an angle bracket, a chevron, or a caret. Thus, to enter a right chevron in the text, your macro would include ^».

You can run one macro in another, just as if you had executed the macro from within Word. To run a macro from within a macro, use any of the methods for running a macro listed above (the Insert command, the name followed by pressing F3, or the key combination assigned to the macro). This is called *nesting* macros. If you have a macro that sorts a table in a particular way and you are writing a macro that cleans up a document before printing it, the cleanup macro can call the sorting macro by name. You can nest macros up to sixteen levels.

If a glossary contains a macro named "autoexec," Word will execute that macro when the glossary is loaded or merged. Thus, if there are commands you want executed each time you run Word, make those commands into a macro and put them into a macro called "autoexec" in your NORMAL.GLY file.

Since you can run a macro while entering text or during command mode (that is, after you have pressed the Escape key and are choosing commands), you must be careful about the initial keys that are in your macro. For example, assume you have a command that gives the **Transfer Save** command (<esc>ts<enter>). If you are in command mode when you give this command, Word exits command mode (from the Esc) and types "ts" followed by a paragraph mark in your document. Since you cannot tell what mode you are in when you start, you can use a special key combination to always put you into command mode. To be sure you go to command mode, use <ctrl esc> instead of <esc>. In version 5, <Ctrl Shift Esc><esc> always starts the macro, regardless of the mode you are in.

Examples   As you are typing in tables, you might want to copy the word from the line above and insert it on the current line. To do so, go up a line, select the next word, copy it to the scrap, return to where you were typing, and insert from the scrap. The following macro would perform those actions:

```
<up><f8><esc>c<enter><down><insert>
```

If you were editing this macro, you could add a comment that describes the macro's action:

```
«Comment Copy a word from the previous line and insert it»
<up><f8><esc>c<enter><down><insert>
```

The REPEAT command is useful for repeating a set of actions a predetermined number of times. For example, if you want to make the first word on each line italicized for a certain number of lines, use the ASK command to get the number and the REPEAT command to perform the looping:

```
«ASK loop = ?How many lines do you want?»
«REPEAT loop»<home><f8><ctrl esc>fc
<tab>y<enter><down>«ENDREPEAT»
```

You can use the WHILE command to check the status of the macro as it executes. For example, assume that you have a style called "LI" used for list items and you want to find each paragraph with this style and put two hyphens at the beginning of the paragraph. The macro would be as follows:

```
<ctrl pgup><esc>fesli<enter>
«WHILE found»<home>--<f10><shift f4>«ENDWHILE»
```

The first line does the initial find. The first time the WHILE command is executed, it checks whether the search was successful. If so, the macro goes to the beginning of the paragraph, types in the two hyphens, selects the whole paragraph (in order for the next find to go beyond this paragraph), and tells Word to repeat the search. Each time the WHILE command is executed, it checks whether the search was successful; if it was not, the macro stops.

You can use the IF command to enhance the previous macro. For example, you may have already added hyphens to some but not all of the paragraphs. The following macro adds hyphens where required:

```
<ctrl pgup><esc>fesli<enter>
«WHILE found»<home><shift right>
«IF selection = "--"»«COMMENT Do nothing»«ELSE»--«ENDIF»
<f10><shift f4>«ENDWHILE»
```

The **R**eplace command in Word replaces only from the current position to the end of the file. The following macro replaces throughout the file without losing your place. This macro, which only works in version 5, would be as follows:

```
«SET sea = ?Search for:»«SET repl = ?Replace with:»
«IF len(selection) = 1»«COMMENT check for selection»
<esc>fksearchrepholder<enter>«COMMENT put down a bookmark»
<ctrl pgup><esc>r«sea»<tab>«repl»<tab>n<enter>
<esc>jksearchrepholder<enter><esc>fk«COMMENT jump back to it»
«ELSE»<esc>r«sea»<tab>«repl»<tab>n<enter>«ENDIF»
```

Warnings   Do not confuse angle brackets (< and >) with chevrons (« and ») in your macros. Angle brackets are used to set off key names; chevrons are used to set off macro commands.

You cannot have either a **T**ransfer **G**lossary **C**lear command or a **T**ransfer **C**lear **A**ll command in a macro since such a command would wipe out the macro that is running. Word ignores such a command in your macros.

If you have a macro called "autoexec" in any glossary file, that macro automatically executes when you load or merge the glossary. This can cause havoc if you have commands in the macro that delete text or add formatting. Generally, you should have an "autoexec" macro only in your NORMAL.GLY file.

Since some of the command dialogs in version 5 have more options than the dialogs in version 4, some macros written for version 4 may not work correctly under version 5. This is especially true of macros that use "< shift tab >" to select fields at the end of dialogs.

Tips   Always put comments in your macros so that you'll later know their purpose. If you are preparing macros for other users, comments help them figure out how they can modify the macros.

If you are converting from version 4, you will notice that many of your old macros do not work. This is due to options changing or moving from one position to another. To convert a version 4 macro to version 5, use the MACROCNV program supplied in version 5. The program will prompt you for the names of the glossary files to convert. Alternately, you may enter the names of the glossary files on the MS-DOS command line for MACROCNV; wildcard characters are acceptable here. Follow the screen prompts for the conversion. There is also an extensive document called MACROCNV.DOC that lists the types of conversions that the program makes.

When naming macros, you may want to add a tag to the name to indicate that the entry is a macro and not a glossary. Microsoft recommends adding ".mac" to the end of the name, although this can be cumbersome. If you add "M." to the beginning of all macro names, they will be grouped together when you press F1 at the Insert command, and will stand out from the glossary names. Add "Z." to the beginning of the names if you want all the macros to be at the end of the enumerated list.

Look at the contents as described above if a macro does not act the way you want. If everything seems correct, try running the macro in step mode. This will enable you to see if you forgot a step, made an incorrect assumption about what a command would do, or discover the mode you are in when the command is given.

When you run macros that include Word commands, Word shows each menu that it is executing. Depending on the speed of your computer, this can significantly slow down the execution of the macro. You may want to turn off the menu display before running the macro or turn it off at the beginning of the macro and turn it on again at the end. Set the *menu* or *show menu* field in the Options command to *No* to prevent the menus from being displayed.

In version 5, you can repeat the last macro by pressing F4. (In version 4, pressing F4 repeats the last instruction in the macro.)

Mailing Labels

Overview   You can create mailing labels with Word using its form letter capabilities. (See Form Letters.) The instructions here cover many kinds of labels; however, there are dozens of brands, many with slight differences in size and shape. Also, some printers handle mailing labels better than others. You will most likely need many trial runs before your labels print out to your satisfaction.

Printing labels can be tricky because you need to know in advance if the types of labels you are using are continuous feed or sheet feed, and whether your labels have one or three labels across. Also, you must set your margins so that Word prints as many labels on the page as possible (this is sometimes difficult with laser printers). Generally, you should use continuous-feed labels on daisy wheel and dot-matrix printers so that the labels will align properly. You should generally use three-across sheet-feed labels on laser printers.

Procedure   The data document for mailing labels has six fields: name, address1, address2, city, state, and zip. This allows for two lines of addresses, such as company name and street address or street address and suite number. If an address does not need both lines, leave the address2 field blank.

The method for setting up the main document depends on the type of labels and whether the labels are sheet feed or continuous. However, the printing portion of the main document is the same for all documents:

```
«name»
«address1»
«IF address2»«address2»
«ENDIF»«city», «state» «zip»
«IF address2»
«ENDIF»
```

For each label, Word prints the name field and address1 field on lines by themselves. The first IF command checks whether there is anything in address2. If so, Word prints it on a line by itself, but does not print anything if the field is empty. It then prints city, state, and zip on a line by themselves. The second IF command checks if address2 is empty; if so, Word prints a blank line. This ensures that each label has exactly four lines in it and that there is no gap between address1 and the city line if address2 is empty.

In these labels, the reason the name field is on the same line as the DATA or NEXT instructions is so that no paragraph mark appears before the first line of each record printed. This is also the reason that there is no paragraph mark between the second ENDIF instruction and the end of file marker.

Continuous-Feed Labels   If you are using continuous-feed labels, set up the margins so that each label is a "page." Thus, you set the page length to 1 in or the height of your label. The settings for the **Format Division Margins** command for 3.5-inch wide by 1-inch-high labels are listed below.

FIELD	VALUE
top	0 in
left	.1 in
right	0 in
page length	1 in
width	3.5 in

The left margin of .1 inch sets the first character of the label close to the edge of the label; adjust this to suit your preference. Figure 52 shows the main document for continuous-feed, 1-across labels.

Figure 53 shows the main document for continuous-feed, 3-across labels. Note that this uses the NEXT command to get the second and third records for the lines across the page. There are three divisions, each with a label. Select all three divisions, give the **Format Division Layout** command, set the *number of columns* field to 3, the *space between columns* field to 0, and the *division break* to *Column*. This creates three labels in three columns in your 1-inch-high pages.

Sheet-Feed Labels   Since most laser printers do not let you print to the edges of the paper, the top and bottom rows of labels are wasted and you cannot get very near the edge on regular labels. For 3-across 1-inch sheet-feed labels, you must have all 27 available labels in your main documents. The top part of the main document looks like Figure 54. To make the main document, enter the label with the DATA instruction followed by 26 copies of the label with the NEXT instructions.

```
«DATA MLLIST.DAT»«name»
«address1»
«IF address2»«address2»
«ENDIF»«city», «state»   «zip»
«IF address2»
«ENDIF»
```

Figure 52

M

```
«DATA MLLIST.DAT»«name»
«address1»
«IF address2»«address2»
«ENDIF»«city», «state»   «zip»
«IF address2»
«ENDIF»
:::::::::::::::::::::::::::::::::::::::::::::::::::
«NEXT»«name»
«address1»
«IF address2»«address2»
«ENDIF»«city», «state»
«zip»
«IF address2»
«ENDIF»
:::::::::::::::::::::::::::::::::::::::::::::::::::
«NEXT»«name»
«address1»
«IF address2»«address2»
«ENDIF»«city», «state»   «zip»
«IF address2»
«ENDIF»
```

Figure 53

The margins you set depend on whether your printer driver takes into account the area at the edge of the document. On most printer drivers, Word takes this into account, so you need not change the page length and width in the Format Division Margins command. Thus, for 1-inch labels, you would format the division as follows:

FIELD	VALUE
top	1 in
bottom	1 in
left	.25 in
right	.25 in
page length	11 in
width	8.5 in

In the Format Division Layout command, set the *number of columns* field to 3 and the *space between columns* field to 0.

124

```
«DATA MLLIST.DAT»«name»
«address1»
«IF address2»«address2»
«ENDIF»«city», «state»   «zip»
«IF address2»
«ENDIF»
:::::::::::::::::::::::::::::::::::::::::::
«NEXT»«name»
«address1»
«IF address2»«address2»
«ENDIF»«city», «state»
«zip»
«IF address2»
«ENDIF»
:::::::::::::::::::::::::::::::::::::::::::
«NEXT»«name»
«address1»
«IF address2»«address2»
«ENDIF»«city», «state»   «zip»
«IF address2»
«ENDIF»
```

Figure 54

Some manufacturers make sheet-feed labels specifically for laser printers. These have .5-inch margins on all sides. See the manufacturer's suggestions for setting up the labels.

Tips

You will probably need to experiment a fair amount before getting your mailing labels to print correctly. Allocate at least one hour and many pages of labels for testing each printer.

To move down the text in a mailing label (for example, to vertically center the text), create a header that appears in the label. In mailing labels, the distance from the top is always 0. Add the header as the first line in the label and use the Format Paragraph command to set the height of the line to get the desired vertical displacement of the text.

Margins

Overview   Setting the margins for a page is usually a straightforward task. Simply determine the text area of your page and set the margins accordingly. When you decide on the margins, leave enough room for the running heads so that they are not too close to either the edge of the page or to the text.

Whether you are going to copy your document onto both sides of a piece of paper and bind it, you must determine how much space to leave for the *gutter*, which is the extra space left for the binding. The gutter is added to the right margin of even-numbered pages and to the left margin of odd-numbered pages. If you are three-hole punching the paper, use a gutter of .625 inches. For other types of binding, determine how much space is taken up by the binding itself and how much extra visual space to add if the pages do not lie flat when the document is opened in the middle. Word adds the gutter automatically so you need not adjust the left and right margins if a gutter is required.

Procedure   To set the margins, use the **Format Division Margins** command shown in Figure 55. Set the *top, bottom, left*, and *right* fields to the amount you wish. If your document will be copied to both sides of a page, set the *gutter margin* field to the amount you want to leave.

You also use the **Format Division Margins** command to set the page length and width. Be sure to set this to the size of printable area of your printer, even if you want your page size to be smaller than the paper you are using. Word sometimes produces unexpected results if you set the page length to something other than the paper size.

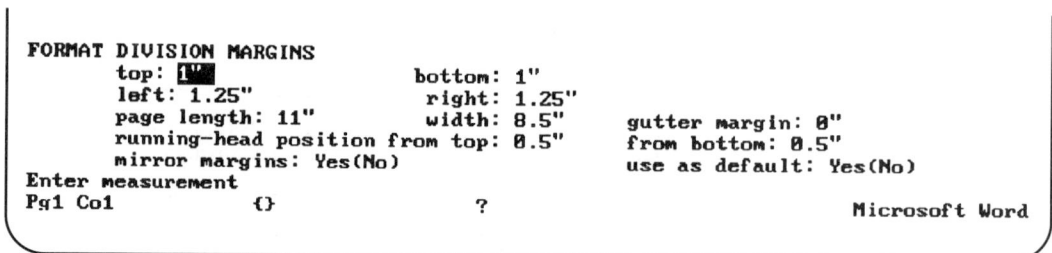

```
FORMAT DIVISION MARGINS
        top: 1"                  bottom: 1"
        left: 1.25"               right: 1.25"
        page length: 11"          width: 8.5"        gutter margin: 0"
        running-head position from top: 0.5"         from bottom: 0.5"
        mirror margins: Yes(No)                      use as default: Yes(No)
Enter measurement
Pg1 Co1              {}                  ?                      Microsoft Word
```

Figure 55

Examples   If you are preparing a booklet that will have pages 5.5 inches wide by 8.5 inches high but are printing on 8.5-inch by 11-inch paper, set the right margin 3 inches wider than the margin you want in the booklet and the bottom margin 2.5 inches taller than the bottom margin you want in the booklet; set the left and top margins as you want them in the booklet. Word will print a small page in the upper-left corner of your paper.

Warnings   Some printers, especially laser printers, do not let you print to the edge of the paper. If you leave the page width and length set to the full size of the paper, Word may not center the available text on the page. If this occurs, consult your printer's user manual for the printer's available print area and set the page width and length accordingly. There are bugs in some of Word's printer drivers, so this adjustment may not always work exactly. You will probably need to experiment to get a full page of text perfectly centered horizontally and vertically.

Tips   Pages with a single-wide column of text usually have equal left and right margins. For pages with headings in the left column and text on the right (such as in this book), some designers use wider margins on the right than on the left to leave more white space and therefore give a better visual balance to the page. If you have a header but no footer, you may want a smaller margin at the bottom of the page.

If your printer has a landscape mode and your pages are 5.5 inches or less, you can print two smaller pages on a sheet of paper by feeding the paper through the printer twice. Set the gutter to a negative number to align the two pages as desired. This process is cumbersome since you need to feed the paper through twice, but it is often easier than cutting and pasting pages side by side.

Math

Overview   Word can perform calculations on numbers in columns and puts the result in the scrap. This feature is useful if you have a column of numbers in a document and want to know the sum, or if you are calculating products of numbers and do not want to use a desk calculator.

Procedure   To perform a calculation, select the numbers you wish and press F2; Word will put the result of the calculation in the scrap. When using Word to add numbers, you need not use arithmetic operators between the numbers to get a sum. Thus, if you select a column (using Shift F6 to turn on column selection) of numbers and press F2, Word provides the sum of the numbers in the column. Note that Word can also add numbers in a sentence.

You must include the operators to perform subtraction, multiplication, division, or percentages. Use a hyphen for subtraction or negative numbers, an asterisk for multiplication, a slash (/) for division, and a percent sign for percentages. You can use parentheses to group numbers together, but a number in parentheses by itself indicates a negative number. Word keeps up to fourteen significant digits in its calculations.

Warnings   Be careful when using parentheses, since a set of parentheses around a number results in a negative number. Thus, "(12*8)" yields 96, but "12*(8)" yields −96.

Measurement.   *See* Options

Microsoft Windows

Overview   Word can be used in conjunction with Microsoft Windows, although it does not use many of Windows' features. When you run Word from Windows, you still see the same screen and use the same actions that you normally do; the principal difference is that you have access to the Windows Clipboard in the glossary. Version 5 offers additional advantages, such as being able to incorporate bitmap graphics from the Clipboard. (See Graphics.) If you are running Word version 4, you might want to run Word with Windows so that you can use Pageview to preview your work or to add graphics from other Windows programs. This section covers Word running under Windows version 2 or Windows/386.

Procedure   **PIFs**   Each program running under Windows should have a PIF (program information file) associated with it. Figure 56 shows the settings in the Word PIF, as displayed by the Windows PIFEDIT command. You can use the PIFEDIT command to change the settings of Word's PIF.

You may want to add /C to the program parameters if you want Word to run initially in text mode (the /K parameter makes Word work correctly with some non-standard keyboards). Word needs a minimum of 256K of RAM, but runs much better if you have 384K. Word only directly modifies the screen, not the other devices. Setting the *Program Switch* field to *Graphics/ Multiple Text* allows you to switch back and forth between Windows and Word without quitting from Word, although this takes up more memory. If you select *Text* for this field, you will be able to switch out of Word only when you are in text mode. Setting *Screen Exchange* to *Graphics/Multiple Text* allows you to read and write graphics in the Windows Clipboard.

Pageview   If you are running version 4, you can use Pageview to preview and print your documents. Pageview runs under Windows, and you can use the Windows Clipboard to put graphics in Pageview documents. You can also use Pageview to crop and stretch the graphics in your documents. If you are running version 5, you probably won't need Pageview.

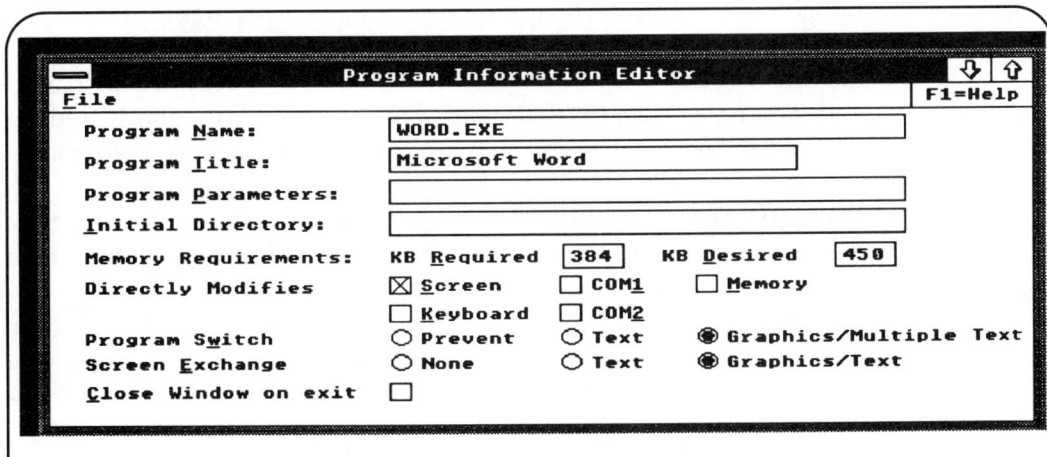

Figure 56

129

Pageview's relationship to Microsoft Windows can be somewhat confusing, since there are two "flavors" of Windows. You can buy the Windows Presentation Manager, which is a package that includes many Windows applications and allows you to run programs such as Word from a graphical user interface. However, you do not need the Windows Presentation Manager to run Pageview. Pageview comes with a program called Pageview Windows, also known as the Windows *runtime module*. This is a subset of the Windows Presentation Manager that allows Pageview to run only under Windows and does not come with the other applications in the Windows Presentation Manager. Thus, Pageview has more capabilities if you also have the Windows Presentation Manager (namely the use of the Clipboard), but the Windows Presentation Manager is not required.

Pageview can read and write Word files directly; there are no special procedures to follow in Word to use Pageview. You can open, save, and print Word files directly. Modifications that you can make to the files are limited to adding or changing graphics, changing the margins and heading positions, and adding or changing page breaks.

To insert a graphic from the Windows Clipboard into your document, use Pageview to insert an empty frame at the desired position, then size the frame. You can clip the picture to be the desired size and move it around on the page. Pageview displays the picture so that you can see how it looks in relation to the other text on the page.

You can immediately see the effects of any changes when you change margins in Pageview. You can change any of the settings for which you would normally use the **Format Division Margins** command by pointing and moving the margins on the screen. When you complete a change, Pageview repaginates the document so that you can see the effects. You can also add and remove page break characters and see the effects very quickly.

Windows Write If you use Windows Write, you can easily exchange files with Word. Since Windows Write has fewer formatting features than Word, some of the formatting will be lost when you open a Word document in Windows Write. Also, Windows Write cannot read styles from style sheets, so any styles you have should be frozen before you open the file in Windows Write. (See Styles.)

To transfer a file from Windows Write to Word, be sure to save it with the Save As command with *Microsoft Word* chosen. This deletes any graphics you have in your Windows Write document but keeps the rest of the formats intact.

Tips Set the *Program Switch* to *Text* in the PIFEDIT program if you need more memory space for other programs. If you do this, however, you must either run Word in text mode or switch back to Windows only by quitting from Word.

Press Alt Space Bar to get the Windows system menu in Word running under Windows. You will now be unable to use Alt Space Bar to remove character formatting; use Alt X Space Bar instead.

Microsoft Word on the Apple Macintosh

Overview Word on the Apple Macintosh has much the same feel as Word on the PC. Although the user interface on the Mac is very different than the user interface on the PC, the two Words have many features in common. Thus, you can move files back and forth fairly easily between the two programs. (See Importing and Exporting Files.)

In addition to user interface, there are many differences between Word on the Macintosh (Word/Macintosh) and Word on the PC (Word/PC). The major differences are listed below.

Common Features That Differ Between Word/PC and Word/Macintosh

- Divisions in Word/PC are called *sections* in Word/Mac.
- Word/Mac has paragraph styles but does not have character and division styles.
- Word/PC style names can be only two characters in length and have restricted characters; style names can be very long and can have spaces and any punctuation on Word/Mac.
- Word/Mac styles can be based on other styles; changing one style can cause automatic changes in other styles.
- Word/Mac styles are kept with a document and not as a separate style sheet.
- On Word/Mac, you search for formats or styles only by selecting them in the document and not by specifying them in the search command; there is no equivalent of Word/PC's **F**ormat s**E**arch command. The same is true of replacing formats and styles.
- Word/Mac does not let you specify a separator for the index.

131

- Print Preview on Word/Mac lets you change the margins; in Word/PC, you can only view the document.
- Word/Mac lets you link many files together in long documents; Word/PC requires that a document be one file.
- Word/Mac graphics are treated like characters instead of paragraphs and can be on the same line as text.
- You can have indents past the margin on Word/Mac; this is not allowed in Word/PC.
- Marking and special characters in tables of contents and index entries are different between the two programs.

Features of Word/PC Not Found in Word/Macintosh

- Print spooling
- Annotations
- Document retrieval
- Revision marks
- Background shading
- Bookmarks
- Selectable decimal character
- Autosave
- Print to a file
- Merge a file into the current one
- Rename a file
- Allsave

Features of Word/Macintosh Not Found in Word/PC

- Character formats: word underline, dotted underline, outline, shadow
- Selectable offset for superscript and subscript characters
- Inter-character spacing (condensed and expanded)
- Tables
- Saving in additional file formats
- Open Mail and Send Mail commands
- Smart quotes
- Customizable menus
- Header and footer windows
- Word Count command

Modes

Overview Word can operate in many modes. Each mode is started and stopped by pressing a key or key combination. The two-letter designator for the mode is displayed near the lower-right corner of the screen. Word's modes are listed below.

MODE	CODE	KEY
Caps lock	CL	Caps Lock
Column select	CO	Shift F6
Extend selection	EX	F6
Line draw	LD	Ctrl F5
Numeric lock	NL	Num Lock
Overtype	OT	F5
Record macro	RM	Shift F3
Revision marks	MR	Format revision-Marks command
Scroll lock	SL	Scroll Lock
Step through macro	ST	Ctrl F3
Zoom	ZM	Ctrl F1

Mouse

Overview Many Word users use the mouse for giving most commands. Word was designed from the start to support a two-button mouse, and is one of the few word processing programs for MS-DOS that addresses the needs of mouse users in a thoughtful way. As more people begin using mice for operating environments such as Microsoft Windows and OS/2 Presentation Manager, they will find that Word's use of the mouse is quite powerful. Although many people find it awkward to take their hands off the keyboard to use a mouse, others prefer pointing at the commands they want rather than typing in characters from the command names.

You can perform most but not all of Word's functions with the mouse. This includes giving any of Word's commands and selecting choices in dialogs. You can also use the mouse for selecting text. For most actions, you will use the left button of the mouse, though the right button is used in many circumstances. The general rule is that the left button selects and the right button acts (or, the left button does something and the right button does more).

Procedure   To execute a command, point at it and click the left button. If the command has subcommands, that menu will appear. If you point at a command and press the right button, Word performs the command with all the current settings. (This is like typing the command's identifying letter and pressing Enter.) To select a value in a field in a dialog, simply point at the value and click the left button; if you press the right button, Word selects that option and completes the command. To cancel a command, press both buttons. In a field where you can press F1 to see a list of possible responses, you can click the right button in that field to see the list. If Word has prompted you with *Enter Y...* you can click the left button instead for "Y" or both buttons to cancel the option.

Using the mouse to select text is easy. Point to the first or last character that you want to select, hold down the left button, then move the pointer to the other end of the text you want to select. If that other end is above or below the text in the window, move to the edge while you hold the button, and Word will rapidly scroll the screen. If you overshoot, pull the pointer back and Word will scroll back.

To extend a selection, use the F6 key. You cannot hold down the Shift key and select more text since Word treats this as speed copying.

You can also use the mouse to directly select blocks of text:

TO SELECT	POINT AT	PRESS
Character	Text	Left button
Word	Text	Right button
Sentence	Text	Both buttons
Line	Selection bar	Left button
Paragraph	Selection bar	Right button
Entire document	Selection bar	Both buttons

To scroll in a document, point to the left edge of the window; the left button scrolls up and the right scrolls down. The amount scrolled is determined by your position in the window: the further down, the more Word will scroll. To scroll a page at a time, put the mouse near the lower left corner of the window. You can also scroll horizontally by pointing to the bottom edge of the window and pressing the left button to scroll left or the right button to scroll right.

Thumbing is scrolling directly to a point of the document. To thumb, point at the left edge of the window and press both buttons. Word will jump to the place in the file that corresponds to the distance from the top of the window to which you are pointing. Thus, to jump directly to the middle of the file, point at the middle of the left edge of the window and press both buttons. Thumbing with the mouse is even faster than scrolling.

You can use the mouse to speed copy and move text without using the scrap. To move selected text, point to the destination spot, then press the Ctrl key and the left button. To copy the selected text, point to the destination spot and press the Shift key and the left button. To copy character formatting, select the text you want to format, point at the character with the format you want, hold down the Alt key, and click the left button. To copy paragraph formatting, select the paragraphs you want to format, point in the selection bar next to the paragraphs with the format you want, hold down the Alt key, and click the right button.

To split the screen horizontally, move the pointer to the right edge of the window and press the left button. To split it vertically, move the pointer to the top edge and press the left button. To close an open window, move the pointer to the top or right edge and press both buttons. To turn a window's ruler on, point in the upper-right corner and click either button; to turn a ruler off, point in the upper-right corner and click both buttons.

If you have more than one window on the screen, you can zoom a window by pointing at its window number in the upper-left corner of the window and clicking the right button. To stretch a window when many windows are on the screen, move the pointer to the lower-right corner, hold down either button, and move to the position in which you want the new corner. To switch between zoomed windows, point at the window number and click the left button.

The mouse takes different shapes depending on where you are pointing in the window. Figure 57 shows the different shapes the cursor can take in a window with no buttons pressed.

Figure 57

Those cursors correspond to the following shapes.

SHAPE	LOCATION	ACTION
↖	Text area	Select text (see above)
↗	Selection bar	Selects text (see above)
□	Top or right window border	Splits window
↕	Left window border	Scroll up or down
↔	Bottom window border	Scroll left or right
✛	Lower-right corner	Resize window
‖‖	Upper-right corner	Turn on or off ruler
↖	Upper-left corner	Zoom or select window

The cursor may change shape when you press one or both of the buttons. These shapes indicate an action in process such as scrolling. The shapes are as follows.

SHAPE	LOCATION	BUTTON	ACTION IN PROCESS
⬚	Top window border	L or R	Vertical window split
⊟	Right window border	L or R	Horizontal window split

SHAPE	LOCATION	BUTTON	ACTION IN PROCESS
⊠	Top or right window border	Both	Window close
↑	Left window border	L	Scroll up
↓	Left window border	R	Scroll down
▶	Left window border	Both	Thumb
←	Bottom window border	L	Scroll left
→	Bottom window border	R	Scroll right
▲	Bottom window border	Both	Thumb

Tips   If you try to select something with the mouse and Word beeps twice quickly but does not select it, you may be recording a macro without realizing it. *RM* will appear on the screen if, in fact, you are recording. You will be unable to perform an action while you are recording.

You should always use the latest version of the mouse driver. In version 4, the MOUSE.SYS file on Printer disk 2 was version 6.11.06 and in version 5, the version is 6.25.21. Using the latest version is especially important if you use a nonstandard mouse or monitor.

Moving Text

Overview   Word allows two methods for moving text. The first method is the scrap, which lets you hold a piece of text and insert it in another location in the document or in a different document. The second method is the mouse, which copies text without affecting the contents of the scrap; Microsoft calls this *speed moving*. (See Copying Text.)

Procedure   To move text using the scrap, use the **Delete** command and press Enter. (See Delete Command.) Once text is in the scrap, you can insert the contents of the scrap in another location in your document or a different document, select the location you want to copy, and give the **Insert** command. The keyboard equivalent of this is the Delete key; the mouse equivalent is clicking on the **Delete** command with the right button.

To use the mouse to speed move text without affecting the contents of the scrap, select the text you want to move, point to the location to which you want to move the text, hold down the Ctrl key, and click the left mouse button. You can also tell Word that you want the text to appear before different blocks of text.

TO MOVE IN FRONT OF	POINT AT	HOLD DOWN THE CTRL KEY AND CLICK THE MOUSE BUTTON
Character	Text	Left
Word	Text	Right
Sentence	Text	Both
Line	Selection bar	Left
Paragraph	Selection bar	Right
Beginning of document	Selection bar	Both

You can use either the scrap or speed moving to copy text from one window to another. Word treats the text as if it were moved from within the document. Thus, the moved text may be formatted differently in the destination document if you have different style sheets attached to the two documents.

Tips If you use a mouse, speed moving is usually more convenient than using the scrap. It is also much faster if you are using a floppy-based system.

MS-DOS Commands

Overview The Library Run command lets you give MS-DOS commands from within Word. You can give standard commands built into MS-DOS, such as COPY and TYPE, as well as batch files and small application programs. This lets you use MS-DOS to perform various functions while editing without having to quit from Word.

This command can be somewhat dangerous and should be used carefully. Limitations in MS-DOS prevent Word from completely protecting itself from injurious effects of other programs. Before you give the Library Run command, always save any open files that you have modified (the Transfer Allsave command is handy for this). Read the warnings below before using the Library Run command.

Procedure After saving all open files, give the Library Run command. Word prompts you for the name of the command you want to run. Type in the command just as you would on the MS-DOS command line and press Enter. Word clears the screen, displays any output from the command, and displays the message *Press a key to resume Word*. To get back into Word, press any key.

138

You may want to run more than one MS-DOS command before returning to Word. If so, enter COMMAND at Word's prompt and press Enter. This loads a copy of the MS-DOS command processor so that you can enter as many commands as you wish. You will see the MS-DOS prompt after you give each command. When you are finished, type EXIT at the MS-DOS prompt and press Enter. When Word prompts *Press a key to resume Word*, press any key.

Some MS-DOS commands have no effect in the **Library Run** command. The CD command will not change Word's default path; you must give the **Transfer Options** command instead. Similarly, entering a command to change the default drive (such as "B:") will have no effect.

If you give the **Library Run** command more than once, Word prompts you with the same command you gave the previous time you ran the command (this is a new feature in Word version 5). Since you may often give the same MS-DOS command to Word, this requires less typing.

If you do not have a hard disk, the **Library Run** command requires that you have a copy of the COMMAND.COM program on your Word disk. Also, if you are running commands that are not internal to MS-DOS (such as the CHKDSK command), the disk with those commands must also have a copy of COMMAND.COM.

When you give the **Library Run** command on a floppy-based system, Word prompts *Replace Word disk if necessary. Enter Y when ready.* This gives you an opportunity to switch diskettes if the command you want to run is on a different diskette.

Examples   To see a list of all the files in the current directory, give the **Library Run** command, type DIR at the prompt, and press Enter. Word clears the screen and shows you the directory. It then displays the message *Press a key to resume Word*. Press any letter or the Space Bar, and your document will reappear.

Warnings   Never delete files with the **Library Run** command; instead, use Word's **Transfer Delete** command. Word might crash if you accidentally erase a file that Word is using (such as a temporary copy of one of your files or a temporary program file). The **Transfer Delete** command will not let you erase files that Word is using.

Do not run programs that stay in memory after the command is finished from within the **Library Run** command; doing so can affect Word's memory usage and possibly crash the system. If you run one of these programs and Word detects it, you must quit immediately. The MS-DOS commands that you cannot run include ASSIGN, GRAPHICS, MODE, and PRINT.

There are many other programs that stay in memory; these are often called "TSRs" or "RAM-resident" programs. Programs such as Sidekick and Ready! are examples of these. In most cases, it is safe to run these programs before running Word, but you cannot run them from the **Library Run** command.

Tips   Since you often want to run more than one command, you should set up a macro that gives the **Library Run** command, types in COMMAND, and presses Enter for you. Remember to type EXIT when you are finished giving commands.

Networks

Overview   To the user, Word on a network looks almost identical to the single-user version of Word. In version 5, the two programs come in the same package, and there are only a few adjustments to make to use Network Word effectively. This section is directed toward network administrators or those people who help beginners use Word on a network.

Procedure   You should explain to network users how Word treats documents in a network environment. Files can be read-write or read-only, and Word treats these types of files very differently. A read-only file is one that is set to read-only from MS-DOS or one that each user opens with the **Transfer Load** command, setting the *read only* field to *Yes*.

If a user opens a read-write (regular) file with the **Transfer Load** command, the file is *locked* and no other user can open it. If a user opens a read-write file with the **Transfer Merge** command, the file is locked until the user saves the document into which the file is being merged. There are no restrictions on the number of people who can read a read-only file.

If someone tries to open a file that is locked, Word displays the message *File is in use*. Note that these same rules also apply to style sheets and glossaries; thus, a read-write style sheet that is attached to a file will become locked when the file is opened. Any file that is opened in read-only mode will have its name displayed in the lower-right corner of the window with an asterisk before it.

You can make a file read-only from the MS-DOS command line with the RDONLY and RDWRITE commands. These commands are supplied with network Word. Give the command and the name of the file you want to be read-only or read-write. The RDONLY and RDWRITE commands can also take file names with wildcard characters. For example, to make the file SPECIAL3.DOC read-only so that many people can view it, at the MS-DOS command enter:

```
RDONLY SPECIAL3.DOC
```

Because of the problem of locking style sheets and glossaries, you should probably make those files read-only and store them in the program directory so that users won't be locked out of them accidentally. If there is no need to share these files at your company, have the users create them on their own disks and be sure that NORMAL.GLY and NORMAL.STY do not exist on the Word directory.

Users should avoid using Word's print queuing on a network because Word keeps hold of the printer from the time the first print job is queued until the printer is no longer running. This should not pose any problems since most networks have their own print queuing facilities.

Tips   Using Word on a network can be confusing for people who are accustomed to single-user systems. It is especially confusing if they are inadvertently sharing a regularly used file such as NORMAL.GLY. If a Network Word user seems to be having problems with Word, check whether Word is giving a message about a file being unavailable or whether a file that the user expected to be available for writing is in fact a read-only file.

Numbering

Overview   Outlines usually have their major headings (and often all headings) numbered sequentially. There are a wide variety of outline styles, but most include separate types of numbering for each level of headings. Adding numbers to an outline can be tedious, and it is easy to make mistakes. Fortunately, Word gives you an easy method not only for numbering but also renumbering. As a result, if you number an outline, then edit it, you can renumber it in a single step. You can also number documents that are not in outline format.

Word determines the kind of numbering you want by example. Thus, if you have a report and want the primary headings numbered with capital Roman numerals and the secondary headings numbered with lowercase letters, simply put the first number of each style at the beginning of the first paragraph of that style, and Word will take those as cues for how to number the rest of your document.

The renumbering scheme is, unfortunately, not perfect. It works much better in outlines than in normal text unless you are simply putting a number at the beginning of each paragraph. The first time you number an outline, Word uses the standard from the *Chicago Manual of Style* unless you give it examples. For regular documents, Word looks at the indentation to determine which paragraphs get numbers. There are six kinds of numbers that Word can use for numbering.

- Arabic numerals (1, 2, 3, . . .)
- Uppercase Roman numerals (I, II, III, . . .)
- Lowercase Roman numerals (i, ii, iii, . . .)
- Uppercase letters (A, B, C, . . .)
- Lowercase letters (a, b, c, . . .)
- Legal format numbers, also called technical numbering (1, 1.1, 1.2, 1.2.1, . . .)

To recognize a number when you renumber your document, Word must begin with the first character in the paragraph unless you begin it with a left parenthesis. Each number must end with a period or right parenthesis (note, however, that legal format numbers cannot end with any punctuation). The period or right parenthesis must be followed by a space or Tab character. When you first number your document, Word formats the new numbers according to the character format of the first letter after the number.

Procedure   The **Library Number** command affords a great deal of flexibility in numbering a document. You can number a section of your document by selecting it and giving the command. If you select only one character, the entire document is numbered. The *number* field lets you specify whether to update the numbers in the document or remove the current numbering. The *restart sequence* field tells Word whether you want to restart the numbering for the selected text.

Warnings   If the selection already contains numbers and you have not selected the beginning of the sequence, be sure to set *restart sequence* to *No*. Since Word's default for this field is *Yes*, you can lose your current numbering and have your overall sequence incorrectly altered if you renumber a section with *restart sequence* set to *Yes*.

Always save a copy of your document before giving the Library Number command the first time. You can sometimes get unexpected results from the first time you number (for example, if some of your headings start with numbers, Word can mistake them for heading numbering). Immediately go through your document after numbering it. If there are major errors, you can reverse the effects of the numbering with the Undo command.

Tips   The Library Number command works much better on outlines. If you use it while viewing the outline in outline view, you can quickly see whether the numbering was done as you expected.

Options

Overview   As you become familiar with Word, there are many choices to make about how Word should look and operate. Some of these are cosmetic, such as the color of the screen; others affect how Word operates (for example, whether Word should print hidden text). The more you use Word, the more strongly you will feel about the settings for these options.

Three commands are used to set options: the Options command, the Print Options command, and the Window Options command. In version 5 only there is no Window Options command: it is part of the Options command. Each time you quit from Word, it saves the current settings of all the options in the Options command as well as some of the options in the Print Options command. (See Printing.)

Procedure   Figure 58 shows the dialog for the Options command for version 5.

```
WINDOW OPTIONS for window number: 1       show hidden text:(Yes)No
        show ruler: Yes(No)     show non-printing symbols:(None)Partial All
       show layout: Yes(No)              show line breaks: Yes(No)
      show outline: Yes(No)               show style bar: Yes(No)

GENERAL OPTIONS mute: Yes(No)             summary sheet: Yes(No)
           measure:(In)Cm P10 P12 Pt       display mode: 5
          paginate:(Auto)Manual                  colors:
          autosave:                 autosave confirm: Yes(No)
         show menu:(Yes)No               show borders:(Yes)No
       date format:(MDY)DMY        decimal character:(.),
       time format:(12)24         default tab width: 0.5"
      line numbers: Yes(No)         count blank space: Yes(No)
      cursor speed: 3              linedraw character: (|)
      speller path: C:\WORD\WORD5\WORD5\SPELL-AM.LEX
Enter number
Pg1 Col         {}                      ?                Microsoft Word
```

Figure 58

The following table is for the window and general options in version 5. Many options work similarly to the way they do in version 4. The window options specifically for version 4 are described in Windows.

FIELD	USE
show hidden text	Specifies whether hidden text is shown. If you choose *Yes*, Word displays hidden text with a dotted underline. Be sure that you are not showing hidden text when you repaginate, since Word will include the hidden text as it determines where text goes on the page.
show ruler	Shows the ruler at the top of the window
show non-printing symbols	Shows graphic characters for special word processing characters. *None* shows none of the characters. *Partial* shows the following characters:

    ¶   Paragraph
    ↓   Newline
    ‑   Optional hyphen
    ↔   Hidden text if the *show hidden text* field is set to *No*.
         All shows the same characters as *Partial*, but also shows:
    →   Tab, shown at the left side of the tab mark. Leader characters are not shown for tabs with leaders.
         Space

O

FIELD	USE
show layout	Shows your document in layout mode with all paragraphs on the page as they will print. Setting *show layout* to *No* puts Word into galley mode. (See Layout.)
show line breaks	Shows lines as they will print. Line breaks change with the setting for the printer in the **Print O**ptions command and the font chosen. Note that setting *printer display* to *Yes* slows down Word's display speed. If set to *No*, Word displays lines as if the text was 10-pitch or 12-pitch, depending on the setting in the *measure* field. This field can also be changed with Alt F7.
show outline	Shows the text in outline view. (See Outlines.)
show style bar	Specifies whether the style bar is shown. The style bar shows the key codes for styles and the type of running head. (See Styles and Running Heads.)
mute	Prevents Word from beeping when you make an error. Setting *mute* to *No* allows normal beeping.
summary sheet	Shows a blank summary sheet each time a file without a filled-in summary sheet is saved. Setting *summary sheet* to *No* causes Word to ignore the summary sheet for new files. If you do not use the document retrieval system, you will probably want to set *summary sheet* to *No*. (See Retrieving Documents.)
measure	Specifies the unit of measurement Word will use. You can choose *In* (inches), *Cm* (centimeters), *P10* (10-pitch characters, or 10 characters per inch), *P12* (12-pitch characters, or 12 characters per inch), or *Pt* (points, or $\frac{1}{72}$ of an inch).
display mode	Selects the mode Word uses to display the screen. The number for graphics modes indicates that you have a graphics adapter and want Word to use the graphics mode. Although this can be slower than text mode, the mouse pointer gives more information. Also, if you have a Hercules Graphics Card Plus, you can better see how your text will print since italicized and boldface words show in those fonts, and superscripts and subscripts are shown as smaller characters. This field can also be changed with Alt F9.
paginate	Tells Word either to repaginate as you work or only when you give a command that would repaginate the document (such as the **Print R**epaginate command). *Auto* indicates automatic repagination, which usually slows Word down; *Manual* indicates no automatic repagination. (See Repagination.)

FIELD	USE
colors	Sets the color for the menu, background, messages, and character formats. The numbers for colors vary with the type of adapter you use. Pressing F1 in this field shows a list of the items for which you can change the colors.
autosave	Tells Word how often to automatically save your document, in minutes. Setting *autosave* to *0* or leaving the field blank indicates that you do not want to automatically save the file. (See Autosave.)
autosave confirm	Specifies that the autosave function will prompt you each time it does an automatic save. Setting *confirm* to *No* tells Word to automatically save the file without prompting you. (See Autosave.)
show menu	Displays the menu at the bottom of the screen. You may want to turn the menu off by setting *show menu* to *No* if you want more space on the screen. As soon as you press the Esc key to give a command, Word shows the menus again so you can give commands. Turning the menu display off during macro execution can also increase the speed of macros.
show borders	Shows the borders of the window. Setting *show borders* to *No* removes the four borders of the window. This also disables some mouse actions that rely on the borders (such as scrolling and thumbing). If you have more than one window on the screen, setting *show borders* to *No* has no effect until only one window is showing, such as in zoom mode.
date format	Specifies the format in which dates are displayed and printed when you use the special glossary entries "date" and "dateprint." *MDY* indicates that Word will print dates with the month first, such as "April 23, 1989." *DMY* indicates that Word will print dates with the day first, such as "23 April, 1989." (See Glossaries.)
decimal character	Specifies the decimal character to be recognized in mathematical calculations and measurements. (See Math.) You can select a period (more common in the United States and Asia) or a comma (more common in many European countries). Note that if you change *decimal character* to a comma, you can no longer separate the fields in form letters with a comma; you must use a semicolon. (See Form Letters.)
time format	Specifies the format in which times are displayed and printed when you use the special glossary entries "time" and "timeprint." A *12* indicates that Word will print times in 12-hour format and include "AM" or "PM," as in "6:00 PM"; *24* indicates that Word will use 24-hour format (sometimes called *military format*), as in "18:00." (See Glossaries.)

FIELD	USE
default tab width	Sets distance between tab stops for all tabs to the right of the furthest set tab. This is usually .5 inches. (See Tables and Tab Stops.)
line numbers	Shows line numbers in the lower-left corner of the screen. If *line numbers* is set to *No*, only the page and column number are shown. The line numbers are affected by the *count blank space* field.
count blank space	Causes the line numbers displayed by the *line numbers* field to represent each line on the page and not just lines with text in them. Setting *count blank space* to *Yes* causes Word to count blank spaces as well.
cursor speed	Sets the speed of the cursor when using cursor repeat (that is, when you hold down one of the cursor control keys). This value will depend on the speed of your computer and your preference for how fast you want Word's cursor to move. The range is 0 (slow) to 9 (fast).
linedraw character	Sets graphics character or character set used for line drawing. You can enter a character that will be used in all directions or press F1 to select a character set or character to use. (See Line Drawing.)
speller path	Shows the location of your spelling program. Word uses this if the spelling program is not in the same directory as Word (an uncommon occurrence). Include the disk name and directory of the speller.

Warnings

Setting *screen borders* to *No* prevents you from using many of the mouse features. This option should be used only if you need the extra two lines and two columns on the screen.

Word was designed to use the period as the decimal character; changing it to a comma can have unpredictable results. If you change *decimal character* to a comma, you will have to change the data documents for any form letters in which you used a comma as a separator.

Tips

Since Word saves the settings for the Options command when you exit, it will start with those settings the next time you run Word. If there are some settings you always want when you start Word, you should set up a macro that automatically executes those settings when you start Word, regardless of how you left Word the last time. (See Macros.)

Note that the line numbers displayed at the bottom-left corner of the screen are lines of text, not lines from the top of the page. For example, if you have paragraphs formatted with one line after (and you therefore

147

cannot put the cursor on the blank line between paragraphs) and have *count blank space* set to *No*, going from one paragraph to the next increases the line count only by 1, not 2. The line count also changes if you have more than one column or absolutely positioned paragraph and are in layout mode. In layout mode, the line number displayed will be the number of lines from the top of the current object. (See Layout and Paragraph Placement.)

Orphans. *See* Keeps

OS/2 and Word

[Version 5 Only]

Overview   Word runs in an OS/2 text window as it does under MS-DOS in text mode. Microsoft distributes the OS/2 version of Word in the same package as Word for MS-DOS. Word under OS/2 runs as an OS/2 application, which means that it does not have to run in OS/2's "compatibility box."

Note, however, that Word does not take advantage of any of OS/2's multitasking features. For example, sorting and repagination do not happen in separate procedure threads. Thus, Word is "OS/2 cognizant" but is not a true OS/2 application. Some of Word's external utilities also run under OS/2, but others are still designed for MS-DOS and must be run in the compatibility box.

There are many circumstances where running Word under OS/2 prevents the mouse from working. If you rely on the mouse when using Word, this may be a significant problem. Future versions of Word and of the mouse driver may fix these problems.

Other Programs

Overview   Since Word is one of the most popular word processing programs for the PC, many other vendors have developed programs that work in concert with it. You will find some of these programs valuable for your daily work,

O

especially if you use Word for high-quality output or do a great deal of writing. This section is written to give you an overview of the types of programs available for Word and give a few examples of each; it is by no means an exhaustive list.

Fonts and Graphics   Word's ability to handle downloadable fonts and laser printers better than almost any other word processor has generated a font industry to grow around Word. If you have either a Hewlett-Packard LaserJet +, LaserJet II, or compatible printer, you will find that there are dozens of high-quality fonts available for Word. These fonts come with pre-configured printer drivers so that Word not only downloads them easily but also accurately reflects line breaks on the screen if you specify printer display in the **O**ptions command. (See Fonts.)

Laser Fonts from SoftCraft, Inc. (16 N. Carroll Street, Suite 500, Madison, WI 53703; 800/351-0500) supplies eighteen fonts and creates printer drivers for you based on the fonts you choose. Since using large printer drivers can take up Word's memory, Laser Fonts lets you create printer drivers as small or as large as you want. Consequently, you can either save memory space or have many fonts available simultaneously if memory space is not important for a particular document. SoftCraft also sells many other fonts that can be used with the Laser Fonts program.

If you have an Epson-compatible dot-matrix printer, you can use SoftCraft's Fancy Word program with Word to produce high-quality output by using the Epson's graphics capabilities. The program allows you to format your document as you normally would (including enhanced graphic capabilities in addition to what Word offers) then print out the document with Fancy Word's special print formatter. The program also helps format for the Hewlett-Packard laser printers.

Now that PostScript printers have become much more popular, software manufacturers are creating utilities that work with PostScript to create more attractive documents. For example, LWPlus from The Laser Edge (360 17th Street, Suite 203, Oakland, CA 94612; 415/835-1581) is a printer driver for PostScript printers that adds many features to Word. LWPlus lets you put words at the tops of boxes, put crop marks on your pages and imbed PostScript commands in your documents. (See Post-Script Printers.)

Lines-Graphs-Symbols from Polaris (613 West Valley Parkway, Suite 323, Escondido, CA 92025; 619/743-7800) contains many common symbols as type characters so that you need not insert a graphic if you want a symbol in line with your text. It also allows you to capture screen images and include them in your Word files. EXACT from TSSI (72 Kent Street, Brookline, MA 02146; 617/734-4130) lets you create and edit scientific and mathematical formulae, and then insert the results in your Word documents. EXACT is much easier to use than manual formatting of equations in Word.

Writing Tools Many people in business are apprehensive about writing original material. Creating a report or even a memo can be frightening to those who have little confidence in their writing skills. To help these people, many companies have created writing tools that analyze documents, help correct common mistakes, and improve poor writing. Although the quality of these programs varies, they are generally becoming better as the language analysis software becomes more advanced. The programs, incorrectly known as "grammar checkers," read the text in a document and perform the following tasks.

- Point out awkward and hackneyed phrases
- Find common punctuation problems
- Highlight jargon
- Determine the education level necessary for understanding the document

These programs are often not as useful as advertised since the rules they use are quite limited relative to the robustness of the English language. However, they can help provide some assurance if you want your writing reviewed before others see it. One of the most popular programs in this category is Rightwriter from RIGHTSOFT (2033 Wood Street, Suite 218, Sarasota, FL 33577; 813/952-9211). Rightwriter can read formatted Word files; make suggestions about grammar, usage, and punctuation; and put corrections back into your document. The newest version of Grammatik from Reference Software (330 Townsend Avenue, Suite 123, San Francisco, CA 94107; 800/872-9933) includes some very advanced capabilities for determining relationships between sentence parts.

O

If you have significant problems with spelling, you may want a program that works more interactively than Word's spelling checker. Microlytics (300 Main Street, East Rochester, NY 14445; 800/828-6293) has created a device that attaches between your keyboard and PC that checks for spelling errors as you type. The device alerts you when you type a word it does not recognize and allows you to change the spelling before you save the document.

Other Tools   Since word processing is the most common use for PCs, many companies have developed auxiliary tools that work with word processors such as Word. These tools are often limited in scope and are targeted at narrow markets of professionals. As Word and other word processing programs incorporate more features, these manufacturers adapt their programs to newer versions of the programs. Microsoft often adds features to new versions of Word that reflect programs that are available in the market; for instance, the first version of Word did not have a spelling checker or thesaurus.

The legal industry uses PC word processing extensively. Although WordPerfect is used by more law offices than Word, Word has a strong following in many large law firms. Other manufacturers have created programs that work with Word to make legal word processing easier. For example, JURISoft (763 Massachusetts Avenue, Cambridge, MA 02139; 617/864-6151) produces CompareRite for comparing two drafts of a document, CiteRite for assuring that citations are in the proper format, and FullAuthority for locating citations in legal briefs.

The movie and television industry has also become very reliant on word processing in the last few years. Since screenplays have a very different format than most documents, formatting them by hand can be difficult. Scriptor from Screenplay Systems (150 East Olive Avenue, Suite 305, Burbank, CA 91502; 818/843-6557) gives Word the power to create scripts using the industry standard formats, while letting you decide on many of the non-standard formatting options such as format for character and scene names.

In the last few years, the software industry has started to pay attention to one of the thorny issues in word processing: How can a group of people edit a single document in a structured fashion? Although annotations help, they do not allow foolproof editing and reviewing by individual writers. (See Annotations.) The first program that works with Word to help this coordination is ForComment from Broderbund (PO Box 12947, San Rafael, CA 94913; 415/492-3500). ForComment allows up to sixteen people to comment on a Word document and keeps track of the revisions.

Tips

Microsoft distributes an advertising booklet with Word called *Microsoft Word Companion Products* that lists some of the products that are known to work with Word. Magazines such as *PC World, PC Magazine*, and *InfoWorld* are also good sources for information on products that work with Word. These magazines often have in-depth reviews and feature articles on word processing tools. Industry-specific journals (such as law journals) also cover some of the products.

Most user groups have libraries of disks that contain public-domain and shareware programs, many of which relate to word processing. Some of these programs work with Word files, but most work only with text-only or DCA-formatted files. Check with the local user group librarian for suggestions about the programs available.

There are also many programs available for translating Word documents into a format usable by other word processing programs and vice versa. (See Importing and Exporting Text.)

Outlining

Overview

Word's integrated outlining gives you a fast, easy method for creating outlines. Even more important, however, it gives you a method for starting a document as an outline and turning it into a regular document by successive editing steps. You first enter and edit the outline as headings; then, as you determine the text that you want under the various levels of headings, you fill those in, leaving the headings in place. The end result is a document that will be better structured than if you had just started from notes.

Using an outline processor during the planning stages of a document gives you a great advantage over normal word processing because you can move groups of headings together automatically. For example, if you have a main heading "Personnel Needed" with subheadings "Accounting," "Support," and "Other," you can select the main heading and the others will be selected automatically. Since it is unlikely that you would want to move a main heading without its subordinate headings, this makes rearranging an outline much quicker.

There are other advantages to using Word's outline method for preparing documents. After you have finished adding in the text (called *body text*) between the headings, you can still switch to outline mode to see the structure of the outline without the text. Thus, you can change the order of your report in outline mode without having to wade through pages of text to find the sections you want to move. You can also have Word hide some of the lower-level headings so that only the major headings show. This is called *collapsing* and *expanding* headings. When you collapse a heading, all headings and body text under it are hidden; Word, however, indicates in the selection bar that more information is hidden. Since the outline is like a formatted table of contents, you can move around easily in an overview of your document without looking at the detail in the body text.

If you wish, Word will create a table of contents from outline headings without requiring that you add special text. (See Tables of Contents.) You can also use the **Library Number** command to number the headings. (See Numbering.)

Since your outline is the same as your document, Word gives you two ways of viewing the same file. *Document view* lets you look at your document as you normally do; *outline view* lets you see your document structured as an outline, with each lower level of heading indented. Thus, outline view lets you see the structure of your document more easily than document view does. Since you probably would not want your printed output to use this indentation, being able to switch back and forth between these two views is a real advantage.

Once you are in outline view, there are two modes to choose from. *Edit mode* lets you edit and add headings and text; *organize mode* lets you move the headings around and change the structure of your outline. The fact that there are two modes in outline view makes using Word's outline processor somewhat awkward since you often think of structural changes you want as you are adding headings. It is quite easy to switch between the two modes, however, so the difference between the two modes should not be a problem.

Procedure To start an outline, open a new document and press Shift F2. Word will display *Level 1* in the lower-left corner of the screen to indicate that you are in edit mode. (When you move from document view to outline view, you are always put into edit mode.) The level indicator shows you the level of the paragraph on which you are editing. To switch back to document view, press Shift F2 again. To move between edit mode and organize mode, press Shift F5. When you are in organize mode, Word displays *ORGANIZE* in the lower-left corner of the window. The relationship between these modes is shown in Figure 59.

Note that in edit mode, you cannot select more than one heading at a time. Thus, to remove two headings, you must select one, delete it, then select the other one and delete it. This makes using edit mode more restricted than document view and can make editing difficult. The only exception to this rule is that you can still select the entire document with Shift F10 (but not by clicking both mouse buttons in the selection bar).

You can, however, use the keyboard to select more than one heading in organize mode. Thus, when you want to perform steps on many headings at once (such as formatting or deleting), switch to organize mode. When you want to edit the text in a heading or body text, switch back to edit mode.

Entering an Outline When you create an outline, be sure that you are in edit mode. Start with a level 1 heading. The lower the number for the level, the more important the heading. A heading can be as long as you like (you are not limited to a single line). Like in a normal paragraph, when you are finished entering the heading, press Enter. Word assumes that you want the next heading to be at the same level (that is, at the same relative

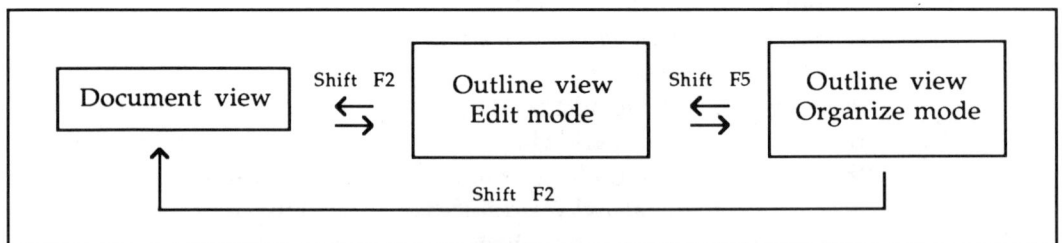

Figure 59

154

level of importance). If you want to make the next heading subordinate to the previous one, press Alt 0. Note that the level indicator in the lower-left corner now says *Level 2* and that the heading is indented from the left margin. If, as you enter the heading text, you decide to make the heading a level 1 heading, press Alt 9.

In edit mode, you can enter headings and edit text within a heading. You can also add body text if you wish. To turn a paragraph into body text, press Alt P. Note that the level indicator in the lower-left corner now says *Text* and the selection bar shows *T*. Body text is formatted with no indentation. Generally, it is easier to view the outline if you add body text after you have entered your headings. If you decide to change some body text into a heading, select it, press Alt 9, then press Alt 9, then press Alt 0 to make it the level desired.

Thus, as you are entering an outline, Alt 0 makes a heading less important, Alt 9 makes a heading more important, and Alt P makes a heading into body text. If you want to add headings between two headings you already have entered, put the cursor at the end of the line before where you want the new heading and press Enter.

Viewing an Outline   Once you have entered an outline, you will want to view it from various levels; viewing is usually easier in edit mode. There are two methods for collapsing and expanding headings: for the entire document or for all headings under the currently selected one. If you are using the keyboard, these actions use the grey keys on the numeric keypad. In this section, "press Keypad +" means pressing the "+" key on the numeric keypad, not the "+" on the top row of the main keyboard. The mouse actions only work in organize mode.

As you collapse and expand headings, you will discover that collapsing and expanding body text is not carried out in parallel with the headings. For example, if you collapse a heading that has body text under it, then immediately expand that heading, the body text is still collapsed. As a result, body text stays collapsed even when you expand the heading above it.

To collapse all the headings under the currently selected heading, press Keypad − or F11 (if you have an extended keyboard). In organize mode, you can collapse with the mouse by pointing at the heading under which you want to collapse and pressing both buttons. When you collapse headings under a heading, Word shows a + in the selection bar. To collapse only the body text under a heading, press Shift Keypad − (or Shift F11). When there is only body text collapsed under a heading, the Selection bar shows *t*.

Expanding headings is similar to collapsing them. Select the heading under which there are collapsed headings and press Keypad *. If you want to only expand one level of headings under the selected heading, press Keypad + (or F12 on the extended keyboard) or, in organize mode, point at the heading and press the right button. To expand body text under a heading, select the heading and press Shift Keypad + (or Shift F12).

When you are viewing an outline as a whole, it is often convenient to collapse or expand all the headings and body text at once. To reduce the number of levels in the entire outline, press Ctrl +. Word prompts *Enter number from 1 to 7*; type the number of the level to which you want to see. For instance, if you enter 3, Word will show you only the level 1 through 3 headings, and will also collapse the body text. Unfortunately, expanding all headings and body text is not as easy. You must select the entire document by pressing Shift F10, press Keypad * then Keypad Shift +.

To summarize the keyboard, then:

KEY	USE
Shift F2	Switch between document view and outline view
Shift F5	Switch between edit mode and organize mode
Alt 9	Make heading a higher level
Alt 0	Make heading a lower level
Keypad − or F11	Collapse heading
Shift Keypad − or Shift F11	Collapse body text
Keypad *	Expand all headings
Keypad + or F12	Expand heading
Shift Keypad + or Shift F12	Expand body text
Control + n	Expand up to level n

Reorganizing an Outline In organize mode, you can only select headings. When you select a heading and copy it or delete it to the scrap, Word acts on all the subordinate headings and body text as well, which makes moving parts of your outline easy. The arrow keys take on a different meaning, which is determined by the relationship between different levels of headings. The arrow keys select as indicated in the list below.

KEY	SELECTION
Up Arrow	Previous heading at the same level, skipping over subordinate headings. If the heading above is a higher level, the selection does not move.
Down Arrow	Next heading at the same level, skipping over subordinate headings. If the heading below is a higher level, the selection does not move.
Left Arrow	Previous heading, regardless of level. F9 performs the same action.
Right Arrow	Next heading, regardless of level. F10 performs the same action.
Home	Previous heading at higher level
End	Last heading subordinate to this heading
F6	Extends the selection to all headings and body text subordinate to this one

To move a heading and subordinate headings and text using the scrap, select the heading and press Delete, move the selection to the heading before which you want the deleted material, and press Insert. In order to not move subordinate headings, you must raise them individually by pressing Alt 9.

If you are using a mouse, you can also use speed copying to move headings and subordinate headings and text. Select the heading, point to where you want the heading to move, press Ctrl, and click the mouse. (See Copying Text.)

Tips

Use style sheets to format outlines. Word predefines "heading 1" through "heading 7" for the seven levels of headings. Word comes with a sample style sheet for outlines called OUTLINE.STY. You can customize this style sheet and attach it to any outline you create, or merge its contents into your NORMAL.STY. (See Styles.)

There are many programs for the PC that only create outlines; these programs are often much easier to use and more powerful than Word's outlining feature. You may want to look into some of these other programs if you do a great deal of outlining.

Page Numbers

Overview Word provides two methods for putting page numbers in your document: in running heads and as page numbers themselves. In a running head, the page number can be part of text (such as "Page 7" or "3-5"), and the position of the page number can be changed based on whether the page is even, odd, or the first page in a division. With direct page numbering, these choices are not available. Thus, it is likely that you will want to use running heads for putting numbers on your pages. (See Running Heads.)

This section describes how to add direct page numbers to a division. You may want to use direct page numbers if you are sure that you want the page number to appear in the same position on each page and that you do not want any text before the page number. Direct page numbering conforms to the way that many other word processors handle page numbers.

Procedure To add page numbers to a division, select any text in that division and give the Format Division Page-numbers command. This command's dialog is shown in Figure 60. Select *Yes* in the first field, then fill in the other fields to specify where you want the page number and in what format.

The choices and meanings for this command are listed below.

FIELD	MEANING
from top	Distance from the top of the paper
from left	Distance from the left side of the paper
numbering, at	*Continuous* indicates that the page numbering should continue from the previous division; *Start* indicates that you want to start the numbering at the number in the *at* field.

```
FORMAT DIVISION PAGE-NUMBERS: Yes No      from top: 0.5"    from left: 7.25"
          numbering:(Continuous)Start     at:           number format:(1)I i A a
Select option
Pg1 Co1              {}                    ?                     Microsoft Word
```

Figure 60

FIELD	MEANING
number format	Format for the page number. The choices are

    1   Arabic numerals (1, 2, 3, . . .)
    I   Uppercase Roman numerals (I, II, III, . . .)
    i   Lowercase Roman numerals (i, ii, iii, . . .)
    A   Uppercase letters (A, B, C, . . .)
    a   Lowercase letters (a, b, c, . . .)

To change the formatting of the page number (such as the font or character format), you must have a style sheet attached to the document. In the gallery, give the Insert command, choose *Character* in the *usage* field, select the *variant* field, and press F1. In the list, select *Page number* and press Enter. Give the Format Character command to set the format you wish and save this as part of your style sheet. (See Styles.)

Examples   To put a page number in the middle near the bottom of an 8.5-inch by 11-inch page, give the Format Division Page-numbers command and set the first field to *Yes, from top* to 10.5, and *from left* to 4.25.

Tips   One good use for direct page numbers is that you can put them in the default division style. (See Styles.) Since you must place running heads by hand, you may want to use page numbers instead by putting the page number in a style that uses the Standard division variant.

Pages.   *See* **Division Formatting**

Paragraph Formatting

Overview   The most important factor in page appearance is the paragraph formatting. If all paragraphs have identical formatting, the page will be visually uninteresting, even if there is a variety of character formats. On the other hand, if each paragraph has a different format, the page will look confusing. Choosing paragraph formats carefully is important to the overall look of your document.

There are five types of paragraph formatting: alignment, indentation, line spacing, keeps, and placement. Alignment refers to how the left and right ends of each line align with the margins. Indentation is the amount of space between the left and right sides of the paragraph and the margins of the page. (See Indentation.) Line spacing tells Word how much space there should be between each line, as well as the amount of white space to put above and below the paragraph. Keeps determine how Word will break paragraphs at the bottom of pages. (See Keeps.) Placement refers to how a paragraph will be placed relative to other paragraphs on a page. (See Paragraph Placement.)

Procedure   Paragraph formatting is performed with the **Format Paragraph** command. Figure 61 shows your choices.

The four choices for *alignment* are *Left, Centered, Right,* and *Justified.* These refer to how the left and right end of the lines align with the margins. The way these choices function are explained in the list below.

CHOICE	ALIGNED WITH LEFT MARGIN	ALIGNED WITH RIGHT MARGIN
Left	Yes	No
Centered	No	No
Right	No	Yes
Justified	Yes	Yes

The *line spacing* field specifies how much space each line gets on the page. You can specify a number of lines that each line will take (such as 2 li for double-spacing) or auto to set the spacing correctly for the largest font size on the line. You can also use auto in paragraphs that have superscript or subscript characters. (See Subscripts and Superscripts.) Using fractional line sizes such as 1.5 li lets you fine-tune the inter-line spacing for the

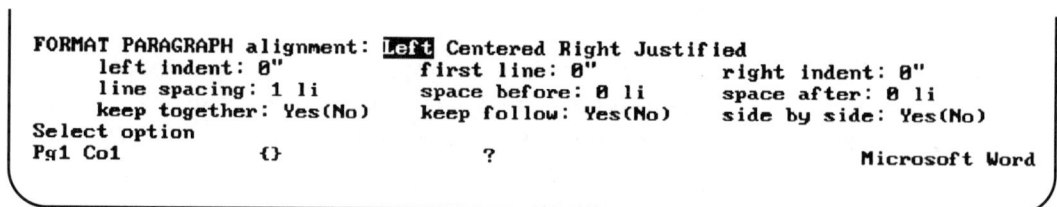

```
FORMAT PARAGRAPH alignment: Left Centered Right Justified
    left indent: 0"          first line: 0"         right indent: 0"
    line spacing: 1 li       space before: 0 li     space after: 0 li
    keep together: Yes(No)   keep follow: Yes(No)   side by side: Yes(No)
Select option
Pg1 Co1              {}                  ?                    Microsoft Word
```

Figure 61

best visual effect. Word always uses ⅙ of an inch as the line height, regardless of the printer or font used.

The *space before* and *space after* fields let you specify a fixed amount of white space to include before and after a paragraph. If you always put a blank paragraph after each paragraph in a letter, it is much better to set *space after* to 1 li instead since a text paragraph may end at the bottom of a page; Word would then put the blank paragraph at the top of the next page. If you specify *space before* or *space after* instead of using blank single-line paragraphs, Word will never put blank space at the beginning or end of a page, and orphan/widow control will work more accurately.

The keyboard equivalents for paragraph formatting are listed below. If any styles attached to your document begin with these characters, you must instead press Alt X and the letter for the keyboard equivalents. For example, if you have a style with the name CG, to center a paragraph you must type Alt XC.

KEY	FORMAT
Alt C	Centered
Alt F	Increase first line indentation by one tab stop
Alt J	Justified
Alt L	Left flush
Alt M	Reduce left indentation by one tab stop
Alt N	Increase left indentation by one tab stop
Alt O	One line after
Alt P	Normal paragraph
Alt R	Right flush
Alt T	Increase hanging indentation by one tab stop
Alt 2	Double space

Examples   If you are using Word version 4, using *space after* is a good way to reserve space for a graphic that is followed by a caption. Since you want to keep the caption on the same page with the graphic, you must format the paragraph that is holding space for the graphic to keep it with the following paragraph. Figure 62 shows how to set the Format **P**aragraph command dialog for the graphic holder paragraph if you want to reserve fifteen lines.

Tips   Instead of specifying 1 li for *line spacing*, it is generally much better to specify auto since this lets you change the size of some of the characters in

```
FORMAT PARAGRAPH alignment:(Left)Centered Right Justified
      left indent: 0"              first line: 0"           right indent: 0"
      line spacing: 1 li           space before: 0 li       space after: 15 li
      keep together: Yes(No)       keep follow: Yes No       side by side: Yes(No)
Select option
Pg1 Co1              {}                    ?                      Microsoft Word
```

Figure 62

the line and still have Word print the line legibly. For instance, you may have a larger-than-normal font for one of your character styles; if you use auto, Word automatically gives enough space above and below the line for those characters.

Some printer drivers use *microjustification*, the insertion of a small space between each word or each letter, for justified paragraphs. Without microjustification, Word puts extra spaces between each word.

Paragraph Placement

Overview   Although most paragraphs follow each other vertically, Word lets you place paragraphs next to each other horizontally; in version 5, paragraphs can be placed anywhere on the page. In tables created with tab stops, only the last column can wrap around. (See Tables and Tab Stops.)

In side-by-side paragraphs, all paragraphs can wrap normally. This gives you much more flexibility when formatting complex documents or laying out brochures. Side-by-side and absolutely placed paragraphs can only be seen as they will be printed in layout and preview modes. (See Layout.)

You can use as many side-by-side paragraphs as you want on a line. To position two or more paragraphs side by side, set the left and right indents of each paragraph so that the indents do not overlap, then set the *side by side* field in the Format Paragraph command to *Yes*. If any paragraph has the *side by side* field set to *Yes*, Word checks whether that paragraph can fit on the same line with the previous paragraph. You need not order the side-by-side paragraphs — simply have them appear before and after one another in the document.

162

Word's absolute paragraph positioning feature in version 5 gives Word very powerful desktop publishing capabilities. An absolutely positioned paragraph consists of a frame and the text that goes in that frame. The frame's definition includes the width of the frame (but not the height, since that is adjusted depending on the amount of text in the paragraph), the frame's horizontal position, and the frame's vertical position. The frame is like a miniature page into which the text fits: all indents for the paragraph are relative to the frame border. All normal paragraphs flow around absolutely positioned paragraphs. For example, if you have a two-column page and a picture in the middle of the page with a frame that is 3 inches wide and 5 inches from the top of the page, the left column will have a "notch" around the left part of the picture, and the right column will have a notch around the right part of the picture. This is shown in Figure 63.

You have a great deal of flexibility in placing absolutely positioned paragraphs on the page. A frame can be horizontally aligned with the frame with the column, margin, page, or an absolute value from the left edge of the page; it can be vertically aligned with the current paragraph, margin, page, or an absolute value from the top edge of the page. Note that these are the alignments of the frame borders and not of the text within the borders. Text within the borders can still be aligned and have indents just as normal paragraphs can. For example, you might align a paragraph frame with the right margin of the page, but the text within that frame can still be centered.

Word automatically resolves conflicts in absolutely positioned paragraphs. For example, you may put a paragraph frame centered 4.5 inches from the top of the page and another one centered 5.5 inches from the top of the page. If the first paragraph is longer than 1 inch, Word simply moves the second one down to fit directly underneath the first. This is especially useful for picture captions or for two paragraphs that must be together: Word always positions the first paragraph it sees, then moves subsequent paragraphs to accommodate paragraphs that are already in place.

Procedure   **Side-by-Side Paragraphs**   To format two paragraphs to be side by side, you must set the indents of each paragraph so that the right indent of the left paragraph is the same as, or to the left of, the left indent of the right paragraph. Two or more paragraphs can be side by side if you set the indents of all the paragraphs so they do not encroach on the indents of the paragraphs to the left and right.

Introduction

Although last quarter was a weak one for our clients, Industrial Refrigeration's sales increased over the same quarter last year. Due to our strong technology and new models, we were able to introduce significant new products to new customers and increase our mainline sales at the same time. With net sales of over $7.3M, this quarter's results indicate that Industrial Refrigeration will finish the fiscal year with a healthy profit.

The restaurant-building market continues to have difficulties, and we scaled back our efforts in the super-restaurant refrigeration units in response. As we did this, we started a new marketing campaign for our smallest cold-storage units aimed at the construction industry. The results were phenomenal, and we were able to increase production of the IR200 series to meet the new demand generated by the marketing campaign.

Management feels strongly about the future of Industrial Refrigeration. President Roger Eisenstadt says, "We are very excited about the new IR800 series. The flexible ventilation system and the easily-removed racks should give us a big advantage in markets with stringent health inspectors. In addition, the development on our laboratory line is almost complete. We will have significant announcements in the coming quarter about a complete scientific refrigeration system that can be installed in new buildings and be retrofitted in rebuilding projects."

Report to Stockholders

Earnings from continuing operations were down slightly due to the process of scaling back the manufacturing of the IR500 series. There was no loss of personnel since the employees were able to move easily to the increased IR200 production. The short-term changeover cost was $120,000 and was easily made up for by the increased sales of the IR200 models.

Research costs were up sharply in the quarter as Industrial Refrigeration finished the development of the IR800 series. The costs were mostly in ventilation fabrication and design, since the IR800 has a very different structure than other models. Research costs for the IRLAB series of laboratory units also increased last quarter, and will continue to increase this quarter as final design and revision is made to the series.

Sales increased by $1.2M over the same quarter last year. Due to a strong marketing push for the IR200 series and advance orders for the IR800, the Industrial

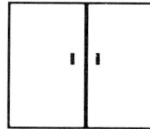

Figure 63

When all the indents are correct, select all the paragraphs and give the Format Paragraph command and set the *side by side* field to *Yes*. You can see the results in layout or preview mode. (See Layout.)

Absolutely Positioned Paragraphs   First, format the text you want to position with the Format Paragraph command, then give the Format pOsition command. The command's dialog is shown in Figure 64. The three fields, *horizontal frame position, vertical frame position*, and *frame width* take many values. To see the possibilities in any of these three fields, select the field and press F1.

The *frame width* field specifies how wide the field will be. The two choices for single-column divisions are *Single Column* and an absolute value. Setting *frame width* to *Single Column* on a single-column page is the same as specifying the area between the margins for the width. If you enter an absolute value, you can enter any amount. If you specify a column wider than the page, Word truncates your text. For divisions with more than one column, you can also specify *Double Column* or *Between Margins*.

The choices for the *horizontal frame position* field are *Left, Centered, Right, Inside*, and *Outside*. These are relative to the column, margins, or page edges, as specified in the first *relative to* field. The choices for the *vertical frame position* field are *In line, Top, Centered*, and *Bottom*. These are relative to the margins or page edges, as specified in the second *relative to* field. *Inside* indicates the left edge of the frame is aligned with the left edge of the *relative to* item on odd pages and the right edge of the frame is aligned with the right edge of the *relative to* item on even pages. *Outside* indicates the left edge of the frame is aligned with the left edge of the *relative to* item on even pages and the right edge of the frame is aligned with the right edge of the

```
FORMAT POSITION
        horizontal frame position: Left        relative to:(Column)Margins Page
        vertical frame position: In line        relative to:(Margins)Page
        frame width: Single Column             distance from text: 0.167"
Enter measurement or press F1 to select from list
Pg1 Co1              {}                  ?                        Microsoft Word
```

Figure 64

relative to item on odd pages. *In line* indicates that the frame should be placed at the spot in the text where the paragraph would appear following the order of the text in the paragraph.

You can also enter an absolute value for the *horizontal frame position* and *vertical frame position* fields. The absolute positions are measured according to the *relative to* fields.

Examples Figure 65 shows the printout of two side-by-side paragraphs. To format the paragraphs, select the first paragraph, give the Format Paragraph command, set *left indent* to 0 in, *right indent* to 4.25 in, and set the *side by side* field to *Yes*. Next, select the second paragraph, give the Format Paragraph command, set *left indent* to 2.5 in, *right indent* to 0 in, and set the *side by side* field to *Yes*.

Figure 66 shows a page that has two absolutely positioned paragraphs. The enlarged quotation is formatted as 24-point boldface type. To format the paragraph, select the paragraph and give the Format pOsition command, set the *frame width* field to 2.5 in, *horizontal frame position* to *Left*, *relative to* to *column*, and the *vertical frame position* field to 5.5 in. The small graphic in the middle of the page was set with *horizontal frame position* set to *Centered*, *relative to* to *page*, the *vertical frame position* to *Centered*, and *relative to* to *page*.

Tips Setting up paragraphs for side-by-side printing is sometimes difficult. Since the *right indent* field is set relative to the right margin, it is not as easy to simply specify the left and right "margins" for each paragraph. It is

The Cars become Boston's first hit band in five years	Formed in Boston during the formative years of New Wave (1975-1978), this band has established many musical idioms. The Cars made tinny synthesizer accompaniment of the lead guitar and unrequited romantic dreams of party girls popular for current bands. Lead singer and song writer Ric Ocasek has also had his own albums become popular.

Figure 65

Introduction

Although last quarter was a weak one for our clients, Industrial Refrigeration's sales increased over the same quarter last year. Due to our strong technology and new models, we were able to introduce significant new products to new customers and increase our main-line sales at the same time. With net sales of over $7.3M, this quarter's results indicate that Industrial Refrigeration will finish the fiscal year with a healthy profit.

The restaurant-building market continues to have difficulties, and we scaled back our efforts in the super-restaurant refrigeration units in response. As we did this, we started a new marketing campaign for our smallest cold-storage units aimed at the construction industry. The results were

> "Industrial Refrigeration will finish the fiscal year with a healthy profit."

phenomenal, and we were able to increase production of the IR200 series to meet the new demand generated by the marketing campaign.

Management feels strongly about the future of Industrial Refrigeration. President Roger Eisenstadt says, "We are very excited about the new IR800 series. The flexible ventilation system and the easily-removed racks should give us a big advantage in markets with stringent health inspectors. In addition, the development on our laboratory line is almost complete. We will have significant announcements in the coming quarter about a complete scientific refrigeration system that can be installed in new buildings and be retrofitted in rebuilding projects."

Report to Stockholders

Earnings from continuing operations were down slightly due to the process of scaling back the manufacturing of the IR500 series. There was no loss of personnel since the employees were able to move easily to the increased IR200 production. The short-term changeover cost was $120,000 and was easily made up for by the increased sales of the IR200 models.

Research costs were up sharply in the quarter as Industrial Refrigeration finished the development of the IR800 series. The costs were mostly in ventilation fabrication and design, since the IR800 has a very different structure than other models. Research costs for the IRLAB series of laboratory units also increased last quarter, and will continue to

Figure 66

helpful to show the ruler with the **Window Options** command (version 4) or the **Options** command (version 5) while setting the indents for side-by-side paragraphs.

Since it is not always easy to set up side-by-side paragraphs, they are good candidates for styles. You can make styles for the elements in a document (such as a text paragraph with a note paragraph to its right), and give them related names such as "NL" and "NR" for "note left" and "note right."

PostScript Printers

Overview   Until a few years ago, almost all printers used with PCs fell into one of three categories: dot matrix, daisywheel, and laser. In 1985, Apple introduced the LaserWriter, the first low-cost laser printer controlled by a language called *PostScript*. PostScript is a *page description language*, which means that you tell the printer how you want the page to look and how text fits within those descriptions rather than specifying where each character or dot goes in a linear fashion. Recently, many other manufacturers have developed PostScript printers, although they still cost significantly more than other laser printers.

If you use Word with a PostScript printer, you might not notice much difference, except that you will have a wider variety of fonts available. Due to the way that PostScript works, you do not need to download fonts for each character size that you use in your document. Thus, printing a document with many sizes on a PostScript printer is faster than on another laser printer. Also, PostScript fonts are scalable, which means that a PostScript printer can create characters of almost any size.

If you are interested, you can see the PostScript commands that Word uses in the output by printing to a file with the **Print File** command and viewing the file with Word. You will see that Word adds a great deal of information to each line that it prints; this additional information enhances the appearance of the output. Note that the **Print Merge Document** command does not put printing commands in a file.

You will probably use Word more than most people if your PostScript printer is the only printer attached to your PC. This is because you will be unable to use standard MS-DOS printing utilities with your PostScript printer. Since most of your day-to-day printing will be done through Word, setting up the standard paragraph and division settings in the NORMAL.STY file will be even more important. (See Styles.) You can set up a style sheet that allows you to open standard ASCII text files and print them easily without having to use any formatting commands.

Printer Drivers

Overview There are hundreds of types of printers available for the PC, and almost every printer has its own way of receiving printing commands. For example, if you have an underlined word in your document, Word needs to know what special sequence of characters it must send to that particular printer to direct it to underline the word. Although some standards have arisen, most printers do not follow them. Consequently, Word needs to know how to direct each type of printer to perform the functions available in Word. To do this, Word uses *printer drivers*, which are special files that tell Word the codes and sequences it must use in order to print correctly. The printer drivers are the files on the Word printers' disks whose extensions are ".PRD." When you run Word's SETUP program, Word copies the printer drivers and associated files to your disk. Some printer drivers are more than a single .PRD file: they include other files that have fonts and other information. These auxiliary files, which must be on the same directory as the .PRD files, have extensions .INI and .DAT.

The printer drivers supplied with Word cover most of the popular printers available today. Of course, there are many printers that could not be included on the two disks. Some printers act just like other printers and therefore can use the printer drivers for the printers that they resemble (this is called *emulation*). For instance, many printers emulate Epson dot-matrix or Diablo daisy wheel printers and therefore can use Word's drivers for these printers. If your printer's manual says that it is Epson-compatible, try the EPSONFX and the EPSONMX printer drivers; if your printer's manual says that it is compatible with the Diablo 630, try the D630 printer driver. Note, however, that many printers that claim to emulate other printers actually do not perform very well and may not work with Word's drivers. Furthermore, you may not be able to take advantage of all of your printer's capabilities in emulation mode.

169

If your printer is not listed among those in the SETUP command or in Word's *Printer Information* guide, there may still be a Word driver for it. Check with the printer's manufacturer and ask if they have a driver available. You can also get drivers from Microsoft on their support system on CompuServe or by calling Microsoft Technical Support. If you still cannot find a driver for your printer, you must use one of Microsoft's generic printer drivers. These printer drivers do not support much character formatting or fonts, but they will at least let you use your printer. The generic drivers are listed below.

DRIVER	USE
TTY.PRD	Standard printer, usually a dot-matrix printer
TTYBS.PRD	Standard printer that can backspace when sent a backspace character. This driver is more powerful than TTY.PRD. Unfortunately, most dot-matrix printers cannot backspace; check your printer's documentation to see how your printer handles backspace characters.
TTYFF.PRD	Standard printer that moves to the top of the next page when sent a form feed character
TTYWHEEL.PRD	Daisy wheel printer

If you are technically inclined, you can change the printer driver for your printer. For example, you may have a newer version of a printer with features that are not available in the printer driver, or you may want to change some of the characters Word uses for creating lines. The MAKEPRD program lets you take a printer driver and convert it into a text format that Word can edit. After editing the text version of the printer driver, you then use MAKEPRD again to change it back into a printer driver that you can use.

There are two main reasons for altering a printer driver: you may want to change the character translation that Word uses to make overstruck characters (such as characters with diacritics), or you may also want to change the sequences that Word sends to the printer to control formatting, especially if you want to add a sequence. Otherwise, it is unlikely that you will ever want to change a printer driver.

Procedure   The two programs you use to change printer drivers are MERGEPRD and MAKEPRD, both of which are automatically copied during installation. Of the two, MERGEPRD is much easier to use and requires less technical knowledge. If you need to change your printer driver, you must be familiar with these programs.

MERGEPRD is used to add and delete features or fonts for a printer driver. It is a menu-driven program and can be learned quickly. MAKEPRD will turn a PRD into a text file and vice versa. To make a change to a PRD with MAKEPRD, you first change the driver to a text file, edit that text file with Word or another editor, and then convert the edited text file into a new driver. The text file is quite difficult to figure out, and it is thus much easier to change font information in MERGEPRD than in MAKEPRD.

Both programs are described in detail in the *Printer Information for Microsoft Word* manual that comes with Word. Be sure to read all the instructions before altering a printer driver since there are many tricks to using the programs.

Warnings   In several early versions of Word, some printer drivers required you to change the page length and width in the **Format Division Margins** command. Later versions of Word changed this to allow you to keep the standard settings. This was especially noticeable to users of the Hewlett-Packard LaserJet printers moving to Word version 4 from Word version 3.1.

Printer drivers tell Word the handshaking protocol (such as "XON/XOFF" or "DTR") to use when talking to the printer. If you cannot get any text out of the printer, check that the printer driver is using the same handshaking for which the printer is set.

Tips   Modifying printer drivers can be tricky and often involves a fair amount of technical knowledge. If you do not want to modify a printer driver for your printer, be sure to check with Microsoft and your printer's manufacturer to see if they might have already done so.

Print Preview. *See* Layout   [Version 5 Only]

Printing

Overview   Word's printing features make it easy to print your documents once you have finished editing them. You can set the options Word will use to print your document from the **Print Options** command, and you can have

171

Word put the files to be printed in a *print queue* so that you can continue to edit while Word prints your document. You can also print out Word's special files such as glossaries and style sheets.

The **Print** command has nine subcommands. The subcommands and their uses are listed below.

SUBCOMMAND	USE
Printer	Prints the document on the printer
Direct	Allows you to send keystrokes directly to the printer
File	Causes Word to send the characters that would have gone to the printer into a file
Glossary	Prints the current glossary. (See Glossaries.)
Merge	Prints form letters. (See Form Letters.)
Options	Sets the options such as choosing the printer driver and defining how much of the document should be printed
Queue	Manages Word's print queue
Repaginate	Repaginates the document. (See Repagination.)
preView	Shows you how the document will look when printed. (See Layout.)

Procedure   You should always give the **Print Options** command before printing a document to be sure that you have the correct printer driver selected and to be sure that you are printing the range of pages you want. After completing the **Print Options** command, Word does not return to your document; instead, it brings you back to the list of **Print** subcommands with the **Printer** subcommand selected; you can then just press Enter to start printing.

Print Options   Figure 67 shows the choices for the **Print Options** command. If you only print to one type of printer, you will probably not change the *printer* and *setup* fields after setting them the first time.

```
PRINT OPTIONS printer: POSTSCRP          setup: LPT1:
       model: PostScript-Single Bin      graphics resolution: 300 dpi
       copies: 1                         draft: Yes(No)
       hidden text: Yes(No)              summary sheet: Yes(No)
       range:(All)Selection Pages        page numbers:
       widow/orphan control:(Yes)No      queued: Yes(No)
       paper feed: Continuous            duplex: Yes(No)
Enter printer name or press F1 to select from list
Pg1 Co1            {}                ?              Microsoft Word
```

Figure 67

The fields for the **P**rint **O**ptions command are listed below.

FIELD	USE
printer	Names the printer driver you want to use. (See Printer Drivers.) To see a list of all printer drivers available, press F1. You should use the SETUP command to copy printer drivers to your disk.
setup	Sets the computer port to which your printer is attached. Your choices are *LPT1:*, *LPT2:*, *LPT3:*, *COM1:*, and *COM2:*.
model	The model of the printer. Press F1 to see the available choices.
graphics resolution	(Version 5 only.) Sets the resolution at which Word will print graphics in the document. Press F1 to see the choices for the printer named in the *printer* field.
copies	Indicates the number of copies you want to print
draft	Specifies whether to print in draft mode or in final mode. Setting *draft* to *Yes* causes Word to print faster than in final mode since Word will not change fonts or use microjustification.
hidden text	Specifies whether Word will print hidden text in your document. Note that you can print hidden text even if it is not visible on the screen.
summary sheet	Tells Word whether you want to print out the document's summary sheet with the document. (See Retrieving Documents.) To have the summary sheet printed before the document, set *summary sheet* to *Yes*.
range	Sets the portion of the document you want Word to print. *All* indicates you want the entire document printed. *Selection* causes Word to only print the portion that is selected. *Pages* causes Word to print only the pages that are listed in the *page numbers* field.
page numbers	Indicates the ranges of pages you want to print. You can specify the ranges as either a single page or a set of pages with either a colon or a hyphen. Each range is separated by a comma. If you want to specify specific pages within a division, give the page number followed by "D" followed by the division number (such as 5D3 for page 5 of the third division). Thus, to print pages 1 through 7, 12, and 20 through 25, enter 1-7,12,20-25 or 1:7,12,20:25.
widow/orphan control	Specifies whether you want widow and orphan control when printing the document. (See Keeps.)
queued	Causes Word to put the file in the print queue

FIELD	USE
paper feed	Controls the printer feed used for the paper. *Manual* indicates that you will insert a piece of paper at the beginning of each page; Word prompts you before printing each page. *Continuous* prints from the main feeder for the printer. If your printer has alternate bins, you can select *Bin1, Bin2,* or *Bin3. Mixed* takes the first page from the first bin and the other sheets from the second bin; this is useful if you have letterhead paper in the first bin and second sheets in the second bin.
duplex	(Version 5 only.) Tells Word whether you want to print on both sides of a single sheet of paper. A few printers allow you to print on both sides of the page. If you are using such a printer and want to print on both sides, set *duplex* to *Yes.*

Using the Print Queue   Word's print queue lets you continue working while you print files. When you print to the queue by setting *queued* field in the **Print Options** command to *Yes,* Word sends characters to the printer as you work. Although this is convenient, it sometimes results in commands that do not flow smoothly. If you have a program in your computer that performs print queuing, use that program instead of Word's queue.

After sending one or more files to Word's queue, you can control the queue with the **Print Queue** subcommands. Use the **Print Queue Pause** command to stop the printer temporarily and the **Print Queue Continue** command to start it again. If you want to get rid of all the print jobs queued, give the **Print Queue Stop** command. If you are printing from the queue and you notice something wrong in the current file printing, use the **Print Queue Restart** command to direct Word to start printing the current document again.

Other Subcommands   The **Print File** command lets you store the characters that Word would have sent to the printer in a file. You can then later print the file by using the MS-DOS COPY command to copy the file to the port on which the printer resides. Depending on the type of printer you are using, the print output file might be quite large relative to the size of the document file.

The **Print Direct** command is useful for putting a short heading on a one-page document without adding the heading in the file or for creating an envelope. Give the **Print Direct** command, type the text you want,

Q

press Enter, then press the Escape key. Those characters will appear on the printer but not on the screen. When you print the rest of the page, Word will begin directly after your heading.

Warnings   If you use the **Print File** command, be sure that you have selected the correct printer driver in the **Print O**ptions command and that the printer you use when you eventually print the file is the same as you specified. The output will probably be garbled if you send a file from the **Print File** command to a different type of printer.

Quit Command

Overview   The **Quit** command returns you to MS-DOS, OS/2, or Windows. Before leaving Word, however, it makes sure that you have saved any changes you made to documents, the glossary, and any open style sheet. It also saves the current settings for many options in a file called MW.INI so that those settings will be used when you start Word again.

It you have made changes to any of the open documents, Word selects the entire changed document and prompts *Enter Y to save, N to lose edits, or Esc to cancel.* Press Y to save the document or N to ignore the changes. Press the Escape key if you change your mind about quitting. Similar prompts appear if you have changed but not saved the glossary or a style sheet.

Word remembers the name of the document in window 1, the selection in that window, whether you were in overtype mode, the current glossary, the last annotation, and the graphics mode you were using. Word also records the values for the following fields in MW.INI file.

COMMAND	FIELD
Library **D**ocument-retrieval **Q**uery	*path*
Library **S**pell **O**ptions (version 5 only)	*user dictionary*
	lookup
	ignore all caps
	check punctuation
	alternatives

COMMAND	FIELD
Options (version 4 only)	*visible*
	printer display
	menu
	menu color
	mute
	display
	screen borders
	line numbers
	date format
	time format
	decimal character
	default tab width
	measure
	linedraw character
	summary sheet
	cursor speed
	speller
Options (version 5 only)	*show hidden text*
	show ruler
	show non-printing symbols
	show layout
	show line breaks
	show style bar
	mute
	summary sheet
	measure
	display mode
	paginate
	colors
	autosave
	autosave confirm
	show menu
	show borders
	date format
	decimal character
	time format
	default tab width
	line numbers
	count blank space
	cursor speed
	linedraw character
	speller path

COMMAND	FIELD
Print Options	*printer*
	setup
	draft
	graphics resolution (version 5 only)
	duplex (version 5 only)
	hidden text
	widow/orphan control
	feed or *paper feed display*
Print preView Options	*display*
Transfer Load command	*read only*
Transfer Options	*setup*
Window Options (version 4 only)	*show hidden text*
	background color
	style bar
	ruler

Note that the *copies, summary sheet, range, page numbers*, and *queued* fields in the **Print Options** command are not preserved. The *outline* field in the **Options** command is not preserved either.

Repagination

Overview   As you enter or edit text in Word, the text that appears on a particular page often changes. For example, when you add text, some text that was on the same page as the new text moves to the next page, some text from that page moves to the next page, and so on. Instead of continuously calculating on which page text will appear, Word usually determines the new page breaks only when you request it to. Version 5 allows you to constantly repaginate the document, although this causes Word to respond more slowly to editing commands.

Automatic pagination also causes problems with page numbering because the **Jump Page** command and the *range* field of the **Print Options** command are reliant on page numbers. Hence, if you repaginate your document after editing it, or if Word constantly repaginates your document, the pages might have different numbers than you expect. Inaccurate page numbering and loss of speed dissuade many people from using automatic repagination.

If you are new to Word version 5, you may want to experiment with both the automatic and manual repagination methods. The repagination in version 5 is significantly faster than in previous versions thanks to a major change in the method Word uses to determine the vertical size of paragraphs. Thus, although repaginating a long document in version 4 might take many minutes, version 5 might take only a few seconds if only a few paragraphs are changed.

Procedure

Use the **Print Repaginate** command to direct Word to repaginate a document. The command's *confirm page breaks* option lets you insert your own page breaks in the document on a page-by-page basis. If you set this field to *Yes*, Word shows you each page break and prompts *Enter Y to confirm or use direction keys*. You can change where Word will break the page by pressing the Up Arrow or Down Arrow. Most of the time, however, you will not want to check each page break and you will set *confirm page breaks* to *No*.

In version 5, use the *paginate* field in the **Options** command to set automatic repagination. The choices are *Auto* and *Manual*. You can still use the **Print Repaginate** command even if you have set the field to *Auto*.

Tips

If you are using automatic repagination, Word usually repaginates only from the recent edits. Thus, if you have a 75-page document and start editing on page 50, the first 49 pages will not be repaginated. However, the actions listed below cause Word to start repaginating from the beginning of a document.

- Loading a document that has not been paginated, such as a text-only file. Since version 5 uses different internal structures for repagination, opening a Word file created in an earlier version of Word causes automatic repagination the first time it is opened.
- Loading a document whose stored printer driver is different than the printer driver currently specified in the **Print Options** command. Since different printer drivers cause lines and pages to break differently, Word assumes that it must repaginate the entire document. Word also starts paginating from the beginning of a document if you change printer drivers in the **Print Options** command.
- Loading a document whose style sheet is more recent than the document itself. Changing the formatting in the style sheet while it

is attached to some other document may affect the pagination. Word also starts paginating from the beginning of a document if you change or delete a style in the style sheet or change the style sheet itself.

- Changing the value of the *hidden text* or *widow/orphan control* fields in the **Print Options** command.

Replacing Text

Overview   Word's **Replace** command lets you change text in your document automatically. It can replace one instance of a word with another, or it can replace text throughout a document. You can also use the **Format repLace** command to replace formatting and styles.

Procedure   The **Replace** command's dialog is shown in Figure 68. In most cases, enter the text you want to change in the *text* field and the replacement text in the *with text* field (up to 40 characters for each field). The default choices for the *confirm, case,* and *whole word* options are usually correct for most of the instances in which you use the **Replace** command.

Word always searches forward in the document. If you have only one character selected when you give the **Replace** command, Word searches and replaces to the end of the document (but not before the selected character). If you have selected more than one character, however, Word searches and replaces only within that selection.

Setting *confirm* to *Yes* causes Word to prompt *Enter Y to replace, N to ignore, or press Esc to cancel* each time it is about to replace characters. Word shows you the change that it is about to make. Set *confirm* to *No* if you want to do the replacements throughout the file.

```
REPLACE text: █                          with text:
         confirm:(Yes)No   case: Yes(No) whole word: Yes(No)
Enter text
Pg1 Co1            {}                ?                    Microsoft Word
```

Figure 68

The *case* option tells Word whether to search only for characters that match the case of the characters you specified in the *text* field, or to find characters that match the *text* field in either uppercase or lowercase letters. Setting *case* to *Yes* indicates that you only want to replace characters that match the case exactly. Often, you want Word to ignore the case since the word you are replacing may or may not be at the beginning of a sentence. As the list below shows, Word matches the capitalization of the characters to be replaced when *case* is set to *No*.

CHARACTERS FOUND	CHARACTERS REPLACING
All uppercase	All uppercase
All lowercase	All lowercase
Initial capital	Initial capital
Mixed cases	Exactly as specified in the *with text* field

The *whole word* option specifies whether the text that is searched for must be a whole word. If you are sure that the text you entered in the *text* field is a whole word and that is all you want to replace, set the *whole word* option to *Yes*. This also makes the replacement process a bit faster.

Special Characters   You can indicate special characters in the search and replace text. For example, you may want to replace all instances of two words that are separated by a tab character. Since you cannot enter a tab character in the text, Word lets you indicate these special characters with the caret character as listed below.

TO INDICATE	USE
Tab character	^t
Newline mark	^n
Paragraph mark	^p
Division mark or forced page break	^d
Column break	^c
Nonbreaking space	^s
Optional hyphen	^-
Caret mark	^^
Any white space	^w

For example, to change instances of "Thus" at the beginning of a paragraph to "Therefore," set the *text* field to ^pThus and the *with text* field to ^pTherefore.

Using "^w" is very useful if you do not know what kind of separation there is between two words. It will match spaces, tab characters, newline marks, paragraph marks, division marks, forced page breaks, and non-breaking spaces, or any combination of them. Note that you cannot use "^w" in the *with text* field.

Replacing Formats and Styles The Format repLace command lets you replace the formatting and styles on characters in your document. It has three subcommands (Character, Paragraph, and Style), and each subcommand has a *confirm* option. With the Character and Paragraph subcommands, choose any format or combination of formats you want to search for, press Enter, and select the format or combination of formats you want to apply. With the Style subcommand, enter keycodes of the styles for which you want to search and replace.

Toggling Case You can change the characters in a selection to be all lowercase, all uppercase, or first letter of each word uppercase. To do this, select the desired characters and press Ctrl F4. Word cycles through the three types of capitalization. This is quite different than using the uppercase character formatting since Word changes the characters, not just the formats.

Warnings If the text in the *text* field does not contain optional hyphens, Word will find all matching text whether or not it has hyphens. However, if the text in the *text* field does contain optional hyphens, Word will match only text that has the optional hyphens in exactly the same place.

Tips Word comes with two macros that use the Replace command. The "repl_w_gloss.mac" macro sets up the Replace command to replace text with the contents of a specified glossary entry, and the "repl_w_scrap.mac" macro sets up the Replace command to replace text with the contents of the scrap. You can create your own macros for advanced searching and replacing. See Macros for an example that replaces throughout the file and keeps your current position.

Retrieving Documents

Overview   Word documents can have a *summary sheet* attached to them that lists pertinent information about the contents of the document. The information in the summary sheets can then be scanned by the Library Document-retrieval commands in order to find documents that meet certain criteria. For example, the *keywords* field of the summary sheet holds key words that are used in the document. To find all documents with those key words, give the Library Document-retrieval Query command and specify the key words in the command's dialog. Word will present a list of all files whose summary sheets include that key word.

Figure 69 shows the fields in a summary sheet. Word prompts for the summary sheet information the first time you save a file unless you have set the *summary sheet* field to *No* in the Options command. You can also update information in a summary sheet or add a summary sheet to a document that does not have one.

The fields in the summary sheet can be filled in any way you want. Use consistent guidelines when filling in summary sheets so that they will be useful when you later search your document. The fields and their uses are listed below.

FIELD	MAXIMUM LENGTH	SUGGESTED USE AND COMMENTS
title	40	Title of the document; topic of a letter or memo; recipient's name
author	40	Your name; your department
operator	40	Name of person who typed the document; name of the editor

```
SUMMARY INFORMATION
   title: █                              version number:
   author:                                 creation date: 03/18/89
   operator:                               revision date: 03/18/89
   keywords:
   comments:
Enter text
Pg1 Co1          {}              ?                    Microsoft Word
```

Figure 69

FIELD	MAXIMUM LENGTH	SUGGESTED USE AND COMMENTS
keywords	80	Important words in the document; main concepts of a paper; recipient's name
comments	256	Other material; since you cannot search for text in this field, no unique information should be listed here.
version number	10	Number of times this document has been revised
creation date	8	Word fills this in automatically, although you can change it.
revision date	8	Word fills this in automatically, although you can change it.

Procedure   The Library Document-retrieval command has six subcommands. Giving the Library Document-retrieval command puts you in document retrieval mode, indicated by *DOCUMENT-RETRIEVAL* in the lower left corner of the screen.

The **Query** subcommand finds the files with which you want to work. After stating the file searching criteria, you are presented a list of files that meet those criteria; you then can select from that list and the selection is used by the other subcommands. In version 4, you can only select one file; in version 5, you can select many. After you have selected a file or files, the four subcommands listed below can act on them.

SUBCOMMAND	USE
Load	Loads the documents as if you had given the Transfer Load command. You can specify whether or not to load the files in read-only mode.
Print	Prints the documents, the summary sheets, or both. You can specify whether to print all the documents or just the selected ones.
Copy (Version 5 only)	Copies the selected files to a different drive or directory. You can also specify that Word should copy the style sheet for the documents. This allows you to create sets of documents on other directories or drives along with all the necessary material associated with them.
Delete (Version 5 only)	Deletes the selected files. You can also specify that Word should delete the style sheet for the documents.

The **View** subcommand lets you change the way the selected files are listed. You can specify a sort order and how much information is given in the list of select files. You can sort by directory, author, operator, revision date, creation date, or file size. The three choices for the views are listed below.

OPTION	MEANING
Short	Only the file and path names are shown. Word uses two columns for the display.
Long	Word shows the file and path name and also shows the sort key in a one-column. If the list is sorted by file, the author is shown.
Full	This shows a list like *Short*, but there is a window with the summary sheet of the selected document in the middle of the screen.

The **Update** subcommand lets you update the information in the selected summary sheets. Choose the **Exit** subcommand to leave document-retrieval mode.

Query Subcommand When you give the **Library Document-retrieval Query** command, Word prompts you for the search criteria. These include the *author, operator, keywords, creation date*, and *revision date* fields from the summary sheets, as well as a path, text from the documents, and case-sensitivity of the document search. Figure 70 shows the choices for the **Library Document-retrieval Query** command. Generally, you will enter words to look for in the summary sheet fields and a set of paths in the *path* field and press Enter to perform the search.

The path is all the paths you want Word to search for documents. You must state the paths exactly, with each path separated by a comma. Word

```
QUERY path: C:\
  author:
  operator:
  keywords:
  creation date:                        revision date:
  document text:
  case: Yes(No)                         marked files only: Yes(No)
Enter search directories separated by commas or press F1 to select from list
                            ?                              Microsoft Word
```

Figure 70

184

will always search the path specified in the **T**ransfer **O**ptions command, but you will probably want to add other paths to this list. Paths can include disk names and can use absolute or relative path names (such as ".." to indicate the directory above the current directory). Since Word saves the path that you use after you quit, you need not reenter the path each time you use Word.

You can enter up to 256 characters for each of the *author, operator,* and *keywords* fields. You can use wildcard characters (* and ?) in the text for which you are searching. For instance, if you enter "chair*n," Word will match with "chairman," "chairwoman," and "chairperson."

You can use logical operators in these fields (as well as the *creation date* and *revision date* fields) to make your search more specific. The logical operators must be used without spaces around them. The logical operators are listed below.

LOGICAL OPERATOR	CHARACTER
OR	, (comma)
AND	& (ampersand) or a space
NOT	˜ (tilde)
less than	<
greater than	>

For example, to find all summary sheets that have either the keyword "mining" or the keyword "tunneling," enter mining,tunneling in the *keyword* field. To find only the summary sheets with both "highlights" and "annual" in the *keyword* field, enter highlights&annual or highlights annual. You can also group logical operators with parentheses. For example, to find all authors with the name "Benson" but not also with "Shirley," enter Benson˜Shirley in the *author* field. To find all revision dates before 3/7/89, enter <3/7/89.

If the text for which you are searching has any of the logical operator characters, you must put the text in quotation marks. If the text for which you are searching has quotation marks, use double quotation marks and enclose the entire string in quotation marks.

Searching through the summary sheets goes fairly quickly, even on floppy-based systems. However, sometimes you want to find information that you know is not in the summary sheets but is in the documents themselves. For that, you must fill in the *document text* field. You can use up to 256 characters in this field and use the logical operators described above. Note, however, that searching for this text can be agonizingly slow if you have many files in your path. The *case* field tells Word whether or not to match case in its search for text listed in the *document text* field.

After pressing Enter, Word searches through the paths for the specified documents and presents a list. If the list is longer than can be seen on the screen, you can use the Home, End, Pg Dn, and Pg Up keys to scroll through the list. In version 4, you select a file by moving the selection to that file's name. In version 5, you can select many files by moving the selection to each name and pressing the Space Bar. Pressing Ctrl Space Bar selects all the files; pressing Shift Ctrl Space Bar deselects all the files. Marked files are indicated by an asterisk next to their name.

In version 5, you can also reduce the list shown to just those marked by selecting *Yes* for the *marked files only field* and pressing Enter.

Warnings   Word looks only on disk for documents. If you are editing a document in Word and have not saved the changes to disk, Word will look only at the copy on disk.

If you are searching for files on network servers or are using Word under Windows, the **Library Document-retrieval Query** command will not detect changes. To update the list so the **Library Document-retrieval Query** command looks at the most current files, press Ctrl F4 before giving a query.

Tips   The dates you enter in the *creation date* and *revision date* fields must be in the same format as the one selected in the *date format* field of the **O**ptions command. If you choose the comma for the *decimal character* in the **O**ptions command, you must use the semicolon as the OR logical operator.

You might have different lists of paths that you use at different times. For example, you might search one set of paths for memos and another set of paths for chapters in a set of reports. You can create macros that fill in the *path* field of the **Library Document-retrieval Query** command so that you need not type the paths in by hand.

Revision Marks

Overview   Producing a document takes many steps. Often, you begin with an outline, then start writing the text. After you are finished entering the text the first time, you go back and begin changing words and sentences, possibly rearranging paragraphs. By the time you have finished editing, your document often looks very different from your first draft. This process is also known as *redlining*.

Tracking the changes you make is not easy. Although you can print out every version of the text or keep copies of the document files when backing up your disks, accurately comparing two documents on paper or on disk is difficult. Word offers revision marks as one method of controlling the editing process. Word's Format revision-Marks command controls the use of revision marks. When you use revision marks, Word indicates where text has been inserted or deleted. You can quickly see where you have changed text by looking for the revision bar in the margin of your document. When you are finished editing, Word updates the document so that all insertions and deletions are reflected in the final document. Figure 71 shows some revised text; the underlined text is new and the struckthrough text is deleted.

Revision marks are truly useful for only one or two steps in the revision process. After that, your document often becomes difficult to read due to the jumble of deleted text and new text. Revision marks can be helpful, however, if someone else is checking your document to ensure that changes were made correctly. If many people are revising a document, you may prefer using a package specifically designed for revisions, such as ForComment. (See Other Programs.)

```
Although last quarter was a weak one for our clients,
Industrial Refrigeration's sales increased over the
same quarter last year. Due to our strongleading-edge
technology and new models, we were able to introduce
significant new products to new customers and increase
our main line sales to our current customersat the same
time. With net sales of over $7.3M, this quarter's
results indicate that Industrial Refrigeration will
finish the fiscal year with a healthy profit.
```

Figure 71

Procedure

To turn on revision marks, use the Format revision-Marks Options command. Select *Yes* for the *add revision marks* field to begin using revision marks. You can also select the format in which the added text is shown and whether you want to see revision bars. Word displays *MR* at the bottom of the screen to indicate that you are adding revision marks. After you turn on revision marks, Word stores the choices you make for the Format revision-Marks Options command in the file.

The choices for the *inserted text* field are *Normal, Bold, Underlined, upper-Case,* and *Double-underlined.* Choose a style that you do not use in your document so that the additions will stand out. Generally, it is useful to see revision bars, and you can specify their position: *None, Left, Right,* and *Alternate* (outside of the page for even and odd pages). Word always displays deleted text with struckthrough characters unless you are using a color adapter, in which case deletions are shown in red.

As you revise your document, Word displays the inserted and deleted text as indicated. If you are using revision marks, you cannot backspace over text you want to remove; instead, you must delete it using one of the other methods described in Deleting Text. You cannot use overtype mode when revising.

After the revision process is complete, you can either accept or reject your changes. To accept changes, select the portion of the document in which you want to make the changes permanent and give the Format revision-Marks accept-Revisions command. The "removing marks" indicate that revision marks were removed when permanent changes were made. To make the changes permanent for the whole document, select the entire document with Shift F10 before giving the Format revision-Marks accept-Revisions command. To reverse your changes, select the changed text and give the Format revision-Marks Undo-revisions command.

Searching for revised text with the Format revision-Marks Search command moves the selection to the next revised text in your document. Since Word keeps the Format revision-Marks command selected, you need only press S again to repeat the search.

Warnings

In version 4, Word does not mark as changed any text that is changed by a Library command. Thus, words changed by the spelling checker or thesaurus are not marked in version 4; they are, however, marked in version 5.

R

Word counts text formatted with the strikethrough format as revised. This is unfortunate, since you cannot use that format in a document with revision marks. If you have text that you have formatted as strikethrough and give the Format revision-Marks accept-Revisions command, Word will delete that text. If you give the Format revision-Marks Undo-revisions command, Word removes the strikethrough formatting.

Ruler

Overview   Each window in Word can display a ruler at the top of the window. The ruler shows the position of the indents and tab stops. As you move the selection from paragraph to paragraph, the ruler changes. In version 4, the ruler shows the number of characters across the page, not the distance; each numerical marking indicates ten characters. In version 5, the ruler shows numbers of inches. The markings on the ruler are based on the *measure* field of the **O**ptions command.

The ruler appears when you give the Format **P**aragraph command or the Format **T**abs command. (See Tables and Tab Stops.) You can also set the ruler to appear all the time. Figure 72 shows a typical ruler. The marks that appear on rulers are listed below.

MARK	MEANING
[	Left indent
¦	First line indent
]	Right indent
L	Left tab
C	Center tab
R	Right tab
D	Decimal tab
|	Vertical tab
.	Leader . before tab
-	Leader - before tab
_	Leader _ before tab

Sliding and Scaling Rulers (Version 5 Only)   In version 5, the ruler has more uses than in previous versions. In layout mode, the ruler becomes *sliding* and *scaling*, which makes it easier to see the relative positions

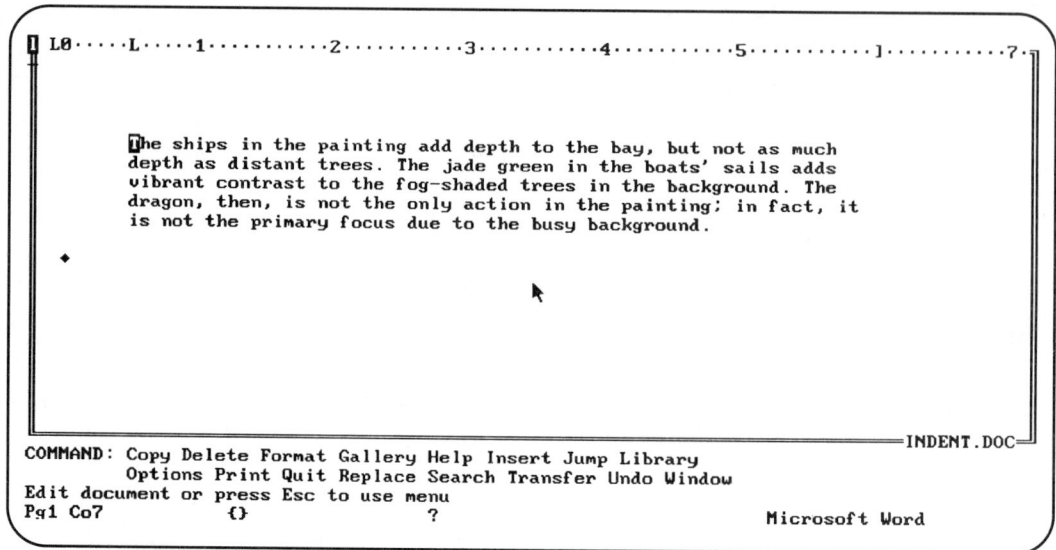

```
  L0·····L····1············2············3·········4············5··········]··········7·

          The ships in the painting add depth to the bay, but not as much
          depth as distant trees. The jade green in the boats' sails adds
          vibrant contrast to the fog-shaded trees in the background. The
          dragon, then, is not the only action in the painting; in fact, it
          is not the primary focus due to the busy background.
       ◆
                                              ▸
                                                                     =INDENT.DOC=
  COMMAND: Copy Delete Format Gallery Help Insert Jump Library
           Options Print Quit Replace Search Transfer Undo Window
  Edit document or press Esc to use menu
  Pg1 Co7            {}              ?                    Microsoft Word
```

Figure 72

of text within objects such as columns and absolutely positioned paragraphs. Sliding and scaling rulers are especially useful for proportional fonts and smaller fonts.

If you have objects such as absolutely positioned paragraphs and columns next to each other, the ruler slides so that the 0 mark is aligned with the left edge of the object with the selection. The paragraph indents are shown for the object's frame, not for the page.

In order to show number of inches correctly, the ruler must scale itself to handle small fonts and proportional spacing. This is important in layout mode so that you can check the position of objects that are on the same line of the position of the columns. The ruler will also be scaled in galley mode if you have printer display set in the Options command.

Procedure   To display the ruler, give the Window Options command (version 4) or the Options command (version 5) and set the *ruler* or *show ruler* field to *Yes*. If you are using the mouse, you can turn on the ruler by pointing in the upper-right corner of the window and clicking the left button. To turn off the ruler, point in the upper-right corner and press both buttons.

190

R

Tips

Viewing the ruler in layout mode gives a good idea of how the objects are laid out. The following macro for version 5 can be used to be sure the ruler is on when you switch to layout mode.

```
<ctrl esc>o<tab 2>y<tab 2>y<enter>
```

Running Heads

Overview

Most books, magazines, reports, theses, and other multi-page documents have information at the top or bottom of the page. This information can be just the page number, but it is also common practice to put the document or chapter title in the header or footer as well. Word makes it easy to insert and control the content of the headers and footers. Since all commands for headers are the same as for footers, Word groups them as *running heads*.

Running heads are treated just like other paragraphs. You can format them with character and paragraph formatting so that you can have part in italics or in boldface. You can even include graphics in a running head, such as an icon representing the subject of a chapter.

To create a running head, enter the text. After entering the text, give the **F**ormat **R**unning-head command to mark the paragraph as a running head and specify its position on the page (top or bottom) as well as the type of page on which it should appear (even, odd, first in the division, or a combination of these three). If this is the first text on the current page, Word begins using that running head immediately; if not, the running head takes effect beginning on the next page.

In the **F**ormat **D**ivision **M**argins command, specify how far from the top and bottom of the paper you want the running heads. Thus, the position of the running heads remains the same if you change the top and bottom margin of the page. You can specify the horizontal position of the running heads from either the edge of the page or from the left margin.

The running heads you specify are only valid for the division in which they are defined. Thus, if you have many divisions in your document, you must put the running heads at the beginning of each division. Since this can get tedious, you will probably want to create a macro that puts the standard running heads at the beginning of a new division. If you break up your division with page breaks and column breaks, you only need the header at the beginning of the division.

Running heads can be multi-line. Since each page can have only one header and one footer, multi-line running heads must be created from a single paragraph. The easiest way to do this is to use the newline character (Shift Enter) to make more than one line. Running heads can also have the page number, date, or other special glossary entries. (See Glossaries.)

If your document will be printed on two sides of a page, you will probably want different running heads for even and odd pages. For instance, in the footer of this book, the page number appears near the outside edge of the page so that you can see it easily when flipping through the book; in the header, the large letter appears on the outside edges and the section names appear on the inside edges.

In books where even and odd pages are different, left-side pages are always even and right-side pages are always odd. You will usually choose *right* for the alignment on odd pages and the first page and *left* for the alignment on even pages. This makes the running heads appear near the outside edge of the pages when printed. The headings are therefore easier to read.

Procedure   Enter the text or graphics you want in the running head and give the **Format Running-head** command. Select either *Top* or *Bottom* for the *position*, and set the *odd pages, even pages*, and *first page* fields. For example, to make a header that appears on the top of all odd pages (but not the first page), *set position* to *Top, odd pages* to *Yes, even pages* to *No*, and *first page* to *No*. You can use Ctrl F2 to make a paragraph a header and Alt F2 to make a paragraph a footer, but Word will use the last settings you used for the options, which may not be what you want.

You will generally want at least one of your running heads to contain the page number. To include the page number, type page and press F3 (since the page number is a special glossary entry). Use the "dateprint" special glossary entry if you want the running head to indicate the date the document was printed. When Word prints your document, it prints the page number in the format you specify in the **Format Division Page-numbers** command. (See Page Numbers.) You can also use compound page numbers (such as "Page 3-5" or "Page Marketing-12") by typing the text preceding the page number, the hyphen, page, then pressing F3.

When you format a paragraph as a running head, Word puts a caret (^) in the selection bar. If you want to see what type of running head a paragraph is, you must display the style bar. If you do not have the style bar shown, give the **Window Options** command (version 4) or **Options** command (version 5) and set *style bar* or *show style bar* to *Yes*. You will see the following styles for running heads.

CODE	TYPE OF RUNNING HEAD
t	Top, odd and even pages
te	Top, even pages
to	Top, odd pages
tf	Top, first page of the division
b	Bottom, odd and even pages
be	Bottom, even pages
bo	Bottom, odd pages
bf	Bottom, first page of the division

If you have made a paragraph a running head and want to change it back to a normal paragraph, give the **Format Running-head** command and select *No* for *odd pages, even pages,* and *first page.* If you are using Word version 5, you can also select *None* in the *position* field.

You must position your running heads both vertically and horizontally. Use the **Format Division Margins** command to position the headers and footers vertically, and use the **Format Running-head** and the **Format Paragraph** commands to place the running head horizontally.

In the dialog for the **Format Division Margins** command, set the distance from the top and bottom edge of the page in the *running-head position from top* and *from bottom* fields. For example, if your top and bottom page margins are .75 inches, you might enter **.5** in for the running head position.

Before positioning a running head horizontally in version 5, decide if you want to position it relative to the left margin or relative to the edge of the page (in Word version 4, you can only position it relative to the edge of the page). If you specify *No* for this field, be sure to check the measurements you choose for the running heads if you change the margins of your document. Next, give the **Format Paragraph** command and select the desired alignment, left indent, and right indent.

Examples   **A Sample Report**   Assume that you have a report that will be printed on both sides of the page after you have printed it. The report is broken into chapters that always begin on an odd page, and the headers have the chapter name. The footers will have the page numbers on the outside edge, and the report title ("Annual Customer Survey") on the inside edge.

You do not want the header with the chapter name to appear on the first page of the chapter, since it would be directly above the chapter title and would seem redundant. You do, however, want the footer to appear on the first page of the chapter. The headers will be aligned with the edge of the pages, 1 inch from each edge.

At the beginning of the first chapter (called "Introduction"), before any of the chapter's text, enter a blank paragraph, select it, and give the Format Running-head command. Select *Top* for the *position* and set *odd pages* to *No*, *even pages* to *No*, and *first page* to *Yes*. This creates the blank running-head that prevents a header from appearing on the top of the first page.

Next, create four paragraphs that look like this:

```
Introduction
Introduction
Annual Customer Survey <tab> Page (page)
Page (page) <tab> Annual Customer Survey
```

Note that the "(page)" was created by typing page and pressing F3. Also note that there is a Tab character between the two parts of the footers. You will use left- and right-aligned tabs to make these tabs appear in the correct position on the page. You will now format the four paragraphs as the odd page header, even page header, odd page footer, and even page footer, respectively.

- Select the first paragraph (the odd header) and give the Format Running-head command. Select *Top* for the *position* and set *odd pages* to *Yes*, *even pages* to *No*, *first page* to *No*, and *align with left margin* to *No*. Give the Format Paragraph command and select *Right* for *alignment* and enter 1 in for the *right indent*.
- Select the second paragraph (the even header) and give the Format Running-head command. Select *Top* for the *position* and set *odd pages* to *No*, *even pages* to *Yes*, *first page* to *No*, and *align with left margin* to *No*. Give the Format Paragraph command and select *Left* for *alignment* and enter 1 in for the *left indent*.
- Select the third paragraph (the odd footer) and give the Format Running-head command. Select *Bottom* for the *position* and set *odd pages* to *Yes*, *even pages* to *No*, *first page* to *Yes*, and *align with left margin* to *No*. (Note that you want to set *first page* to *Yes* so that the footer appears at the bottom of the first page of the chapter). Give

the Format Paragraph command and select *Left* for *alignment*, enter 1 in for the *left indent*, and enter 1 in for the *right indent*. Now give the Format Tabs Set command, and set a right tab at the right margin, which is shown on the ruler as a right square bracket (]).

- Select the fourth paragraph (the even footer) and give the Format Running-head command. Select *Bottom* for the *position* and set *odd pages* to *No, even pages* to *Yes, first page* to *No*, and *align with left margin* to *No*. Give the Format Paragraph command and select *Left* for *alignment*, enter 1 in for the *left indent*, and enter 1 in for the *right indent*. Now give the Format Tabs Set command, and set a right tab at the right margin, which is shown on the ruler as a right square bracket (]).

You can adapt this procedure when experimenting with running heads. For example, to position the report title in the center instead of on the inside of the page, add a tab before the title and add a centered tab to the middle of the two footer lines. You can also experiment with changing the formatting and margins for the headers and footers.

Warnings   If Word stops printing headings in your document, be sure that you did not accidentally add a division mark in the middle of the document. Also be sure that each division has the running heads immediately after the division mark.

If you use the *align with left margin* field in the Format Running-head command and change the left margin, the position of your running head will change. Thus, this field is useful for aligning text with the left margin of the text (such as the outside of even pages or the inside of odd pages) but not with text that is meant to be aligned with the right margin (the inside of even pages or the outside of odd pages).

When you format running heads with the Format Paragraph command, Word displays the heading on the screen as if you had indented it from the left and right margins, not the left and right page edges. As a result, the running heads may appear improperly positioned when you look at the screen. Don't trust the screen—use the Print preView command (in version 5).

Tips   One of the most common frustrations in formatting a document is getting the running heads in exactly the right position. Positioning them so that they are neither too close to the edge of the paper nor to the print on the page often takes a few tries. When you are experimenting, it is best to use the **Print pre**View command (if you are using Word version 5) or Pageview (if you are using Word version 4 under Windows). If you cannot use either of these, use the **Print O**ptions command to specify two representative pages on which the running heads appear and only print those until you have the positioning correct.

If you are creating a document with many divisions, you must copy the running heads to the beginning of each division. Since this is often time-consuming, you may want to create a macro that inserts a division marker, types in the standard headers and footers, and formats each running head paragraph correctly. Then, to create a new division, simply run the macro and change any wording in the running heads if necessary.

The F4 (repeat formatting) key makes formatting running heads less tedious. Once you give the formatting for one running head, select the next one, press F4, then change any of the formatting differences. If you are formatting many headings, format the first one, select all the others, press F4, then change any desired formatting.

Saving. *See* Transfer

Scrap

Overview

The scrap is very useful as a temporary holder for moving text in your document. You can move text to the scrap with the **C**opy command or the **D**elete command, and you can copy text from the scrap to your document with the **I**nsert command. For any of these commands, Word displays { } as the default choice when it prompts you for the location. The curly braces indicate the scrap.

The scrap holds only one chunk of text at a time. You can replace but not add to the text in the scrap. However, the scrap is flexible; in the gallery, you can copy or delete styles to the scrap. (See Styles.) When you perform mathematical calculations in Word, the result is put into the scrap. (See Math.) You can read the contents of the scrap into a variable in macros.

The contents of the scrap are shown at the bottom of the screen, between the braces. If the scrap has more than sixteen characters, Word displays the first six and last six with ellipses between them. If the text you selected has special characters, Word displays them with the graphics symbols listed below.

SYMBOL	MEANING
↔	Beginning or end of hidden text
◙	Dateprint glossary entry
§	Division mark
▍	End of row in column selection
♠	Footnote reference
↓	Newline character
–	Optional hyphen
◙	Page number glossary entry
¶	Paragraph mark
·	Space
→	Tab character
♥	Timeprint glossary entry

Procedure   To delete selected text from your document and put it into the scrap, use the **Delete** command or press the Delete key. To make a copy of the selected text into the scrap, give the **Copy** command. To copy the text from the scrap into your document, use the Insert command or press the Insert key. If you have selected text and you want the contents of the scrap to replace the selected text, press Shift Insert.

Warnings   The **Transfer Clear All** command empties the scrap. Be sure you do not want to save the text in the scrap before you give the command. Also, using Word's mathematical calculations puts the results into the scrap, replacing whatever was there before.

Tips   Each character in the scrap takes up part of Word's memory. If you have a large selection in the scrap and Word indicates that it is running low on memory, you may want to clear the scrap by selecting a single character and copying it to the scrap.

Scrolling and Selecting

Overview   Word gives you many choices about how to move from place to place in your text. Scrolling is one technique. You will find that most of your time editing a document is spent scrolling with both the keyboard and the mouse. This section gives brief summaries of the scrolling actions. (See Keyboard and Mouse.)

Procedure   The following keys move the cursor.

KEY	MOVEMENT
Up Arrow	Up
Down Arrow	Down
Left Arrow	Left
Right Arrow	Right
Home	Beginning of line
End	End of line
Pg Up	Up a windowful
Pg Down	Down a windowful
Ctrl Up Arrow	Beginning of previous paragraph
Ctrl Down Arrow	Beginning of next paragraph
Ctrl Left Arrow	Beginning of previous word
Ctrl Right Arrow	Beginning of next word
Ctrl Home	Top of window
Ctrl End	Bottom of window
Ctrl Pg Up	Top of document
Ctrl Pg Down	Bottom of document

The following keys are used for selecting.

KEY	SELECTION
F7	Previous word
F8	Next word
F9	Previous paragraph
F10	Next paragraph
Shift F7	Previous sentence
Shift F8	Next sentence
Shift F9	Current line
Shift F10	Entire document

To scroll with the mouse, point at the left border of a window and press the left or right buttons to scroll up or down. To thumb to a specific spot in a document, point at the left border of a window and press both buttons. To scroll horizontally, point at the bottom border of a window and press the left or right buttons.

The following mouse actions are used for selecting.

TO SELECT	POINT AT	PRESS
Character	Text	Left button
Word	Text	Right button
Sentence	Text	Both buttons
Line	Selection bar	Left button
Paragraph	Selection bar	Right button
Entire document	Selection bar	Both buttons

When you type text on the last line of the window and Word needs to go to a new line, Word scrolls all the lines up one and starts the new line. You may want Word to scroll up half the window instead, leaving a blank half window in which to type. To implement this, run Word with the /Y option. From MS-DOS, give the command WORD /Y. Word will then continue to use half-screen scrolling each time you run Word until you start Word with the /Z option, which reverts Word back to its normal scrolling.

Tips

In version 5, you can scroll and thumb using the mouse even if you have borders turned off for the window. Simply point in the first column of the window and use the same buttons shown above.

You can make a macro that scrolls down through your text until it gets to the end. This lets you start the macro, sit back and watch the text, then press Esc to stop it at any time. The macro is simply

```
«while selection<>""»<down>«endwhile»
```

Searching

Overview   Word's Search command lets you find text anywhere in your document, even if you are not completely specific when specifying the text you want. You can also use the Format sEarch command to search for formatting and styles.

Procedure   The Search command's dialog is shown in Figure 73. In most cases, you enter the text for which you want to search in the *text* field (up to 40 characters). The default choices for the *direction, case,* and *whole word* options are usually correct for most of the instances in which you use the Search command.

Word lets you choose which direction from the current position to search in the *direction* field. The *case* option tells Word whether to search only for characters that match the case of the characters you specified in the *text* field, or to find characters that match the *text* field in either upper-case or lowercase letters. Setting *case* to *Yes* indicates that you want to search only for characters that exactly match the case of the characters in the *text* field. Often, you want Word to ignore the case since the word for which you are searching may or may not be at the beginning of a sentence.

The *whole word* option specifies whether the text that is searched for must be a whole word. If you are sure that the text you entered in the *text* field is a whole word and that is all you want to find, set the *whole word* option to *Yes*. This also makes the searching process a bit faster.

Special Characters   You can indicate special characters in the search text. For example, you may want to search for two numbers separated by

```
SEARCH text: █
        direction: Up(Down) case: Yes(No) whole word: Yes(No)
Enter text
Pg1 Co1            {}                    ?                    Microsoft Word
```

Figure 73

a Tab character. Since you cannot enter a Tab character in the *text* field, Word lets you indicate these special characters with the caret character.

TO INDICATE	USE
Tab character	^t
Newline mark	^n
Paragraph mark	^p
Division mark or forced page break	^d
Column break	^c
Nonbreaking space	^s
Optional hyphen	^-
Caret mark	^^
Any white space	^w

For example, to search for "Finally" at the beginning of a paragraph, set the *text* field to ^pFinally.

Using "^w" is very useful if you do not know what kind of separation exists between two words. It will match spaces, tab characters, newline marks, paragraph marks, division marks, forced page breaks, and non-breaking spaces, or any combination of them.

Searching for Formats and Styles   The Format sEarch command lets you search for text based on the formatting and styles on characters in your document. It has three subcommands (**C**haracter, **P**aragraph, and **S**tyle). With the **C**haracter and **P**aragraph subcommands, choose any format or combination of formats you want to search for. With the **S**tyle subcommand, enter the key codes of the styles for which you want to search.

Warnings   If the text in the *text* field does not contain optional hyphens, Word will find all matching text whether or not it has hyphens. However, if the text in the *text* field does contain optional hyphens, Word will match only text that has the optional hyphens in exactly the same place.

Selecting.   *See* **Scrolling and Selecting**

Sequences

Overview

Reports and papers often contain figures and tables, both of which are numbered sequentially starting with 1 for the first figure. This numbering system becomes a problem in long documents if you add or delete a figure in the middle of the document and therefore need to renumber all the following figures.

Word's sequencing feature allows automatic numbering of figures and tables. Because the numbering is determined when you print, you can add items to the middle of the sequence without needing to change anything else in the document. You can have up to ten sequences in a document.

You can use sequences with Word's cross-referencing feature. (See Cross-References.) For example, you can refer by name to an element in a sequence somewhere else in the document. Since the cross-reference is by name, Word finds the correct sequence number and inserts it at the place of reference.

Procedure

Each sequence must have a sequence name that identifies it. You then include *sequence holders* in your document to indicate where you want the number to appear. When Word encounters a sequence name that has not appeared earlier in the document, it begins numbering that sequence at 1. The next time it sees a sequence holder with that name, it numbers it as 2, and so on. Sequence names can be up to 31 characters and can contain letters, numbers, periods, hyphens, and underscores (but not spaces).

To enter a sequence holder, type the sequence name followed by a colon and press F3. Word displays this in parentheses to indicate that it is a special mark similar to the special glossary marks. Each sequence has a different name.

You may want Word to skip numbers in the sequence. To do this, type the sequence name followed by two colons and press F3. This causes Word to increment the sequence number without printing anything.

You may choose any number to begin a sequence or to reset the numbering in a sequence. To do this, enter the sequence name followed by two colons and a number that is one less than the value you want for the next instance of the sequence. For example, if you want to start a sequence at 6, enter the name followed by ::5 before the first occurrence of the sequence.

Examples   Assume that your paper has both figures and tables. Each figure and table has a caption that has the number and some text. For instance, a figure caption might be "Figure 6. New Building Plans for the Proposed Site."

You will use two sequences called "figure.number" and "table.number." You can enter the caption text without the sequence name, then add the sequence name after. For the above example, type the caption `Figure . New Building Plans for the Proposed Site.` Use the Left Arrow to move the cursor to the first period, type `figure.number:`, and press F3. Figure 74 shows the result.

Tables are entered the same way. For the caption of a table, type the caption text with the sequence name. First type `Table table.number:` and press F3. Then type `. Work Allocation By Month.`

When you print the document, Word replaces this first occurrence of "figure.number" with 1, the next occurrence of "figure.number" with 2, and so on. The printed output of the example figure caption is shown in Figure 75.

Tips   Using meaningful names for your sequence holders will help someone unfamiliar with the document determine the use of each sequence.

Remember that you can create tables of figures with Word's table of contents feature. (See Tables of Contents.)

```
          .G.D:\NEWBUILD.PCX;5.5";2.468";PCX
Figure (figure.number:). New Building Plans for the
Proposed Site.
```

Figure 74

Figure 4. New Building Plans for the Proposed Site.

Figure 75

S

Shading

Overview   If you use Word to prepare brochures and advertising material on a laser printer, you may have noticed that your pages often have a great deal of white space. Many designers working with typesetting and pasteup sometimes use gray shading on some headings to avoid the appearance of too much white. Word allows you to put shading over a paragraph with the Format Border command.

When you print, paragraph shading overlays your paragraph with dots. You specify the density of the dots as a percentage of black: 0 indicates no shading, 50 indicates half gray, and 100 indicates completely black. Word rounds whatever values you give to 0, 10, 40, 70, or 100.

Procedure   To add shading to a paragraph, give the Format Border command and enter a number for the *background shading* field. Lower numbers indicate less shading.

Examples   Figure 76 shows samples of headlines shaded with 0, 10, 40, 70, and 100 percent shading.

Tips   Shading generally looks good only on laser printers and very high quality dot-matrix printers. On most dot-matrix printers, shading either obscures

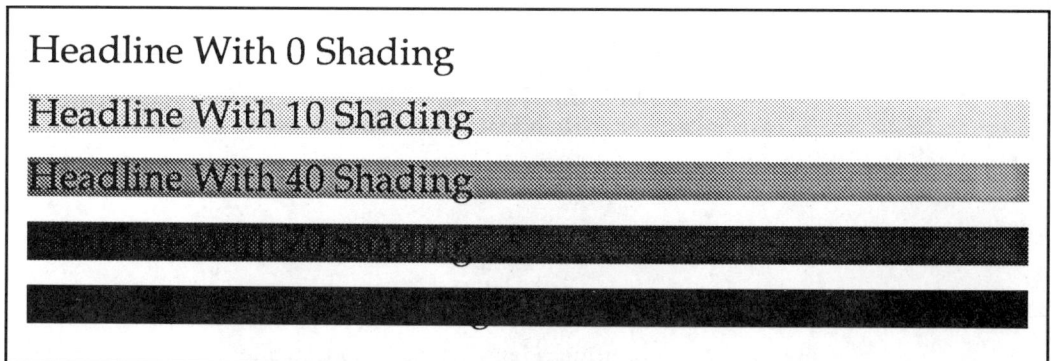

Headline With 0 Shading

Headline With 10 Shading

Headline With 40 Shading

Figure 76

the text or makes it look messy. Experiment with shading on your printer before using it in final output.

If your printer has IBM graphics characters but no graphics capabilities, Word overlays the three shading characters (ASCII 176, 177, and 178) for the different shading amounts. Using more than 40 percent shading uses the middle-weight character, which is usually too dark for most applications.

Sorting

Overview   Typing lists in sorted order is tedious if the list from which you are work-ing is not already sorted. This task is especially difficult if you want to sort a table based on a column in the middle of the table. Fortunately, Word can sort your unsorted lists and tables. You can sort into ascending or descend-ing lists, and can also specify the column on which you want to sort.

Word's sorting can be either alphabetic or numeric. The ASCII sequence handles the alphabetic sorting and is shown in Figure 77. Word ignores diacritical marks, but sorts international characters in the positions they would occupy in a Roman alphabet. Numeric sorting sorts numbers by their value. Numeric values can include decimal points, dollar signs, per-cent signs, minus signs, commas, and parentheses.

Word sorts paragraphs unless you have a column selected with the column select feature (Shift F6). Thus, if you are sorting a table or an outline, each line that you want to be sorted should be a paragraph unless you have selected only one column.

```
space
! " # $ % & ' ( ) * + , - . /
: ; < = > ? @
A B C D E F G H I J K L M N O P Q R S T U V W X Y Z
[ \ ] ^ _ `
a b c d e f g h i j k l m n o p q r s t u v w x y z
{ | } ~
```

Figure 77

205

Procedure   Use the Library Autosort command to sort the selected text. Figure 78 shows the Library Autosort command dialog. Select the type of sort you want to perform in the *by* field and the order you want for the list in the *sequence* field.

Setting *case* to *No* tells Word to ignore case when it sorts. You can use this setting if you have mixed-case words (such as proper names and uncapitalized words) and do not want Word to differentiate them based on case.

If you select entire paragraphs, Word sorts based on the first letter of the paragraphs. If you select a column, Word bases the sort on that column. For example, in Figure 79, you may want to select whole paragraphs in order to sort by the person's name, or you may want to select only the second column in order to sort by the birthdates.

If you set *column only* to *Yes*, Word sorts the column without moving the other rows. This is rarely what you want since it changes the contents of each line of the table. For example, if you select the birthdates column in the above table and set *column only* to *Yes*, Word changes the birth years.

To sort a table by two columns, select the less important column, give the Library Autosort command, select the more important column, and give the Library Autosort command again. For example, assume you have a table of names with first name in the first column and last name in the second. You want to sort the table so that it is in order by last name, and

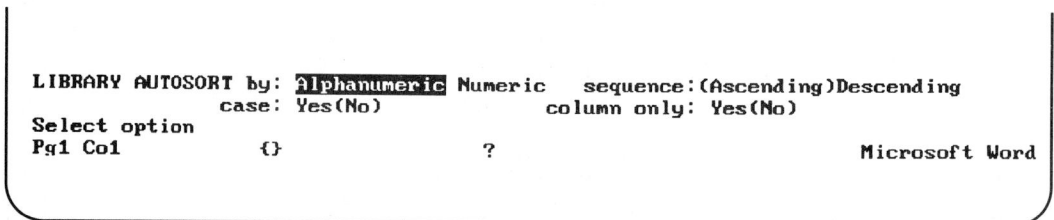

```
LIBRARY AUTOSORT by: Alphanumeric Numeric   sequence:(Ascending)Descending
                case: Yes(No)               column only: Yes(No)
Select option
Pg1 Co1            {}                 ?                      Microsoft Word
```

Figure 78

Phelps, Ellis	1954
Bandow, Carolyn	1962
Vishniac, Avi	1951
Nelson, Chris	1953

Figure 79

also with first names sorted when two or more people have the same last name. Select the column with first names, sort, then select the column with last names, and sort again.

Warnings   The difference between alphabetic and numeric sorting is important. If you sort a list of numbers using alphabetic sorting, the numbers will probably not be in the correct order. For example, if you sort the list "32, 178, 59" using alphabetic sorting, the resulting list will be "178, 32, 59" because "1" comes before "3" in alphabetic sorting.

Tips   Word may run out of memory when sorting a large selection. To give the sorting function as much memory as possible, save the document, clear Word's memory with a **Transfer Clear All** command, load the document again, make your selection, and give the **Library Autosort** command.

Spelling

Overview   People with poor spelling (such as this author) face daily embarrassment. A misspelled word in a document often greatly detracts from the message; many misspellings suggest that the writer was rushed or simply sloppy. When spell-check programs became available for PCs, many poor spellers were able to write with more confidence, knowing that most of their spelling mistakes would be found by the program. Spell-check programs are not panaceas, however, since they have many faults.

Basically, a spelling checker looks at every word in your document and compares it to words that it knows are spelled correctly. If it finds a word that it does not know (called a *suspect* word), it assumes that it is a misspelling and alerts you. You can then correct the spelling (if it is indeed misspelled) or tell the program that this is a correctly spelled word that it should add to its dictionary of words. Some spelling checkers, such as Word's, have extra features such as the ability to look at a misspelled word and guess what you actually wanted in its place.

You cannot rely on a spelling checker to find all of your errors, however. Just because a word exists in the spelling checker's dictionary does not mean that it is correct. You may have accidentally substituted a homonym (such as "We decided not to go their") or simply made a typing error that resulted in an obscure but correctly spelled word (such as "He was selfish and geocentric"). There is still no substitute for careful proofreading of a document; however, if you cannot easily spot a misspelled word, spelling checkers can certainly improve your spelling.

When the program flags words that are actually spelled correctly, you will want Word to remember those words and not flag them in the future. The *standard* dictionary is Word's main dictionary and contains all words known to Word. The *user* dictionary is one you create for groups of documents such as memos or reports. Since there are words that are acceptable in one type of writing but not in others, you will probably have many user dictionaries. A *document* dictionary, which is only used with one particular document, holds words that the speller recognizes when checking that document.

Unlike version 4, in version 5, the speller works correctly with documents that have revision marks turned on. Word knows that text with no spaces that has part inserted and part deleted is actually two words and thus checks for two words instead of one.

The interface to Word's spelling checker changed significantly from version 4 to version 5. In version 4, the spelling checker took the whole screen, did not use graphics, and used a command structure that was not the same as Word's; in version 5, the spelling checker appears as a window at the bottom of the screen and uses commands in a fashion similar to Word. Invoking the spelling checker in Word now puts you into spell mode instead of running a separate program. This section mainly describes the actions in version 5.

Procedure   To start Word's speller, give the **Library S**pell command or press Alt F6. If you are on a floppy-based system, you may have to shuffle disks in order to get the spelling program and data into Word.

If you have only a single character selected, Word starts checking either from the word on which the selection resides or from the word immediately preceding that if the selection is on a space, tab, paragraph mark, or end mark. If more than one character is selected, the speller only checks the selected words. Thus, if you want to check the spelling of only one word, select the word by pressing F7 and start the speller by pressing Alt

F6. To check the spelling of a word at the end of a document as you are typing, just start the speller. To check the spelling of the entire document, go to the beginning of the document by pressing Ctrl PgUp, then start the speller.

Figure 80 shows what the screen looks like when you are in spell mode. When you enter spell mode, Word zooms the document window and puts the spell window at the bottom of the screen. The spell window has two parts: the top is used for suggesting alternatives to misspelled words, and the bottom is used for messages.

The speller immediately begins looking for suspect words. When it finds one, it scrolls the document and highlights the suspect word. This lets you see the word in context so that you can remember what you were trying to say. As in gallery mode, the commands change to only spell commands and can be selected by pressing their first letters, or pressing the Escape key first. To stop the speller as it is searching for suspect words, press the Escape key and give the Exit command.

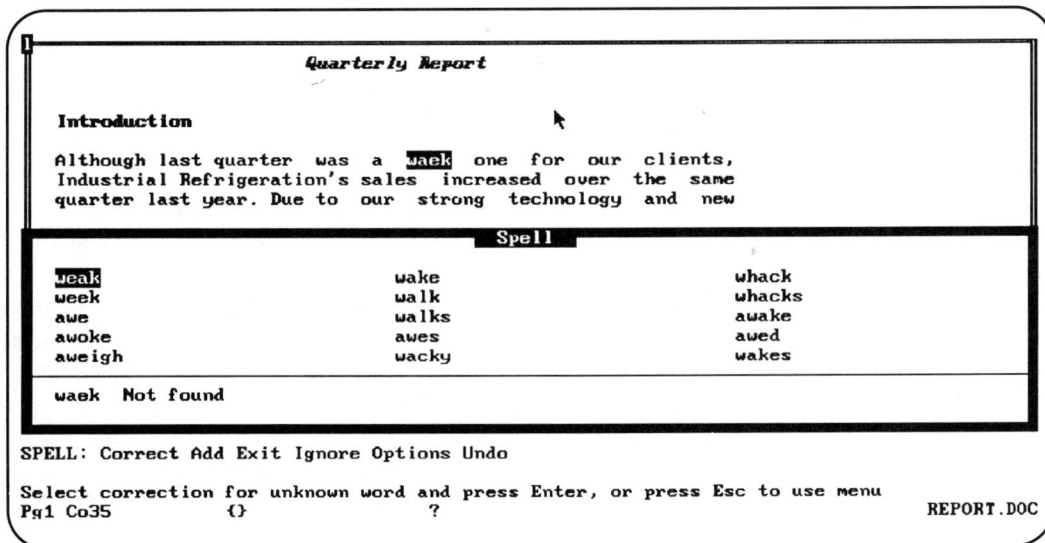

```
┌─────────────────────────────────────────────────────────────────────┐
│                     Quarterly Report                                  │
│                                                                       │
│  Introduction                              ▶                          │
│                                                                       │
│  Although last quarter  was  a  waek  one  for  our  clients,         │
│  Industrial Refrigeration's sales  increased  over  the  same         │
│  quarter last year. Due to  our  strong  technology  and  new         │
│ ┌──────────────────────────── Spell ─────────────────────────────┐   │
│ │ weak            wake            whack                           │   │
│ │ week            walk            whacks                          │   │
│ │ awe             walks           awake                           │   │
│ │ awoke           awes            awed                            │   │
│ │ aweigh          wacky           wakes                           │   │
│ ├─────────────────────────────────────────────────────────────── │   │
│ │ waek  Not found                                                 │   │
│ └─────────────────────────────────────────────────────────────── │   │
│  SPELL: Correct Add Exit Ignore Options Undo                          │
│                                                                       │
│  Select correction for unknown word and press Enter, or press Esc to use menu │
│  Pg1 Co35           {}                ?                  REPORT.DOC    │
└─────────────────────────────────────────────────────────────────────┘
```

Figure 80

The commands and actions of the spell mode are listed below.

COMMAND	ACTION
Add	Adds a word to one of the three dictionaries (*Standard, User*, and *Document*). This action tells Word that the selected word is in fact spelled correctly and that you want it remembered for use in the future.
Correct	Corrects the misspelled word. If you have set the *alternatives* field in the **Op**tions command to *Auto*, the suggested alternatives are shown in the top part of the spell window and the suggested alternative is selected.
Exit	Exits from the speller and unzooms the document if necessary. The cursor is left at the last misspelled word.
Ignore	Ignores the suspect word. Use this to prevent Word from stopping at that word again during this session. (This command does not add the word to a permanent dictionary.)
Options	Sets spelling options. The fields are as follows:

FIELD	MEANING
user dictionary	Gives the name of the user dictionary. The user dictionary is usually kept in the same directory as Word.
lookup	Sets the amount of checking Word does when looking for alternatives. *Quick* causes Word to find the list of alternatives faster, but the list is shorter than if you choose *Complete*.
ignore all caps	Specifies whether to stop for suspect words in all caps. You may want to set this to *No* if your document contains many acronyms.
check punctuation	Specifies whether to look for improper punctuation. Word looks for punctuation not followed by a space (such as ",which") and other suspect uses of punctuation.
alternatives	Sets whether Word should look immediately for alternatives when it finds a suspect word. Setting this to *Yes* makes the speller work more slowly when a suspect word is found but prevents you from having to ask for the alternatives each time. If you have a fast PC, the time needed to look up alternatives is usually also quite short.

Undo   Reverses the last spelling change or dictionary addition and lets you specify again what action to take. Unlike version 4, version 5 cannot undo more than the last change.

When you reach the bottom of a document, Word prompts *Enter Y to continue spelling from top of document, N to exit, or Esc to cancel.* This allows you to continue checking if you did not begin at the top of the document. If you enter N, Word returns to the place from which you started the speller.

Correcting Misspelled Words   You have three choices when Word finds a suspect word: tell Word that it is a real word with the **A**dd command, correct the spelling of the misspelled word in your document with the **C**orrect command, or tell Word to ignore that word for now with the **I**gnore command.

To correct a word that you recognize as misspelled (or to see what Word can suggest for alternative spellings if you have set the *alternatives* field in the **O**ptions command to *No*), give the **C**orrect command. If you find the word you want in the list of alternatives, simply select that word with the cursor keys and press Enter, or point at the word with the mouse and press the right button. If the correct spelling is not in the list of suggested spellings but you think that it is in the dictionary, press F4 to get Word to try harder at the list of alternatives.

If Word does not find the correct spelling but you know what it is, give the **C**orrect command and type the word at the prompt. When you press Enter, Word changes the spelling of that word in your document.

If Word finds the misspelled word again as it is scanning your document, it will prompt you with the previous correction that you gave. Press Enter to accept that correction. If the misspelling is one that you commonly make, set the *remember correction* field to *Yes*. This causes Word to put the pair of words in the file called REMEM-AM.COR and use that as the suggested correction in the future.

Correcting Mispunctuation   Word automatically checks for punctuation marks that are not followed by a space. For instance, the words ",full" or "fu,ll" would both be wrong. Word normally looks for these misplaced punctuation marks and alerts you if it finds them. It will flag #, %, &, *, +, =, @, or _ if they are not followed by a space, and will flag numbers that are not followed by a space or punctuation mark.

To turn off Word's punctuation checking, give the Library Spelling Options command and set *check punctuation* to *No*. You may want to do this if you have a document in which you know that there are many instances of this type of punctuation but it is correct, such as examples of computer output.

Warnings   There is a bug in version 4 that sometimes causes the spelling checker to take many minutes to start up. If the directory in which you keep Word has over 125 files, the spelling checker becomes incredibly slow. To avoid this problem, move files not associated with Word (such as documents) out of the directory. This bug does not exist in version 5.

Tips   To save space, list in the standard dictionary only words that you will use in all your documents. If you are only going to have one user dictionary, putting all additions there is safe. Document dictionaries are not very useful since you might change the name of the document and forget to change the name of the dictionary.

If you have added words to the user or document dictionaries and later decide that you do not want those words in the dictionary, you can remove them easily with Word or a text editor. The user and document dictionaries are simply text files with lists of acceptable words. Open up the file, delete the words you no longer want, and save the files as text only.

Spreadsheets

Overview   Since reports and papers often include tables, many people use a spreadsheet program such as Lotus 1-2-3 or Microsoft Excel to prepare tables for use in their Word documents. Instead of saving the spreadsheet as a text-only document and importing it to Word, you can use Word's spreadsheet importing feature to integrate directly from the spreadsheet file. This capability allows you to keep the information in the spreadsheet up-to-date and separate from the document. If you use the spreadsheet program to update the values in the spreadsheet, you need not change the values in the Word document that integrates the spreadsheet. Thus, the data in the document is *dynamic*.

Word can use spreadsheet data from Lotus 1-2-3, Microsoft Multiplan, and Microsoft Excel. It can also read files that are compatible with these spreadsheets, such as those written by VP-Planner and Twin. Many spreadsheet and database programs can write out files in 1-2-3 format (also called "WKS" and "WK1" format). Word can read almost all of these files.

The methods for specifying the data you want to integrate differ for the three spreadsheets, but are similar in nature. Basically, you name the spreadsheet and the area of the spreadsheet you want to include in your document. Word reads the current values for the data when you first integrate the spreadsheet with the Library Link command; you can make the data current any time by selecting the data and giving the Library Link command again.

If you wish, you can detach your document from the spreadsheet so that updates to the spreadsheet will not be reflected in your document. For example, if the spreadsheet is used by many people, you may want to "freeze" the values in your document so that changes others make to the spreadsheet do not change the values in your document. You can, of course, always relink to the spreadsheet if you want to make the data dynamic again.

Procedure   Put the cursor at the position you want the spreadsheet data and give the **Library Link S**preadsheet command. In the *filename* field, enter the name of the spreadsheet file from which you want to read. You should specify the full path name for the file, although you can use a relative path name if you wish. However, Word uses relative path names in reference to the path in the **Transfer O**ptions command. You can see the names of all the files in the default path by pressing F1.

Enter the range that you want to use in the *area* field. You can enter a range name or a range of cells; if you want the entire spreadsheet, leave this field blank. To see a list of named ranges in the spreadsheet, select this field and press F1. If you enter a range that is protected, Word prompts you for the password. To enter a range, you must use the correct format as indicated below for the spreadsheet.

SPREADSHEET	FORMAT
Excel	RC format, such as "R7C3:R9C4", or corner format, such as "C7..D9"
Multiplan	RC format, such as "R7C3:R9C4"
1-2-3	Corner format, such as "C7..D9"

When you press Enter, Word reads the spreadsheet file, finds the area, and puts the data in your document as a single paragraph. Word surrounds the data with hidden tag text so that it knows that the data is to be updated when you open the file again. The leader tag text consists of a leading ".L.*filename,area*" followed by a newline character; the trailer tag consists of ".L." followed by a paragraph mark. You can see these tags if you set *show hidden text* to *Yes* in the **W**indow **O**ptions command (version 4) or the **O**ptions command (version 5). If you later want to move the spreadsheet data to some other part of your document, be sure to move the two tags with it.

To update the information in an integrated spreadsheet, select the entire paragraph in which the data resides and give the **Library Link S**preadsheet command again. Do not fill in the fields; simply press Enter. Word prompts *Enter Y to update, N to skip, or Esc to cancel.* Press **Y**, and Word updates the information. If you select more than one integrated spreadsheet in your document, Word prompts you for each spreadsheet. Thus, you can bring all the spreadsheets in a document up to date by selecting the entire document and giving the **Library Link S**preadsheet command.

To unlink an integrated spreadsheet from the spreadsheet file, simply delete the header and trailer tags. Word then views the data just like data you enter manually. To relink it, delete the data and give the **Library Link S**preadsheet command again, specifying the spreadsheet name and desired range.

Warnings   In version 4, Word could not read all date formats in Lotus 1-2-3 files correctly. It also had problems with some integer formats in Multiplan.

When you update spreadsheet data, Word preserves the paragraph formatting that you applied to the paragraph, but loses any character formatting that you added to data in the spreadsheet. Thus, you should probably add character formatting only when you are sure you will not be updating the spreadsheet or when you are about to print. If you update the information fairly often and you have added many formats, you may want to write a macro that adds the formats to the correct fields to help automate the process.

Tips   Word preserves the number format of the data it reads, but does not preserve any character formatting stored in the spreadsheet. If you want the data to have character formatting, you must add it yourself after integrating the spreadsheet.

When Word reads fields with currency values, it uses the value specified in your version of MS-DOS (except in MS-DOS version 2.0, which uses only $). If you are using MS-DOS version 2.1, Word uses the currency symbol built into MS-DOS. If you use MS-DOS version 3 or later, Word uses the currency associated with the MS-DOS COUNTRY environment variable.

Styles

Overview   Direct formatting attaches formats to the text in your document. If you do not like the format you gave to a paragraph, you can change the format by selecting the paragraph and giving the Format Paragraph command again. If you give a particular set of formatting instructions throughout a long document and decide to change them, you must select each element with that formatting and change it. Even with macros and the Format repLace command, this process can be tedious and lead to accidental format changes.

Using direct formatting can lead to other problems. For example, if two people are working together on a document and one person uses a different set of formatting instructions, it is difficult to merge their work. Even if only one person is working on a document, he or she may forget the set of formatting instructions used for a particular type of text and might inadvertently change them halfway through editing the document.

Word's solution to these problems is *styles*. A style is a description of a repeating element in your document (such as bulleted lists, book titles, or warning paragraphs) and the formatting you want to go with the element. Thus, if you want every paragraph in a bulleted list to have the left indent .5 inches, first line − .5 inches, right indent .5 inches, and space after 1 line, you would create a style for all bulleted list items and describe that format. The list of styles for a document is called a *style sheet*, named after the sheets used by newspapers and magazines to assure that all similar elements in the publication look the same.

Styles are stored in files separate from documents. A style sheet file (which has the extension .STY) holds a group of styles and can be attached to any Word document. One style sheet can be attached by many documents; in fact, you will probably use only a few style sheets for all your work. Any change made to the style sheet is immediately reflected in any document that has the style sheet attached.

Formatting with styles is much easier than direct formatting because you do not need to think about formatting as you write. Content is much more important than format, and using style sheets lets you concentrate on the content.

Each style in a style sheet has four elements. Those elements and their uses are listed below.

ELEMENT	USE
Key code	A two-letter code that identifies the style in the document. When you format your document with styles, select the text to which you want to apply a style, hold down the Alt key, and type the key code. If you have set *style bar* or *show style bar* to *Yes* in the **W**indow **O**ptions command (version 4) or the **O**ptions command (version 5), you will see each paragraph key code listed in the style bar.
Usage	The type of style. A style may have either character, paragraph, or division usage. Styles with character usage can have any set of character formatting; styles with division usage can have any type of division formatting. Styles with paragraph usage can have both character and paragraph formatting. You will find that the majority of styles you define will be paragraph styles.
Variant	Each usage type has many variants, so you can have many different character styles, paragraph styles, and division styles. There are some predefined variants that Word uses; for example, the "Line Number" character variant is applied whenever you use Word to number the lines in your document. (See Line Numbering.) Each variant within a usage is unique.
Remark	An optional comment. You should fill in the remark for each style you create so that you can later remember the use for that style.

Each style has a set of formatting instructions associated with it. Simply set the formatting just like you do with direct formatting, and all formatting that is performed with direct formatting will be available in the styles.

To get a feeling for the power of styles, assume that you have created a long report and have formatted it with styles instead of direct formatting. As a draft of the report is being reviewed, most people think that you should change the font and sizes used in the headings. Instead of needing to find each heading and change the fonts, simply open the style sheet, select the heading style, and change its formatting. When you return to editing the document, you will see that Word has automatically changed the formatting for all of the headings in the document. If you create a style for book titles, changing all the book titles from underline to italic can be performed in one quick step, and you do not have to worry about accidentally changing other parts of your document that you may want to leave as underlined text.

If many people are working on a document, using styles prevents almost all accidental misformatting. Instead of having to give many formatting commands for items such as headings, each person simply needs to know kinds of items in the document and the key code for each item. This is especially helpful for people who are not very familiar or comfortable with Word.

Word loads the style sheet called NORMAL.STY when you start Word. If there are styles that you want to use often, you should store them in NORMAL.STY. You can create as many style sheets as you want, and you can merge styles from one style sheet into another.

Using styles does not preclude you from also using direct formatting. The two are not mutually exclusive, although you can usually reduce or eliminate your reliance on direct formatting once you start using styles. A good example of where you might still want to use direct formatting is on the title page of a report where it would be a waste of time to create a style that would be used only once in the report. (On the other hand, you may indeed want to create a style for the report title so that someone else using your style sheet can create a similar title page without having to guess what formatting to use in the report title.)

Consider all the types of items in your document before you start creating a style sheet. Make a list of each type and include some suggested formatting for each. Every document should have a "standard paragraph" style for all paragraphs that are regular text; multi-division documents will probably have a "standard division" as well. Word has many predefined variants, which are described below. Some of the other style items you might have in a document are listed here; you will certainly be able to think of others for your specific documents.

USAGE	ITEM
Character	Title reference (book, magazine, other company documents)
	Emphasis
	Names of keys on the keyboard
Paragraph	List items (numbered, bulleted)
	List titles
	Headings (each level of heading)
	Name and address for letters (sender's, recipient's)
	Complimentary close for letters
	Tables (financial, names)
	Table headings
	Notes (warnings, suggestions)
	Quotations (long, short)
Division	Front matter (title page, verso)
	Table of contents
	Appendixes
	Index
	Page-wide headings

Procedure   Give the **G**allery command to create or modify a style sheet. This command takes you to gallery mode in which you can edit and change style sheets but not documents. You can also add a style to the current style sheet with the **F**ormat **S**tylesheet **R**ecord command. You can add and modify styles any time you want. To attach a style sheet to a document, use the **F**ormat **S**tylesheet **A**ttach command.

Creating a Style Sheet   Enter gallery mode by giving the **G**allery command. Figure 81 shows the screen in gallery mode. The commands you can give in gallery mode are very similar to the commands in normal mode. Those commands and their uses are listed below.

COMMAND	USE
Copy	Copies the selected style to the gallery scrap
Delete	Deletes the selected style to the gallery scrap
Exit	Leaves galley mode
Format	Adds or changes formatting to the selected style
Help	Gives help on gallery commands
Insert	Adds a new style to the style sheet or copies the style from the scrap
Name	Changes the information in the selected style

COMMAND	USE
Print	Prints the style sheet
Transfer	Loads, merges, and saves style sheets
Undo	Undoes the last Copy, Delete, Format, Insert, Name, Transfer Merge, or Undo command

To start a style sheet, give the Insert command. Figure 82 shows the Insert command's dialog. Fill in the fields and press enter. The fields are as follows.

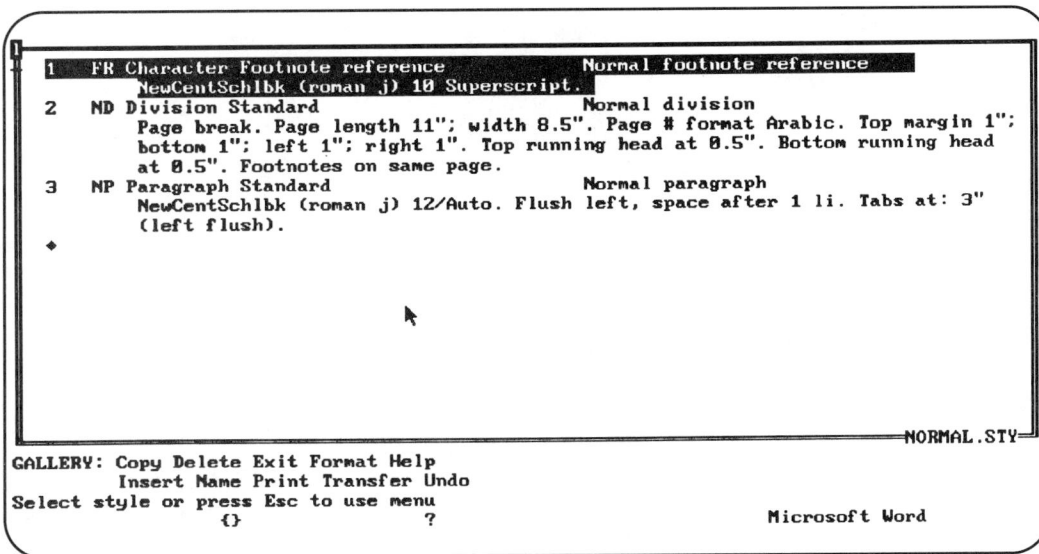

Figure 81

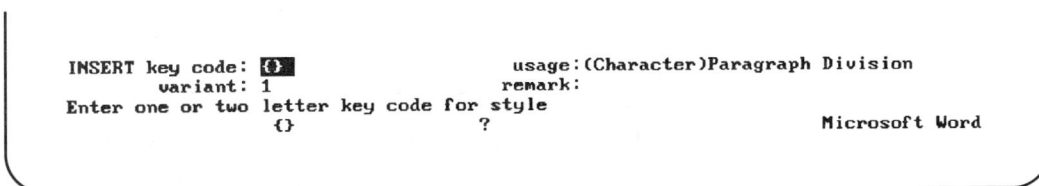

Figure 82

FIELD	COMMENTS
key code	A one- or two-character code. The first letter should not be "X" for reasons described below. It is generally better to have two-character key codes so that you have a wider range of possible key codes. Use key codes which might be mnemonic such as "LI" for "list item." Generally, two-letter key codes are preferable. If you have a two-letter code such as "LI," you cannot later name a style with the one-letter code "L."
usage	Either *Character, Paragraph,* or *Division*. Once you assign a usage to a style, you cannot change the usage with the **N**ame command.
variant	The name or number for the style. Choose either one of Word's defined variants or an unused variant number; you can press F1 to see a list of choices of the variants for the usage you choose. The variants are as follows:

	Character	Page number
		Line number
		Footnote ref
		Summary info
		Line draw
		Annotation ref
		1 through 23 (your variants)
	Paragraph	Standard
		Footnote
		Running head
		Heading level 1 through 7
		Index level 1 through 4
		Table level 1 through 4
		Annotation
		1 through 55 (your variants)
	Division	Standard
		1 through 21 (your variants)

remark	A comment. Enter a meaningful comment, with a maximum of 28 characters.

When you press Enter, Word adds the style to the gallery mode window. The first line of each entry shows a style number (not used by anything in Word), the key code, the usage, the variant, and the remark; the lines following it show the formatting.

To change the formatting of a style from the default, select the style and give the **F**ormat command. If the style is a character style, Word brings up the character formatting dialog. If the style is a paragraph style, you can add character formatting, paragraph formatting, tabs, border, or absolute positioning. If the style is a division style, you can add margins, page numbers, layout, or line numbers. Each time you add formatting, Word shows that formatting in the gallery window.

Save your style sheet with the **T**ransfer **S**ave command. If you are editing your NORMAL.STY file or another style sheet, Word will prompt you with the file's name. For convenience, store the style sheet in the same directory as your document or in the directory in which you store Word.

If you are editing a document with direct formatting and want to turn some formatting into a style, select the formatted text and give the **F**ormat **S**tylesheet **R**ecord command or press Alt F10. Enter the style information in the dialog box and press Enter; Word adds the style to the attached style sheet. This method is not used much, however, since you usually do not use styles in a document with much direct formatting.

Formatting with Styles   In regular edit mode, you can add styles using Alt key combinations. First, use the **F**ormat **S**tylesheet **A**ttach command to be sure the desired style sheet is attached to your document. Select each item to which you want to attach a style, hold down the Alt key, and type the key code. For example, to attach a paragraph style whose key code is "MA," select any part of the paragraph, hold down the Alt key and type MA. To attach a character style, select only the characters you want with that style, hold down the Alt key, and type the key code. You can also add styles with the **F**ormat **S**tylesheet **C**haracter, **F**ormat **S**tylesheet **P**aragraph, and **F**ormat **S**tylesheet **D**ivision commands, although this is usually not as convenient as using the Alt key combinations.

You can, of course, add styles to more than one paragraph at a time. You may want to do this when formatting a table or many list entries. Simply select all the paragraphs and use the Alt key combination. This is also useful for adding a style to a group of divisions.

If you are adding styles to a document that already has direct formatting, you should remove all direct formatting first. The fastest way to do this is select the entire document with Shift F10, set plain character formatting with Alt Space Bar, and set plain paragraph formatting with Alt P. If you have a paragraph style that will apply to most of the paragraphs in your document, you may want to add it to the whole document first by selecting the whole document and adding the style.

There is a side effect of attaching a style sheet to a document: the Alt key formatting commands may no longer work unless you press Alt X first. This is true when you have a style name that begins with the same letter as the letter in the Alt key formatting command. Thus, after you have attached a style sheet which has a style name that begins with a C, Alt C will no longer center a paragraph; you must use Alt XC. This is why the first letter of the key code cannot be "X."

Editing a Style Sheet To edit a style sheet, simply enter gallery mode. To edit a style sheet other than the one that is attached to the current document, use the gallery **T**ransfer **L**oad command in gallery mode.

To change the formatting for a style, select the style and give the **F**ormat command. To add a style, give the **I**nsert command. To change the key code, variant, or remark of a style, select the style and give the **N**ame command.

If you want to make a style that is similar to another style already in the style sheet, select the style and give the **C**opy command. Press the Insert key to copy the style into the scrap, press Enter to copy the style into the style sheet, and then give the **N**ame command to change the key code and the variant (Word will not let you save a style sheet that contains two entries with the same key codes or variants).

To read in styles from another style sheet, use the **T**ransfer **M**erge command. This may bring in styles with the same key codes or variants; you must change them with the **N**ame command before saving the merged style sheet. You can change the order of the styles in the style sheet by deleting styles to the scrap with the **D**elete command or the Delete key and inserting them in other positions with the Insert key. This change is only cosmetic, but it can help make a style sheet easier to read. You can print a style sheet with the **P**rint command.

When you are finished editing a style sheet, be sure to save your changes to the style sheet with the **T**ransfer **S**ave command.

Predefined Variants The following variants are predefined in Word and are used for some elements of formatting whether or not you have styles that use them. To change the formatting for any variant, simply define a style that uses that variant and add your own formatting. The variants and their uses are as follows.

USAGE	VARIANT	USE
Character	Page number	Page numbers shown with the **Format Division Page**-numbers command
	Line Number	Line numbers shown with the **Format Division** line-**Numbers** command
	Footnote ref	Reference marks for footnotes
	Summary Info	Document summaries shown by the **Library Document**-retrieval command
	Annotation mark (version 5 only)	Reference marks for annotations
Paragraph	Standard	All paragraphs that do not have a style attached. This is very handy for defining a font and standard paragraph attributes for all unstyled text.
	Footnote	Footnotes
	Running Head	Running heads. If you use this to define a standard set of tab stops for running headers and the margins or page size of your document change, you only have to change this one style to fix the running headers.
	Heading level 1 through 7	Outline levels
	Index level 1 through 4	Index entries if you set the *use style sheet* field in the **Library Index** command to *Yes*
	Table level 1 through 4	Table of contents entries if you set the *use style sheet* field in the **Library Table** command to *Yes*
	Annotation	Annotations
Division	Standard	All divisions that do not have a style attached. This is useful for defining margins and other division attributes for all unstyled text.

Freezing Styles   Once you have added styles to a document, you may want to turn the formatting created by the styles into direct formatting. This is called freezing the styles since it removes the attachments between the style sheet and the document but leaves the formatting intact. For example, if you have an application that can read Word files with direct formatting but not with styles, you may want to freeze the styles so that the other program can use the formatting information.

To turn style formatting into direct formatting, select the styled text and give a direct formatting command that sets a style not used in the text. Thus, if you have a paragraph that is formatted with a style and you want to freeze that style, select the paragraph, give the **Format Paragraph** command, and set a style that is not used in that paragraph to *No*. For example, small caps is a character format that is rarely used; border right is a paragraph format that is rarely used.

To freeze the format for an entire document, select the entire document by pressing Shift F10, give the **Format Character** command, select a style that is not used anywhere in the document (such as *small caps*), set it to *No*, and press Enter. Give the **Format Border** or **Format Paragraph** command, select a style that is not used anywhere in the document (such as *right*), set it to *No*, and press Enter. Give the **Format Division** command, select a style that is not used anywhere in the document (such as *Line-number*), set it to *No*, and press Enter. When you save the document, all style formatting will be lost but the direct formatting will remain.

Warnings When you freeze styles, Word forgets all the styles in the document. You should save the frozen document under a different name so that you can preserve your styled document.

The "freeze _ style.mac" macro that comes with Word does not work if you have double-underline or keep follow formats in your document.

Tips Using the "Standard" paragraph and division variants in your default style sheet lets you specify your preferred formatting. For example, if you like .75 inch margins for most of your documents, add a style to your NORMAL.STY that uses the "Standard" division variant formatted for those margins. Similarly, if you want to use a standard font, add a style with the "Standard" paragraph format.

There are very few companies that sell pre-made style sheets, although some exist. Some people have put their style sheets on networks such as CompuServe. An excellent book on style sheets, which includes dozens of style sheets and extensive tips on creating style sheets, is *Microsoft Word Style Sheets* by Peter Rinearson and JoAnne Woodcock (Microsoft Press, 1988).

When using styles, it is usually best to show the style bar by setting the *style bar* or *show style bar* field in the **Window Options** command (version 4) or the **O**ptions command (version 5) to *Yes*. If you often need to show and hide the style bar due to long lines running off the right side of your screen, you may want to make a macro that toggles this field. An asterisk in the style bar indicates a paragraph for which a style is specified, but that style does not exist in the current style sheet. For more screen space, you can toggle the *outline* or *show outline* field of the **Window Options** command (version 4) or the **O**ptions command (version 5) at the same time. You can also toggle the *show borders* option.

Macros work well with style sheets. For example, assume you have a table with three columns that is made with three side-by-side paragraph styles. You might want to make a macro that applies the left style to the current paragraph, selects the next paragraph and applies the middle style, and selects the next paragraph and applies the right style, and moves the selection to the next paragraph.

Subscripts and Superscripts

Overview   Most character formatting involves adding emphasis to characters by changing their appearance. You can, however, also change their position on a line with the *position* field in the **Format Character** command. This command lets you create superscripts, which are often used in reports for footnote references, and subscripts, which are often used in formulae in scientific papers.

Procedure   Select the characters that you want to appear above or below the line and give the **Format Character** command. Set the *position* field to *subscript* to put the characters below the line; set it to *superscript* to put the characters above the line.

You cannot specify the distance that characters will move up or down; that is set in the printer driver. If you want to change the distance, you must modify the printer driver. All superscript or subscript characters must be at the same height. (See Printer Drivers.)

Tips   Since you generally use subscripts and superscripts for specific items, you may want to create character styles for those items. Word has predefined styles for footnote references, but you can add other styles to suit your particular uses of subscripts and superscripts. (See Styles.)

Tables and Tab Stops

Overview　　Many documents include tables. Tables are laid out by separating the contents of each column with tab stops. Since Word has many different types of tab stops, you have a great deal of flexibility in designing tables. If you use styles to create your tables, changing the format of a table is quite easy.

Word's column handling also aids in setting up tables. To change the order of columns in a table, you can select a column, delete it to the scrap, and insert it at a different location. You can also sort tables by columns. (See Sorting.)

Word's tab stops are set similarly to tab stops on a typewriter. In the **Format Tabs Set** command, you place a tab at a specific position on the ruler. Since tabs are paragraph formatting, you only need to set the tabs once for a paragraph. Tab positions are set relative to the left margin; you can have a maximum of nineteen tab stops per line.

The four types of tabs are left-aligned, right-aligned, center-aligned, and decimal-aligned (there are also vertical tabs, which act differently and are described later). Each type of tab affects the text that follows it. For example, if you have a left-aligned tab stop set at 2 inches, text that is preceded by a tab would begin 2 inches from the left margin. The tabs and their actions are listed below.

TAB	ACTION
Left	Aligns the left side of the following text to the right of the tab stop
Right	Aligns the right side of the following text to the left of the tab stop
Centered	Aligns the middle of the following text with the tab stop
Decimal	Aligns the decimal point of the following text with the tab stop; if there is no decimal point, this acts the same as a right-aligned tab

You can still use tab stops even if you do not set your own tabs. Word has preset tab left-aligned stops set at regular intervals (you can change the interval with the *default tab width* field in the **O**ptions command). Even if you set tab stops, Word uses the preset tab stops for the area to the right of your rightmost tab stop. For example, if you set a tab stop at 1.5 inches and another one at 2.6 inches, entering three Tab characters would move

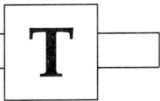

you 3 inches from the margin since that is the first preset tab stop past your rightmost tab stop.

Vertical tabs do not act like other tabs since they do not affect placement of text. A vertical tab simply causes Word to draw a vertical line at the position indicated. Vertical tabs are very useful for creating boxes and for making columns in tables more distinct.

Leader characters are text that Word inserts in the blank space before a tab stop. Leader characters are most useful in tables of contents or in widely spaced tables. You can use periods, dashes, or underscores for leader characters. For example, most tables of contents use a right-aligned tab with a leader character of periods.

Figure 83 shows examples of each type of tab stop. Figure 84 shows a table with left-aligned, decimal-aligned, right-aligned, and vertical tabs at the same position, all of which are the tabs you will most often use.

Procedure   To set tabs, use the **Format Tabs Set** command or press Alt F1. Word displays the command's dialog shown in Figure 85 and the ruler. As you add tabs, Word displays them on the ruler. Remember that Word automatically uses the preset tabs to the right of your rightmost tab.

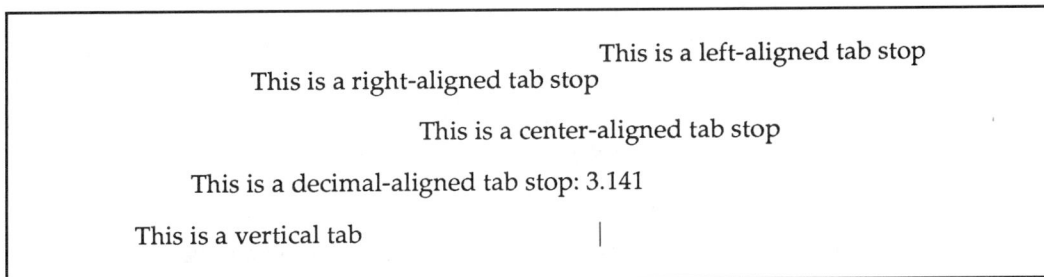

This is a left-aligned tab stop
                                    This is a right-aligned tab stop

                        This is a center-aligned tab stop

        This is a decimal-aligned tab stop: 3.141

    This is a vertical tab |

Figure 83

Name	Company	Amount owed	Date
Bill Garcia	Hughes Electric	1423.82	3/29/89
Norman Yee	self-employed	225.00	4/15/89
Tom Ianson	Remington	88.11	3/15/89

Figure 84

227

```
FORMAT TAB SET position: █
      alignment:(Left)Center Right Decimal Vertical    leader char:(Blank). - _
Enter measurement
Pg1 Co1              {}                ?                        Microsoft Word
```

Figure 85

If you are using the keyboard, enter the desired location for the tab stop in the *position* field and make selections in the *alignment* and *leader char* fields. To select from a position on the ruler, move the selection to the *position* field and press F1. You can then move back and forth on the ruler with the Left Arrow and Right Arrow keys. When you have set the tab stop you want, press Insert. Set each tab stop in this fashion, and press Enter when finished.

If you are using the mouse, you can place tabs on the ruler by specifying the *alignment* and *leader char* fields, pointing at the desired position, and pressing the left button. Be sure to make the settings before placing the tab; otherwise, Word will use the default settings (left-aligned tab with no leader).

To delete a tab stop that you have placed, give the Format Tabs Set command and enter its position in the *position* field (or move around the ruler by pressing F1 and the Left Arrow and Right Arrow keys) and press the Delete key. If you are using the mouse, point at the tab stop on the ruler and press both buttons. To clear all the tabs at once, use the Format Tabs Reset-all command.

You can move a tab around on the ruler with the mouse. In the Format Tabs Set command, point at the tab stop you want to move, hold down the right button, move to the new location, and release the button. You cannot move tabs with the keyboard; you must remove the tab and place a new one.

Setting Tabs in Version 5   The user interface in version 5 makes it easier to set tabs from the keyboard. When you give the Format Tabs Set command and press F1 in the *position* field, you have more power as you move back and forth along the ruler. To set a tab at the current position, press L, R, C, D, or V to set left-, right-, center-, decimal-aligned, or vertical tabs. To make a leader character, move to the desired tab and press the period, hyphen, or underscore keys.

To move tabs, put the cursor over the desired tab stop and press Ctrl Left Arrow or Ctrl Right Arrow. You can quickly delete all the tab stops to the right of your current position by pressing Ctrl Delete.

Decimal-aligned tabs also work slightly differently in version 5. Numbers in decimal-aligned tabs will always align on the tab stop, even if there are punctuation marks such as parentheses at the right side of the number.

Moving Columns in a Table   Word's column selection feature lets you move vertical blocks of text around in a table. To select a column, first select a character in one corner of the desired column. Press Shift F6; Word displays *CS* at the bottom of the screen. Extend the selection to the opposite corner of the column and select the character in the space to the right of the text, which is the Tab character. Give the **D**elete command to delete the column to the scrap, move to the upper left corner of where you want the column to be (which should be on the leftmost character in a column), and give the Insert command.

Copying columns can be tricky if the text in the columns is not evenly lined up. If you are selecting any column other than the far right column, you must select at least one "blank" column to the right of the text. It is safe to select all the text up to the beginning of the text in the next column if that column is left-aligned. If the next column is right- or center-aligned, you can select up to it as long as the two columns do not overlap, as they might.

Selecting from a center-aligned or right-aligned column is almost impossible since you are likely to get part of the tabs from the column to the left. Instead, change the tab stop to left-aligned, select and move the column, and restore the original format after you have moved the column.

Warnings   Tabs on the screen do not match tabs in your printout if you use proportional fonts or fonts other than 10-pitch. For example, assume you are using Word's preset tabs of .5 inches and a proportional font. Typing five characters on the screen and entering a Tab character moves you on the screen to the 1-inch mark. However, if the characters you entered are thin (such as the letter "i"), you may only be at the .5-inch mark on your printout.

Tips   If you are using version 5 or Pageview, always preview your printout if you plan to check whether the tabs lined up correctly in your tables.

If your table does not look correct after you edit it, you may have used spaces instead of tabs in some places in the table. Use the *visible* (version 4) or the *show non-printing symbols* (version 5) field in the **O**ptions command to see all the characters on the screen so that you can determine if there are any spaces before or after Tab characters.

Not all tables are created with tab stops; you can also create a table with side-by-side paragraphs as described under Paragraph Placement. Use tabs if all columns other than the right column in every entry are a single line long; use side-by-side paragraphs if any column other than the right column has more than one line in an entry.

Tables of Contents

Overview   Most readers start reading a report or book at the table of contents. A good table of contents shows the structure of the document, the subjects covered, and the flow of the information. Word's Library **T**able command lets you create a table of contents very easily. You can either use heading styles that you add or that Word automatically adds when you use the outlining feature, or you can add hidden characters to mark table of contents entries. Using styles is usually much more convenient.

Creating a table of contents in Word is similar to creating an index. (See Indexes.) As you edit your document, you either set paragraph styles that correspond to "Heading level *n*" usages (by adding styles or using Word's outline feature), or you flag words that you want in the table of contents with special codes that are in hidden character format. When you are finished marking table of contents entries, you give the Library **T**able command and Word compiles the table of contents and places it at the end of your document in its own division (you can move it to wherever you want after it is created). Word also adds hidden text at the beginning and end of the table of contents so that it can replace the current table of contents if you give the Library **T**able command a second time.

Each line in your table of contents should be a paragraph, usually a heading. You can use text that is shorter than a paragraph. In the interest of clarity, however, the text in the table of contents should match the text in your document. Since the entries in the table of contents have styles, you can format them easily and consistently if you are using style sheets.

After Word creates a table of contents, you can format it in any way you want. You can use direct formatting or, if you have told Word that you want your table of contents entries to be in predefined styles, you can change the formatting in the gallery. You can also add a chapter heading to a table of contents. Note, however, that unless you are careful where you put it, Word will delete that heading if you recreate the table of contents. Since Word wipes out all lines in the table of contents when you recreate it, you should probably only add direct formatting after the last time you create the table of contents.

Procedure   **Creating Table of Contents Entries with Styles**   If you use Word's outlining feature to create the headings in your document, you need not do anything else before creating a table of contents. Word uses the automatic styles "Heading level 1," "Heading level 2," and so on when you create an outline. The Library Table command uses these styles to create the table of contents.

If you did not use the outlining feature but still want to use styles to create your table of contents, add styles with the "Heading level" variants to the style sheet attached to your document and apply those styles to the paragraphs you want in the table of contents. For example, you might create styles with key codes "H1," "H2," and so on, and apply them to each heading. Of course, you can apply any formatting you wish to the styles at the same time and use the style formatting instead of direct formatting.

Marking Table of Contents Entries   If you do not use styles, you must mark each heading you want in your table of contents. All marks are entered in hidden text, so it is likely that you will want to make hidden text visible when you are adding your table of contents entries by setting the *show hidden text* field to *Yes* in the **Window Options** command (version 4) or the **Options** command (version 5).

To mark an entry, add the *table code* before the entry and the *endmark* after the entry. If the end of the entry is the end of the paragraph, you need not include the endmark, but may do so if you wish. For first-level entries, the table code is ".c." and the endmark is ";"; both of these are in hidden text. (You can use a letter other than "c" if you wish; see below for an example of why you might change this.) To mark the heading "Research and Development Studies" you would follow these steps.

1. Place the cursor on the "R" of "Research."
2. Press Alt E or give the **Format Character** command and set *hidden* to *Yes*.
3. Type `.c.`, which should show with dotted underline (indicating that it is hidden).
4. Move the cursor to after the "s" in "Studies."
5. Press Alt E or give the **Format Character** command and set *hidden* to *Yes*.
6. Type `;`, which should show with dotted underline (indicating that it is hidden) if you are in graphics mode.

Clearly, it would be better to combine these actions into macros. (See Macros.) A common practice is to define one macro to insert a hidden ".c." at the current location and another to add a hidden ";" at the current location. You can assign these macros to keys that are easy to remember (such as Ctrl C and Ctrl ;). You can also use the glossary to hold the hidden ".c." and ";". (See Glossaries.)

So far, you have only seen how to mark entries for a one-level table of contents. Most tables of contents in longer works are generally two or three levels. The table of contents might have the first-level entry aligned with the left margin, the second-level entries indented slightly, and so on. Another common practice is to have all entries left-aligned, but with first-level entries in a larger font and boldface.

To mark a second-level heading, enter `.c.:`; the endmark is the same (a hidden semicolon). For example, to mark "Protein Studies" as a second-level heading, use the marking shown in Figure 86. Third-level headings are marked with `.c.::`, and so on.

If you want some of the entries in your table of contents not to have page numbers, simply add a colon before the endmark. In the above example, you can prevent the entry from showing a page mark in the table of contents by changing it to the text shown in Figure 87.

.c.:Protein Studies;

Figure 86

If you are marking with hidden text, you must be careful if the entry you want has a colon, a semicolon, or a quotation mark (you need not worry about these if you are using styles). Since Word uses these as special characters, you must take extra steps when you mark your entry. If the entry contains a colon or semicolon, enclose the entire entry in hidden quotation marks. If the entry contains a quotation mark, enclose the entire entry in hidden quotation marks. For example, assume you want to mark the following headings:

```
Financing a Growth Phase: Problems and Solutions
Keeping "Hard" Clients Happy
```

You would mark them as shown in Figure 88.

Creating the Table of Contents   You can compile the table of contents after your document has the styles attached or is marked. Be sure hidden text is not shown. If the hidden text is shown, Word will include the hidden text when it paginates, which results in incorrect page numbers in the table of contents. You should also be sure that you have specified the appropriate printer driver and model in the **Print Options** command so that Word knows how to determine the page sizes.

Give the Library **Table** command, and you will see the dialog in Figure 89. After selecting the options, press Enter. If the document already has a table of contents, Word asks if you want to replace the existing table of contents; press Y to create the new table of contents. The choices for the Library **Table** command are as follows.

```
                    .c.:Protein Studies:;
```

Figure 87

```
    .c."Financing a Growth Phase: Problems and Solutions";
    .c."Keeping "Hard" Clients Happy";
```

Figure 88

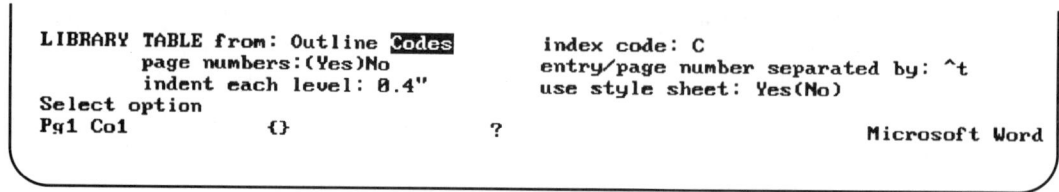

```
LIBRARY TABLE from: Outline Codes          index code: C
            page numbers:(Yes)No           entry/page number separated by: ^t
            indent each level: 0.4"         use style sheet: Yes(No)
Select option
Pg1 Co1                    {}              ?                    Microsoft Word
```

Figure 89

FIELD	MEANING
from	You must specify whether Word should create the table of contents from styles (*Outline*) or from your hidden text markings (*Codes*).
index code	If you did not use "c" for the code, you must specify the letter you used here.
page numbers	You can prevent Word from including page numbers in the table by setting *page numbers* to *No*.
entry/page number separated by	This is the character(s) that you want to separate the entry and the page number. Word's default is a Tab character.
indent each level	For direct formatting, this field tells Word how much to indent subentries from the preceding level.
use style sheet	It is often convenient to use a style sheet for the table of contents entries. If you select *Yes* for this field, Word formats each entry as "Table level 1," "Table level 2," and so on instead of using direct formatting. You can then change the appearance of the lines in the table of contents in the gallery.

When you execute the command, Word compiles the entries and puts them at end of the document. It also puts a division mark before the table of contents and inserts hidden text *.Begin Table C.* before the table of contents and hidden text *.End Table C.* after the table of contents.

Formatting and Moving the Table of Contents   To add a heading to the table of contents, you must first create a table of contents and show the hidden text. Place your heading after the division mark but before the hidden text *.Begin Table C.* When Word recreates the table of contents, it will only delete the text between (and including) the hidden text. If you want running heads in that division, you should put them before your heading. If you want to change the styles of some of the entries, you can use either direct character formatting or character styles.

You will probably want to move the table of contents to near the beginning of your document. When you do, be sure to move the division mark and hidden text. The next time you generate a table of contents, Word will place it in its new position.

Warnings   If you add hidden text for the table of contents entries, hide the hidden text, then continue to edit your document, you can accidentally alter the table of contents marks. Once you hide the hidden text, you will not know if you are adding before or after the hidden text if you later insert text at the location of the hidden text. Thus, once you have added table of contents entries, you should either edit with the hidden text shown or review the contents of your document with hidden text showing before generating the table of contents.

If you want running heads in your table of contents, you must add them yourself after you give the Library Table command. Since Word adds a division mark before the table of contents and running heads are active only in the division in which they are defined, you must add your own for your table of contents.

Tips   Using style sheets with a table of contents facilitates reformatting each level of the table of contents because you can quickly change the way each level uses the Tab characters and fonts.

You can change the letter used for the table code to something other than C, I, L, or P if you want to compile figure tables. Mark all your figure captions with ".f." and give the Library Table command. Set the *index code* field to F and execute the command. Word creates a table of figures separate from your table of contents.

Thesaurus

Overview   Dictionaries are useful both for finding the correct spelling of a word and its definition, but you often want more than a definition for a word when you are writing. If you have used a particular word many times in a document, you might want a synonym to give some variety to your writing. In that case, a thesaurus is much more useful than a dictionary.

A thesaurus gives you synonyms and related words for a particular word. Since many words in English act as more than one part of speech, the entry in a thesaurus covers all uses of the word. For example, the entry for the word "first" would show words that relate to "first" as a noun (such as "demo" and "model") and as an adjective (such as "supreme" and "advanced").

Since Word's thesaurus lets you look up words as you type and also after entering them in your document, it is useful both during entering and editing. You will find that using a thesaurus is especially helpful for finding alternate adjectives and adverbs.

Procedure   Select the word you want to look up and give the Library thEsaurus command or press Ctrl F6. If you are on a floppy-based system, you may have to shuffle disks in order to get the thesaurus program and data into Word. Word opens up the thesaurus window shown in Figure 90, and you are in thesaurus mode.

Your choices are listed below.

KEY	ACTION
Direction	Moves the selection over the words in the thesaurus window. Use this to select words to insert in your document or to continue your search.

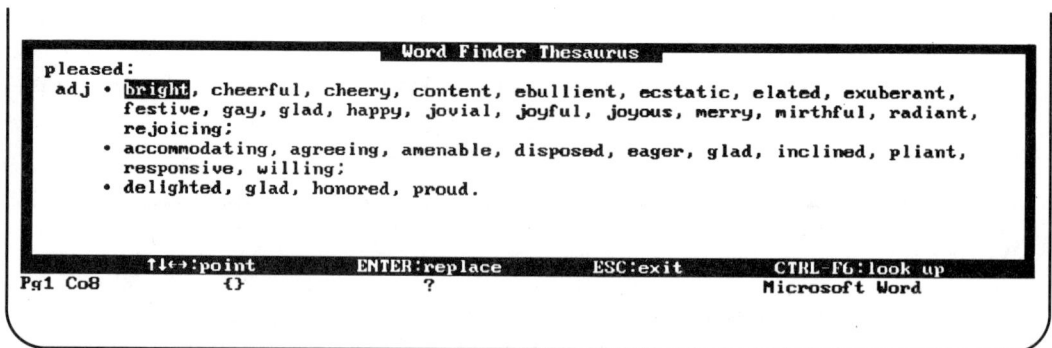

```
                          Word Finder Thesaurus
pleased:
  adj • bright, cheerful, cheery, content, ebullient, ecstatic, elated, exuberant,
        festive, gay, glad, happy, jovial, joyful, joyous, merry, mirthful, radiant,
        rejoicing;
      • accommodating, agreeing, amenable, disposed, eager, glad, inclined, pliant,
        responsive, willing;
      • delighted, glad, honored, proud.



      ↑↓←→:point          ENTER:replace      ESC:exit        CTRL-F6:look up
Pg1 Co8              {}                 ?                      Microsoft Word
```

Figure 90

236

KEY	ACTION
Enter	Replaces the selected word in your document with the word selected in the thesaurus
Esc	Leaves the thesaurus
Ctrl F6	Looks up a synonym for the word selected in the thesaurus window

You can use the thesaurus to browse and let your chain of thought lead you around. As you find words that are interesting, use the thesaurus to find synonyms for those words, and then for synonyms of the synonyms, and so on. Simply select the word for which you want to find a synonym and press Ctrl F6. Continue this as long as you like, and press the Esc key to get back to editing your document.

Tips

Do not rely on the thesaurus to find the "right" word for you. Although it can give you suggestions about what might be a good replacement for the word you have entered, it cannot rate how well the suggestion fits your document. If you replace one of your words with an alternative from the thesaurus, close the thesaurus and read the sentence or paragraph again to be sure that the word you chose is appropriate for the context of the sentence.

Transfer Command

Overview

Word performs almost all of its reading from and writing to the disk with the **Transfer** command. The subcommands allow you to open, close, and save files, as well as to set the standard directory on which Word looks for documents and style sheets. There is also a **Transfer** command in the gallery. (See Styles.)

Figure 91 shows the **Transfer** command menu.

The subcommands and their uses are listed below.

COMMAND	USE
Load	Opens files for editing
Save	Saves files to disk

```
TRANSFER: Load Save Clear Delete Merge Options Rename Glossary Allsave

Loads named document
Pg1 Co8              {}                    ?                  Microsoft Word
```

Figure 91

COMMAND	USE
Clear	Clears the current document from the window (**Transfer Clear Win-dow** command). The **Transfer Clear All** command clears all open windows, glossaries, and style sheets.
Delete	Deletes a file from disk. This is useful if you have run out of space on a disk and want to save your current work.
Merge	Combines a document into the current document after the selection
Options	Sets the default directory for searching
Rename	Renames the current file
Glossary	Merges, loads, or clears glossary entries. (See Glossaries.)
Allsave	(Version 5 only.) Saves all open documents to disk

Procedure

To load a file, use the **Transfer Load** command or press Ctrl F7. In the command, you can specify that the file is read-only so that you will not be able to modify the file.

To save a file to disk, use the **Transfer Save** command or Ctrl F10. Word normally saves files in its own format; you can specify differently in the **Transfer Save** dialog. In version 4, setting the *formatted* field to *No* in-structed Word to save the file as text only with carriage returns at the end of each paragraph. In version 5, you can set the *format* field to *Word, Text-only, RTF,* and *Text-only-with-line-breaks.* (See Importing and Exporting Files.)

Sometimes Word gets low on memory, especially if you have been doing a great deal of editing without saving your changes to disk. Word will display *SAVE* in blinking letters at the bottom of the screen as it gets close to running out of memory. You should immediately save any open documents to disk. This both prevents loss of data if Word fails to recover from the low memory and clears out space in memory for you to continue.

238

The **T**ransfer **O**ptions command tells Word where to look for documents for which you do not give complete path names. This should be set to the directory in which you keep the documents on which you are currently working. In version 5, you can specify that you want Word to remember the setting in the **T**ransfer **O**ptions command when you quit from Word. You generally only want to save this if you almost always use the same directory for your document files.

New Features in Version 5   The **T**ransfer **A**llsave command saves all open documents, all attached style sheets, and the current glossary. If you have many files open, using this command is, of course, much faster than changing windows and saving each file. It is a good way to ensure that you have saved all changes when you have edited many files.

Word can save the current file automatically after a specified amount of time. (See Autosave.)

Warnings   Since you might have many files with the same name in many directories on your system, always use a full path name with the **T**ransfer **D**elete command. Do not rely on the setting of the **T**ransfer **O**ptions command or assume that Word is deleting from the "current" directory.

Undo Command

Overview   Word was one of the first popular word processing programs to include an undo feature. When you give an editing command, you can almost always reverse the action by giving the **U**ndo command. Think of the **U**ndo command as a safety net when you are editing.

Note that you can only undo the last edit you made. If you delete some text, move the cursor, and start editing again, you can no longer undo the deletion. The **U**ndo command also undoes Word commands that change formatting.

The **U**ndo command has a second purpose: you can use it to experiment with some changes and reverse the changes if you do not like them. If you give the **U**ndo command after giving the **U**ndo command, Word redoes the change (that is, it switches back and forth between the edited and unedited state). You can use this to compare the effects of an edit. For

239

example, if you want to see how adding boldface changes the appearance of a paragraph, add the formatting, then give the Undo command and note the change. Keep giving the Undo command again until you have decided which formatting you prefer.

If you undo typing or an Insert command, Word simply removes the text. If you undo a Delete command or a Copy command, Word undoes the action and restores the contents of the scrap. Word can undo the following commands.

- Copy
- Delete
- most Formats
- Insert
- Library Autosort
- Library Hyphenate
- Library Index
- Library Number
- Library Table
- Library Thesaurus
- Replace
- Transfer Merge
- Undo

The Undo command cannot undo all commands and actions. For example, it cannot undo moving the cursor, regardless of whether you move the cursor with the mouse, the keyboard, the Jump commands, the Format sEarch commands, or the Search command. It also cannot undo changes in the gallery. It also cannot undo the following commands.

- Format Stylesheet Attach
- Library Run
- Library Spell
- Options
- Print Options
- Print Repaginate
- any Transfer commands other than Transfer Merge
- Windows

Procedure   Give the **U**ndo command or press Shift F1 if you make a mistake. If the last change cannot be undone or you have not edited anything, Word prompts *No edit to Undo*.

          The **L**ibrary **S**pell command has its own **U**ndo command. (See Spelling.)

Warnings   Always check the results of the **U**ndo command before continuing to edit. If you are using the **U**ndo command to replace text that you have typed in and backspaced over, the results might not be what you expected. For example, if you format some text, move the cursor, type in five characters, press Backspace five times, and give the **U**ndo command, Word undoes the formatting rather than the backspacing.

Versions of Word

Overview   Microsoft made significant enhancements to Word version 4 when it released Word version 5. These changes include new commands, greater keyboard usefulness, and a more consistent user interface. This section lists the major features added to version 5 and the place in this book in which these features are discussed.

- Absolutely positioned paragraphs. (See Paragraph Placement.)
- Annotations. (See Annotations.)
- Automatic saving of text. (See Autosave.)
- Background repagination. (See Repagination.)
- Bookmarks. (See Bookmarks.)
- Borders: new thick line style. (See Borders.)
- Case of characters can be changed with the Ctrl F4 key. (See Replacing Text.)
- Color: better integration of color (see Graphics Adapters) and font colors (see Character Formatting)
- Column breaks and pages with more than one type of columns. (See Columns.)
- Cross-references. (See Cross-References.)
- Document retrieval: added **C**opy and **D**elete commands. (See Document Retrieval.)
- Duplex printing. (See Printing.)

- File name enumeration: more options. (See F1 Enumeration.)
- Glossaries: **Transfer Glossary Load** command. (See Glossaries.)
- Graphics: formats not tied to the printer; ability to preview in Word; specify printing resolution; capturing screens from other applications. (See Graphics.)
- Help: better interface. (See Help.)
- Layout mode. (See Layout.)
- Macros: new predefined variables (save, window, echo, wordversion) functions; logical expressions (AND, OR, NOT); using variables in prompts. (See Macros.)
- Networks: part of the basic Word package. (See Networks.)
- Options: *count blank space*. (See Options.)
- OS/2. (See OS/2 and Word.)
- Preview mode. (See Layout.)
- RTF files. (See Importing and Exporting Files.)
- Running heads: align with left margin. (See Running Heads.)
- Saving all files at once. (See Transfer Command.)
- Scrolling: can now scroll with the mouse with window border turned off. (See Scrolling and Selecting.)
- Shading of paragraphs. (See Shading.)
- Speed: improvements in printing, indexing, generating tables of contents, and sorting
- Speller: only takes part of the screen; more alternative guesses for unknown words, now part of Word program; much better interface. (See Spelling.)
- Spreadsheets: reads dates and integers better. (See Spreadsheets.)
- Tabs: better interface for **Format Tabs Set** command; better lining up of decimal-aligned. (See Tables and Tabs.)
- Text only files with line breaks. (See Importing and Exporting Files.)
- Thesaurus: much better interface. (See Thesaurus.)
- **Transfer Options** command setting can be saved when quitting. (See Transfer Command.)

Tips   If you have not yet updated your copy of Word to version 5, you should do so in order to take advantage of these new features. You can find out more information on updating by calling Microsoft Customer Service at 800/426-9400.

Widows. *See* Keeps

Windows

Overview

Using many windows at once allows you to move text between documents and between different parts of a Word document. You can also easily compare the contents of two files. You can have up to eight windows open, but it is unlikely that you will use more than four or five. Since the scrap is not associated with a window, you can use it to move text between windows; you can also use speed copying and moving between windows. (See Copying Text and Moving Text.)

Word uses *tiled* windows on its screen. Tiled windows sit next to each other on the screen and share edges. If you are familiar with the Macintosh or Microsoft Windows version 2, you know that these environments use *overlapping* windows.

At any time, only one window is *active*. This means that you cannot edit in two windows at the same time; instead, you have to select the window in which you want to work and make it active. Word makes this easy to do.

Procedure

To split a window, use the **Window Split Horizontal** or **Window Split Vertical** command. The *at line* field is filled in with the number of the line on which the cursor is on, but you can change this to any number. If you want to open a blank window instead of seeing two views of the current file, set the *clear new window* field to *Yes*. You can also split a window with the mouse by pointing at the right border and pressing the left button (to split and open another window in this document) or the right button (to open a blank window). To open the footnote window in a document, use the **Window Split Footnote** command or at the top border (hold down the Alt key if the ruler is visible). (See Footnotes.)

You can move from window to window by pressing F1. This makes the window with the next higher number active. To move to the window with the next lower number, press Shift F1. You can move between windows with the mouse simply by clicking in the desired window.

To close a window, use the **Window Close** command. If you are using the mouse, you can close a window by pointing to its right border and pressing both buttons. If there is only one window on the screen and you close it, Word clears the window but it will still show.

Since Word's windows are tiled, you cannot really move them. Instead, you can only move the lower-right corners of windows, which in turn moves other windows that share edges with that corner. For example, Figure 92 shows three windows. If you move the corner of window 1 to the right and down, you move windows 2 and 3 to make room. If you move the corner of window 1 down, window 3 grows as well.

To move the lower-right corner of a window, use the **Window Move** command. Fill in the *to row* and *to column* fields with the desired locations. To move the corner with the mouse, simply point at the corner, hold down the left button, move to the desired location, and release the button.

If you have a few small windows in different documents on the screen, you may want to enlarge them to full size and be able to flip through them. Microsoft calls enlarging a window *zooming*. To zoom the active window, press Ctrl F1 (Word displays *ZM* at the bottom of the screen when you have zoomed the windows). In effect, this zooms all windows. When you

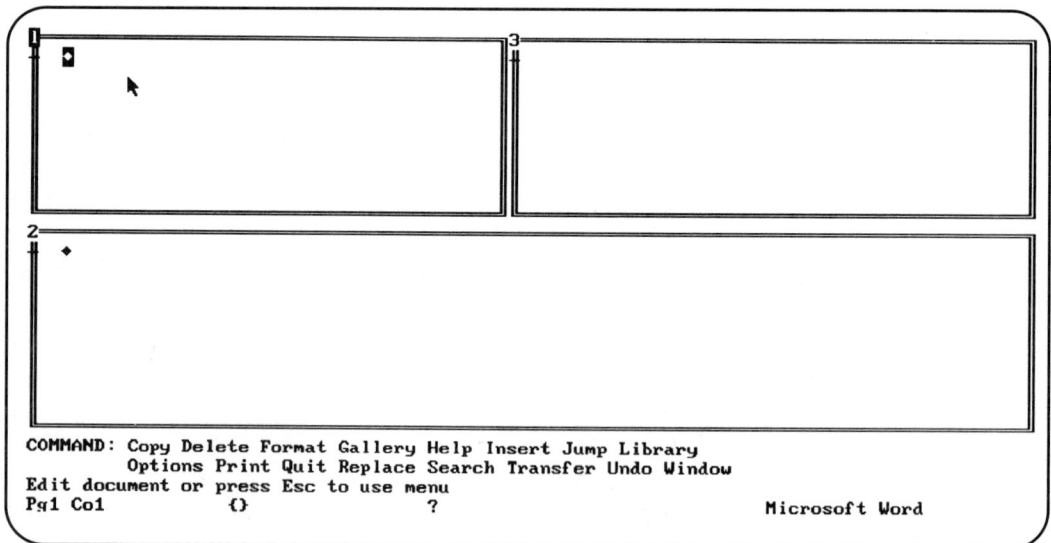

```
COMMAND: Copy Delete Format Gallery Help Insert Jump Library
         Options Print Quit Replace Search Transfer Undo Window
Edit document or press Esc to use menu
Pg1 Co1              {}              ?              Microsoft Word
```

Figure 92

press F1 or Shift F1, the next or previous window will be selected and will already be zoomed to full height. To return the windows to their previous sizes, press Ctrl F1 again.

To zoom with the mouse, point at the window number and click the right button. To select the next window, point at the window number and click the left button; to select the previous window, point at the window number, hold down the Shift key, and click the left button. To return the windows to their previous sizes, point at the window number and press the right button again.

The **W**indow **O**ptions command in version 4 lets you specify what is or is not shown in a window. The field choices and uses for the **W**indow **O**ptions commands are listed below.

FIELD	USE
outline	Shows the text in outline view. (See Outlines.)
show hidden text	Specifies whether hidden text is shown. If you choose *Yes*, Word displays hidden text with a dotted underline. Be sure that you are not showing hidden text when you repaginate, since Word will include the hidden text as it determines where text goes on the page.
background color	Sets the color for the background of the window. Press F1 for a list of the choices of color for your adapter. (See Graphics Adapters.)
style bar	Specifies whether the style bar is shown. The style bar shows the key codes for styles and the type of running head. (See Styles and Running Heads).
ruler	Shows the ruler at the top of the window

For version 5, see Options.

Warnings   You cannot split or resize a zoomed window. Once you have zoomed a window, you must reduce it back to normal size in order to split windows again.

Tips   If you are visually comparing the contents of two windows, scrolling them at the same time is convenient. The following macro, which only works in version 5, does that for you.

```
<pgdn>
«SET currwin = window»
«IF currwin = 1»«SET window = 2»«ELSE»«SET window = 1»«ENDIF»
<pgdn>
«SET window = currwin»
```

You can split the screen in two windows and view a document's outline in one and the document itself in the other. (See Outlines.) You can also use split screens to view a form letter and its associated data document. (See Form Letters.)

Appendices

Appendix A: Edit Menu Commands

Copy
        to:

Delete
        to:

Format
    Character
        bold: Yes No
        italic: Yes No
        underline: Yes No
        strikethrough: Yes No
        uppercase: Yes No
        small caps: Yes No
        double underline: Yes No
        position: Normal Superscript Subscript
        font name:
        font size:
        hidden: Yes No
    Paragraph
        alignment: Left Centered Right Justified
        left indent:
        first line:
        right indent:
        line spacing:
        space before:
        space after:
        keep together: Yes No
        keep follow: Yes No
        side by side: Yes No
    Tab
      Set
        position:
        alignment: Left Center Right Decimal Vertical
        leader char: Blank . - _
      Clear
        position:
      Reset-all

Border
    type: None Box Lines
    line style: Normal Bold Double Thick
    left: Yes No
    right: Yes No
    above: Yes No
    below: Yes No
    background shading:
Footnote
    reference mark:
Division
  Margins
    top:
    bottom:
    left:
    right:
    page length:
    width:
    gutter margin:
    running-head position from top:
    from bottom:
  Page-numbers
    : Yes No
    from top:
    from left:
    numbering: Continuous Start
    at:
    number format: 1 I i A a
  Layout
    footnotes: Same-page End
    number of columns:
    space between columns:
    division break: Page Continuous Column Even Odd
  line-**N**umbers
    : Yes No
    from text:
    restart at: Page Division Continuous
    increments:

Running-head
    position: Top Bottom None
    odd pages: Yes No
    even pages: Yes No
    first page: Yes No
    align with left margin: Yes No

Stylesheet
  Attach
  Character
  Paragraph
  Division
  Record
    key code:
    usage: Character Paragraph Division
    variant:
    remark:

s**E**arch
  Character
    direction: Up Down
    bold: Yes No
    italic: Yes No
    underline: Yes No
    strikethrough: Yes No
    uppercase: Yes No
    small caps: Yes No
    double underline: Yes No
    position: Normal Superscript Subscript
    font name:
    font size:
    hidden: Yes No
  Paragraph
    direction: Up Down
    alignment: Left Centered Right Justified
    left indent:
    first line:
    right indent:
    line spacing:

    space before:
    space after:
    keep together: Yes No
    keep follow: Yes No
    side by side: Yes No
  Style
    key code:
    direction: Up Down
rep**L**ace
  Character
    confirm: Yes No
    bold: Yes No
    italic: Yes No
    underline: Yes No
    strikethrough: Yes No
    uppercase: Yes No
    small caps: Yes No
    double underline: Yes No
    position: Normal Superscript Subscript
    font name:
    font size:
    hidden: Yes No
  Paragraph
    confirm: Yes No
    alignment: Left Centered Right Justified
    left indent:
    first line:
    right indent:
    line spacing:
    space before:
    space after:
    keep together: Yes No
    keep follow: Yes No
    side by side: Yes No
  Style
    key code:
    with:
    confirm: Yes No

revision-**M**arks
   Options
      add revision marks: Yes No
      inserted text: Normal Bold Underlined upperCase
         Double-underlined
      revision bar position: None Left Right Alternate
   accept-**R**evisions
   Undo-revisions
   Search
p**O**sition
      frame position horizontal:
      vertical:
      frame width:
Annotation
      mark:
bookmar**K**
      name:
Gallery (See Appendix B.)
Help
   Exit
   Next
   Previous
   Basics
   Index
   Tutorial
      Lesson
      Index
   Keyboard **M**ouse
Insert
      from:
Jump to:
   Page
      number:
   Footnote
   Annotation
   bookmar**K**
      name:

Library
    Autosort
        by: Alphanumeric Numeric
        sequence: Ascending Descending
        case: Yes No
        column only: Yes No
    Document-retrieval
        Query
            path:
            author:
            operator:
            keywords:
            creation date:
            revision date:
            document text:
            case: Yes No
            marked files only: Yes No
        Exit
        Load
            filename:
            read only: Yes No
        Print
            : Summary Document Both
            range: Selection All
        Update
            filename:
            title:
            version number:
            author:
            creation date:
            operator:
            revision date:
            keywords:
            comments:
        View
            : Short Long Full
            sort by: Directory Author Operator Revision _ date
               Creation _ date Size

Copy
>   marked files to drive/directory:
>   copy style sheet: Yes No

Delete
>   style sheet with document: Yes No

Hyphenate
>   confirm: Yes No
>   hyphenate caps: Yes No

Index
>   entry/page # separated by:
>   cap main entries: Yes No
>   indent each level:
>   use style sheet: Yes No

Link
>   **D**ocument
>>   filename:
>>   bookmark:
>   **G**raphics
>>   filename:
>>   format:
>>   alignment:
>>   graphics width:
>>   graphics height:
>>   space before:
>>   space after:
>   **S**preadsheet
>>   filename:
>>   area:

Number
>   : Update Remove
>   restart sequence: Yes No

Run

Spell
>   **C**orrect
>>   remember correction: Yes No
>   **A**dd
>>   **S**tandard
>>   **U**ser
>>   **D**ocument

Exit
Ignore
Options
 user dictionary:
 lookup: Quick Complete
 ignore all caps: Yes No
 check punctuation: Yes No
 alternatives: Auto Manual
Undo
Table
 from: Outline Codes
 index code:
 page numbers: Yes No
 entry/page number separated by:
 indent each level:
 use style sheet: Yes No
thEsaurus
annOtation
 filename:
 indent annotation text:
Options

 show hidden text: Yes No
 show ruler: Yes No
 show non-printing symbols: None Partial All
 show layout: Yes No
 show line breaks: Yes No
 show style bar: Yes No
 mute: Yes No
 summary sheet: Yes No
 measure: In Cm P10 P12 Pt
 display mode:
 paginate: Auto Manual
 colors:
 autosave:
 autosave confirm: Yes No
 show menu: Yes No
 show borders: Yes No
 date format: MDY DMY

        decimal character:
        time format: 12 24
        default tab width:
        line numbers: Yes No
        count blank space: Yes No
        cursor speed:
        linedraw character:
        speller path:

Print
    Printer
    Direct
    File
        name:
    Glossary
    Merge
        Printer
        Document
            filename:
        Options
            range: All Records
            record numbers:
    Options
        printer:
        setup:
        copies:
        draft: Yes No
        graphics resolution:
        duplex: Yes No
        hidden text: Yes No
        summary sheet: Yes No
        range: All Selection Pages
        page numbers:
        widow/orphan control: Yes No
        queued: Yes No
        feed: Manual Continuous Bin1 Bin2 Bin3 Mixed
Queue
    Continue
    Pause

Restart
Stop
Repaginate
    confirm page breaks: Yes No
pre**V**iew
  Exit
  Jump
    Page
    bookmar**K**
  Options
    display: 1-page 2-page
  Print
    Printer
    Options
Quit
Replace
    text:
    with text:
    confirm: Yes No
    case: Yes No
    whole word: Yes No
Search
    text:
    direction: Up Down
    case: Yes No
    whole word: Yes No
Transfer
  Load
    filename:
    read only: Yes No
  Save
    filename:
    format: Word Text-only RTF Text-only-with-line-breaks
  Clear
    All
    Window
  Delete
    filename:

Merge
    filename:
    annotations only: Yes No
Options
    setup:
    save between sessions: Yes No
Rename
    filename:
Glossary
  Load
    filename:
    read-only: Yes No
  Merge
    filename:
  Save
    filename:
  Clear
    names:
Allsave
Undo
Window
  Split
    Horizontal
      at line:
      clear new window: Yes No
    Vertical
      at column:
      clear new window: Yes No
    Footnote
      at line:
  Close
    window number:
  Move
    lower-right corner of window #:
    to row:
    column:

Appendix B: Gallery Menu Commands

Copy
Delete
Exit
Format
    Character
            bold: Yes No
            italic: Yes No
            underline: Yes No
            strikethrough: Yes No
            uppercase: Yes No
            small caps: Yes No
            double underline: Yes No
            position: Normal Superscript Subscript
            font name:
            font size:
            hidden: Yes No
    Paragraph
            alignment: Left Centered Right Justified
            left indent:
            first line:
            right indent:
            line spacing:
            space before:
            space after:
            keep together: Yes No
            keep follow: Yes No
            side by side: Yes No
    Tab
        Set
            position:
            alignment: Left Center Right Decimal Vertical
            leader char: Blank . - _
        Clear
            position:
        Reset-All

Border

        type: None Box Lines

        line style: Normal Bold Double Thick

        left: Yes No

        right: Yes No

        above: Yes No

        below: Yes No

        background shading:

Division

  Margins

      top:

      bottom:

      left:

      right:

      page length:

      width:

      gutter margin:

      running-head position from top:

      from bottom:

  Page-numbers

      : Yes No

      from top:

      from left:

      numbering: Continuous Start

      at:

      number format: 1 I i A a

  Layout

      footnotes: Same-page End

      number of columns:

      space between columns:

      division break: Page Continuous Column Even Odd

  line-**N**umbers

      : Yes No

      from text:

      restart at: Page Division Continuous

      increments:

pOsition
> frame position horizontal:
> vertical:
> frame width:

Help

Insert
> key code:
> usage: Character Paragraph Division
> variant:
> remark:

Name
> key code:
> variant:
> remark

Print

Transfer
> **Load**
> > style sheet name:
> > read only: Yes No
>
> **Save**
> > style sheet name:
>
> **Clear**
>
> **Delete**
> > filename:
>
> **Merge**
> > style sheet name:
>
> **Options**
> > setup:
> > save between sessions: Yes No
>
> **Rename**
> > style sheet name:

Undo

Appendix C: Keyboard Commands

Alt 2	Double space
Alt B	Boldface
Alt C	Centered
Alt D	Double underline
Alt E	Hidden
Alt F	Increase first line indentation by one tab stop
Alt I	Italic
Alt J	Justified
Alt K	Small caps
Alt L	Left flush
Alt M	Reduce left indentation by one tab stop
Alt N	Increase left indentation by one tab stop
Alt O	One line after
Alt P	Normal paragraph
Alt Q	Increase left and right indent by one stop
Alt R	Right flush
Alt S	Strikethrough
Alt T	Increase hanging indentation by one tab stop
Alt U	Underline
Alt X	Prefix if style sheet is attached
Alt +	Superscript
Alt -	Subscript
Alt Space Bar	Normal character
F1	Next window
Alt F1	Format **Tab Set**
Ctrl F1	Zoom window
Shift F1	**Undo**
F2	Calculate
Alt F2	Format **Running-head** *position Bottom*
Ctrl F2	Format **Running-head** *position Top*
Shift F2	Outline view on/off
F3	Expand from glossary
Alt F3	Copy

Ctrl F3	Step macro
Shift F3	Record macro on/off
F4	Repeat last editing or inserting command
Alt F4	**O**ptions *layout Yes/No*
Ctrl F4	Toggle case
Shift F4	Repeat last search
F5	Overtype on/off
Alt F5	**J**ump
Ctrl F5	Line drawing on/off
Shift F5	Outline edit on/off
F6	Extend selection on/off
Alt F6	**L**ibrary **S**pell
Ctrl F6	**L**ibrary th**E**saurus
Shift F6	Column selection on/off
F7	Previous word
Alt F7	**O**ptions *printer display* (version 4) or *show line breaks* (version 5) *Yes/No*
Ctrl F7	**T**ransfer **L**oad
Shift F7	Previous sentence
F8	Next word
Alt F8	**F**ormat **C**haracter *font name*
Ctrl F8	**P**rint **P**rinter
Shift F8	Next sentence
F9	Previous paragraph
Alt F9	**O**ptions *display*
Ctrl F9	**P**rint pre**V**iew
Shift F9	Current line
F10	Next paragraph
Alt F10	**F**ormat **S**tylesheet **R**ecord
Ctrl F10	**T**ransfer **S**ave
Shift F10	Select entire document
F11	Collapse heading
Shift F11	Collapse body text
F12	Expand heading
Ctrl F12	Expand all

Shift F12	Expand body text
Down Arrow	Down
Ctrl Down Arrow	Beginning of next paragraph
Left Arrow	Left
Ctrl Left Arrow	Beginning of previous word
Right Arrow	Right
Ctrl Right Arrow	Beginning of next word
Up Arrow	Up
Ctrl Up Arrow	Beginning of previous paragraph
End	End of line
Ctrl End	Bottom of window
Home	Beginning of line
Ctrl Home	Top of window
Pg Down	Down a windowful
Ctrl Pg Down	Bottom of document
Pg Up	Up a windowful
Ctrl Pg Up	Top of document
Backspace	Erase left
Del	Erase selection to scrap
Shift Del	Erase selection
Ins	Copy from scrap
Shift Ins	Erase selection and copy from scrap

Index

Index

Absolute paragraph positioning
  feature, 163, 165–166
  frame width, 165
  horizontal frame position, 165, 166
  vertical frame position, 165, 166
Alignment, 160
Angle brackets (< and >), 120
Annotations
  cautions about, 7
  character format, 5, 6
  footnotes in document with, 39
  Format Annotation command, 3–4, 5
  hidden text method, 5, 6, 7
  Jump Annotation command, 4
  listing to another file, 4
  macros, 4, 5
  merging, 4
  removing, 5
  sorting, 5
  style sheet for, 6–7
  tips about, 7
  usefulness of, 3, 7
  viewing list of, 5
Arithmetic. See Math
ASCII code, special characters and codes, listing of, 86
ASCII files. See Importing/Exporting files
ASK instruction, merging, 47, 48
AUTOEXEC.BAT
  graphics adapter, environment command, 65
  installation of Word, 88
Automatic numbering, footnotes, 35–36
Automatic repagination
  Jump Page command and, 91
  problems related to, 177
Autosave
  cautions about, 9–10
  failure recovery, 9
  setting feature, 8

Boldface, character formatting, 15–18
Bookmarks
  changing name of, 11
  copying text with, 11
  creation of, 10–11
  Format bookmarK command, 11
  Jump bookmarK command, 10, 11
  Library Link Document command, 11
  macros, 11
  size of, 10
  tips about, 11–12
  usefulness of, 10
Borders and boxes
  cautions about, 14
  format border command, 12–14
  line styles, 12
  printer and, 14
  tips about, 14
Boxes. See also Borders and boxes
  line drawing, 102–105
Bulleted lists, 109, 110
Bullet marks, 109
  dingbats, 110

Calculated fields, form letters, 49
Capital letters
  hyphenation and, 70
  small, character formatting, 15–18
Captions
  graphics, 60
  keeps, 92
  tables/figures, 203
Capture program
  graphics, 61–62
  memory space, 61
  modifying saved screen, 62
Case of letters
  formatting, 17
  hyphenation and, 70
  replacing text and, 180
  small capital letters, 15–18
  toggling case, 181
Changing. See Replacing
Character formatting, 52

annotations, 5, 6
  categories of, 15
  caution about, 17
  examples of, 17
  Format Character command, 15, 16
  hidden formatting, 16
  keys for, 16, 94–95
  removing, 15
  screen display, 17
  special purposes, 15
  spreadsheets, 215
  style sheets, 16, 17–18
  usefulness of, 15
Character styles, copying formats, 22
Chevrons (<< and >>), 40, 120
CiteRite, 151
Clipboard, Microsoft Windows, 129
Collapsing headings, outlining, 153, 155–156
Columns
  column break, 19
  defining columns, 18, 19
  examples of, 19–21
  Format Division Layout command, 19, 21
  newspaper columns, 18
  printing, 21
  screen display, 18–19
  tables, moving, 229
  tips about, 21
  wrapping text, 19
Comments, macros, use in, 120
CompareRite, 151
Continuous feed labels, 122–123
Conversion programs, 75
Copy command
  copying text, 23
  executing command, 21
  function of, 21
Copying formats
  character styles, 22
  macros, 22
  mouse, 22
  repeat action key (F4) method, 22

Copying text
  Copy command, 23
  mouse, 23
  speed copying, 23
Cross-referencing
  examples of, 25
  figure/page numbers, use of, 25,
    26
  Format bookmarK command, 24,
    25
  sequences and, 24, 202
  tips about, 26
  usefulness of, 24
Currency values, spreadsheets,
  215
Cursor, keys to move cursor, 93

Data document, form letters, 41–42,
  44–45
DATA instruction, merging, 45
DCA (Document Context
    Architecture), importing/
    exporting files, 72, 73–74
Delete command, 26
Delete text
  execution of, 26
  options for, 26
Dialogs, keyboard, use in, 96, 97
Directory
  listing files in, 139
  navigation through, 31
Division formatting, 52
  choices/actions, 27–28
  Format Division command, 27
  Format Division Layout
    command, 27
  procedure in, 27–28
  scope of, 27
Document dictionary, 208, 212
Double underline, character
    formatting, 15–18

Editing software, programs used
    with Word, 152
Edit mode, outlining, 153, 154, 155
ELSE instruction, merging, 46
Emulation, 169
ENDIF instruction, merging, 45
EXACT, 150

Expanding headings, outlining, 153,
  155–156
Exporting files. *See* Importing/
  Exporting files
Expression, macros, 117

F1 enumeration
  fields for enumeration, 28–30
  mouse, 28
  procedure, 30–31
  usefulness of, 31
Fancy Word, 149
Fields, form letters, 40
Figures
  cross-referencing, 25, 26
  numbering of, sequences,
    202–203
  table of figures, 235
Finding. *See* Searching
Floppy-based system, installation of
    Word, 87, 88
Fonts
  cautions about, 35
  downloadable fonts, 34–35
  Format Character command,
    33–34
  generic font names, 32–33
  line drawing, 103
  manufacturers of, 34
  multiple printers and, 32
  tabs and printing, 229
  tips about, 34–35
  types available for Word, 149
Footers. *See* Running heads
Footnotes
  annotations in same document,
    39
  automatic numbering, 35–36
  cautions about, 39
  footnote mark, 36
  Format Division Layout
    command, 37, 39
  Format Footnote command, 36
  glossary, 39
  Jump Footnote command, 37
  moving text with, 39
  placement of, 36
  printing, 37–38
  repetitive footnotes, 39

  in short documents, 39
  style sheets, 36
  symbols, 36
  tips about, 39
  types of, 36
  viewing, 36
  Window Split Footnote
    command, 36–37
ForComment, 152, 187
Foreign characters. *See also* Inserting
    text fonts, 33
Format Annotation command, 3–4,
    5, 53
Format bookmarK command, 53
  bookmarks, 11
  cross-referencing, 24, 25
Format Border command
  borders and boxes, 12–14
  shading, 204
Format Character command
  character formatting, 15, 16
  fonts, 33–34
  line drawing, 104
  page numbers, 159
  subscripts and superscripts, 225
Format command
  display of settings, 52
  subcommands of, 52
Format Division Command,
    division formatting, 27
Format Division Layout command
  columns, 19, 21
  division formatting, 27
  footnotes, 37, 39
  mailing labels, 123, 124
Format Division line-Numbers
    command, line numbering,
    105–106
Format Division Margins command
  importing/exporting files, 72, 73
  mailing labels, 123, 124
  running heads, 191, 193
Format Division Page-numbers
    command
  page numbers, 158, 159
  running heads, 192
Format Footnote command, 36, 53
Format Paragraph command
  graphics, 60, 62

Format Paragraph *continued*
  indentation, 75–76
  keeps, 91, 92
  mailing labels, 125
  paragraph formatting, 160–161
  Ruler, 189
  running heads, 193, 195
Format repLace command, 53
  replacing text, 181
Format revision-Marks
    accept-Revisions command,
    188, 189
Format revision-Marks command,
    53, 187
Format revision-Marks Option
    command, 188
Format revision-Marks Search
    command, 188
Format revision-Marks
    Undo-revisions command,
    189
Format Running-head command,
    191, 192, 195
Formats
  copying, 22
  replacing, 181
  searching, 201
Format sEarch command, 53
  searching, 200, 201
Format Stylesheet Attach
    command, style sheet, 218,
    221
Format Stylesheet command, 53
Format Stylesheet Record
    command, 221
Format Tabs command, Ruler, 189
Format Tabs Set command, 226–228
Formatting. *See also* Character
    formatting; Division
    formatting; Paragraph
    formatting
  direct formatting, problems of,
    215
  style sheets, 53
  types of, 51, 52
Form letters
  calculated fields, 49
  cautions about, 50–51
  data document, 41–42, 44–45

field, 40
header documents, 45
limitations, 51
main document, 40–41
marking main document, 40
merging, 42–43, 45–49
Print Merge command, 40, 42, 43,
  47, 48
Print Merge Document
    command, 40, 42
Print Merge Options command,
    40, 42, 43
Print Merge Printer command,
    40, 42, 43
record numbers field, 40
records, 40
separators, Tab characters, 42, 50
special characters, 50
tips about, 51
Frame width, absolute paragraph
    positioning feature, 165
Freezing styles, 223–224
FullAuthority, 151
Functions, macros, 117

Gallery command, 6
  style sheet, 218
Galley mode, 97, 98 *See also*
    Layout
  example of, 100
  graphics, 59
  selection of, 98
  use of, 97
Generic font names, 32–33
Glossaries
  cautions about, 56–57
  changing text in entry, 55
  creating entries, 54–55
  file extension .GLY, 54
  footnotes, 39
  length of entry names, 54
  management of file, 55–56
  Print Glossary command, 34, 56
  replacing current glossary with
    new glossary, 56
  several glossaries on disk, 56
  special entries, 55
  tips about, 57

Transfer Glossary Clear
    command, 56
Transfer Glossary Load
    command, 56–57
Transfer Glossary Merge
    command, 54, 56
Transfer Glossary Save
    command, 56, 57
usefulness of, 54, 57
Grammar checkers, programs used
    with Word, 150
Grammatik, 150
Graphics
  captions, 60
  capturing screens, 61–62
  cautions about, 63
  creation off, 59–60
  examples of, 62
  Format Paragraph command, 60,
    62
  formats read by Word, 58
  Library Link command, 58, 59, 60,
    62
  Microsoft Windows, 130
  printing, 59, 61, 63
  Print Options command, 61
  programs used with Word, 150
  screen display modes, 59
  size and position, 60
  style sheets, 63
  tips about, 63
Graphics adapter
  color of menu, changing, 65
  environment commands for
    AUTOEXEC.BAT, 65
  graphics to text mode, switching,
    64
  options for MS-DOS command
    line, 64
  tips about, 65

Hanging indent, 75
Hard disk, installation of Word, 88
Header documents, form letters, 45
Headers. *See* Running heads
Headings
  indexes, 82
  keeps, 92
  tables of contents, 234

INDEX

Help
  with commands, 66
  mouse, 66
  navigation options, 66–67
  tutorial and, 67
Hidden formatting, uses of, 16
Hidden text
  annotations, 5, 6, 7
  indexes, 79, 82–83
  tables of contents, 231, 232, 233, 235
Horizontal frame position, absolute paragraph positioning feature, 165, 166
Hotshot, 61
Hyphenation
  appearance of document and, 70–71
  em dash, 71
  function of hyphens, 69
  hyphenate caps option, 70
  Library Hyphenate command, 69–70
  nonbreaking hyphens, 69
  normal hyphens, 68–69
  optional hyphens, 69, 70
  search and, 201

IF instruction, merging, 45–46
Importing/exporting files
  cautions about, 74
  conversion programs, 75
  documents formatted for DCA, 72, 73–74
  documents formatted for RTF, 72, 74
  Format Division Margins command, 72, 73
  macros, 73
  Print File command, 71, 72, 73
  text files, 72–73
  tips about, 75
  Transfer Load command, 72
  Transfer Merge command, 72
  Transfer Save command, 71, 73, 74
  for Word/Macintosh, 73
INCLUDE instruction, merging, 48
Indentation, 160

convention for, 78
examples of, 77
Format Paragraph command, 75, 76
hanging indent, 75
keyboard equivalents, 77
lists, 110
outdent, 75
positive/negative measurements, effects of, 76
side-by-side paragraphs, 163, 165
tips about, 77–78
types of, 75
Indexes
  cautions about, 82–83
  compiling index, 79, 81–82
  formatting index, 79, 82
  heading, 82
  hidden text, 79m 82–83
  Library Index command, 79, 81–82, 83
  macro, 80
  marking index entries, 79–80
  multi-level indexes, 80
  printer driver, 81
  see references, 83
  special characters, 81
  style sheets, 83
  tips about, 83
Insert command
  insertion capability, 84
  line drawing, 104
  macros, running, 84
  style sheet, 219, 222
  viewing contents of scrap, 84
Inserting text
  cautions about, 87
  overtype mode, 85
  special characters, ASCII code list of, 86
Installation of Word
  AUTOEXEC.BAT, 88
  floppy-based system, 87, 88
  hard disk, 88
  network, 87, 89
  printer drivers, 89
  program directory, 89
  SETUP program, 87–89

Italic, character formatting, 15–18

Jump Annotation command
  annotations, 4
  general use of, 90
Jump bookmarK command
  bookmarks, 10, 11
  general use of, 90
Jump Footnote command
  footnotes, 37
  general use of, 90
Jump Page command
  automatic repagination and, 91
  caution about, 91
  general use of, 90–91
JURISoft, 151

Keeps, 160
  cautions about, 92
  captions, 92
  Format Paragraph command, 91, 92
  headings, 92
  keep follow, 91, 92
  keep together, 91, 92
  meaning of, 91
  Print Options command, 91, 92
  tips about, 92
Keyboard
  dialogs, use in, 96, 97
  indentation, 77
  keyboard commands, 95–96
  keys to format characters, 94–95
  keys to move cursor, 93
  keys to select text, 93–94
  macros, 96
  scrolling, 198
  selecting, 198

Labels. See Mailing labels
Landscape mode, margins, 127
LaserFonts, 149
Layout
  galley mode, 97, 98
  layout mode, 97–98
  preview mode, 97, 99–100
  tips about, 100, 102
Layout mode, 97–98
  example of, 101

269

graphics, 59
  selection of, 98
  use of, 97, 98–99, 102
Leader characters, tabs and, 227
"Learning Microsoft Word"
  program, 67, 87
Legal word processing, programs
  used with Word, 151
Library Autosort command
  annotations, 5
  sorting, 206, 207
Library commands, listing of, 102
Library Document-retrieval
  command, subcommands of,
  183–184
Library Index command, 79, 81–82,
  83
Library Link Document command,
  bookmarks, 11
Library Link Spreadsheet
  command, 213
Library Number command,
  numbering outlines, 142–143
Library Run command
  macros and, 118
  MS-DOS commands, 138–140
Library Spell command
  speller, 208
  undo command, 241
Library Spelling Options command,
  speller, 212
Library Table command
  options for, 234
  tables of contents, 230, 231, 233,
  235
Line drawing. See also Borders and
  boxes
  arrow keys, 103
  best results, tips for, 104–105
  character options, 103
  exiting mode, 104
  Format Character command, 104
  Insert command, 104
  linedraw character field, 104
  Options command, 104
  printing, 102–103, 104
Line numbering
  cautions about, 106
  defaults, 106

empty lines, handling, 106
  example of, 107
  Format Division line-Numbers
  command, 105 106
  use of, 105
Lines-Graphs-Symbols, 150
Line spacing, 160
  auto option, 161–162
Lists
  bulleted lists, 109, 110
  indentation, 110
  lists within lists, 109
  numbered lists, 109, 110
  paragraph formatting, 110
  plain lists, 109
  types of, 109
Loading documents. See Transfer
  command
Logical operators, listing of, 185
Lotus 1–2-3, 213
LWPlus, 149

Macintosh
  importing/exporting files, 72, 73
  Word/Macintosh compared to
  Word PC
  different features, 131–132
  missing features, 132
MACROCNV program, 120–121
MACRO.GLY, 4, 5, 73
Macros
  annotations, 4, 5
  bookmarks, 11
  cautions about, 120
  comments, use in, 120
  copying formats, 22
  editing macros, 113–114
  examples of use, 119–120
  functions, 117
  importing/exporting files, 73
  indexes, 80
  keyboard, 96
  key combinations, 111
  macro commands, 114–115
  macro conditions, 116, 117
  macro instructions, 114
  macro variables, 115–117
  Microsoft macros, 111
  naming macros, 111, 113, 121

recording macros, 111–112
  replacing text, 181
  Ruler, 191
  running, insert command, 84
  running macros, 113, 121
  running one macro into another,
  118
  scrolling, 199
  spreadsheets, 215
  style sheet, 225
  symbols in, 118, 120
  tables of contents, 232
  Transfer Glossary Load, 111
  typing in macros, 112–113
  and version of Word, 120–121
  windows, 245–246
Mailing labels
  centering text, 125
  continuous feed labels, 122–123
  Format Division layout
  command, 123, 124
  Format Division Margins
  command, 123, 124
  Format Paragraph command, 125
  printing, 122
  setup for, 122
  sheet-feed labels, 123–125
  sorting addresses and, 51
  tips about, 125
Main document, form letters, 40–41
MAKEPRD, printer drivers, 170–171
MAKEVID program, 64
Management of file, glossaries,
  55–56
Margins
  examples of, 127
  Format Division Margins
  command, 126
  gutter, setting, 126, 127
  landscape mode, 127
  printing and, 127
Marking main document, form
  letters, 40
Math
  cautions about, 128
  operators/symbols, 128
  procedure for calculations, 128
Measurement. See Options
Menus, color, 65

MERGEPRD, printer drivers, 170–171
Merging
  annotations, 4
  ASK instruction, 47, 48
  DATA instruction, 45
  ELSE instruction, 46
  ENDIF instruction, 45
  error messages, 43
  form letters, 42–43, 45–49
  IF instruction, 45–46
  INCLUDE instruction, 48
  NEXT instruction, 48
  SET instruction, 47–48
  SKIP instruction, 46–47
  stopping process, 43
Microjustification, 162
Microlytics, 151
Microsoft Excel, 213
Microsoft Multiplan, 213
Microsoft Pageview, 97
Microsoft Windows
  Clipboard, 129
  graphics, 130
  Pageview, 129–130
  program information file (PIF), 129
  tips about, 131
  version of Word and, 128
  Windows Write, 130
Microsoft Word Companion Products, 152
Modes of Word, listing of, 133
Mouse
  buttons, rules for, 133–134
  copying formats, 22
  copying text, 23
  cursor/shape correspondences, 136
  double beep and, 137
  executing commands, 134
  F1 enumeration, 28
  mouse driver, 137
  outlining, 157
  scrolling, 134–135, 198
  selecting, 199
  shapes/functions, 136–137
  speed move, 135, 137–138
  splitting screen, 135

tabs, 228
text selection, 134
thumbing, 135
tips about, 137
windows, 245
zooming window, 135
Moving text
  scrap, 137, 138
  speed move, 137–138
MS-DOS commands
  cautions about, 138, 139–140
  commands not running, 140
  Library Run command, 138–140
  loading several commands, 139
  tips about, 140
MW.INI, 175

Negative numbers, indentation, 76
Networks
  installation of Word, 87, 89
  procedure for use, 140–141
  RDONLY command, 141
  RDWRITE command, 141
  read-only files, creating, 141
  Transfer Load command, 140
  Transfer Merge command, 140
  unavailable files and, 141
Newspaper columns. *See* Columns
NEXT instruction, merging, 48
Nonbreaking spaces, 85
NORMAL.GLY file, 120
Numbering
  numbered lists, 109, 110
  page numbers, 158–159
  sequences, 202–203
Numbering outlines
  Library Number command, 142–143
  numbers used, 142
  renumbering, 142
  restart sequence, 143
  saving document before numbering, 143

Options
  automatic save of, 147
  cautions about, 147
  commands to set options, 143
  listing of options, 144–147

Options command
  dialog for, 143–144
  line drawing, 104
Organize mode, outlining, 153, 154
Orphan, 91 *See also* Keeps
OS/2, use with Word, 148
Outdent, 75
Outlining
  collapsing headings, 153, 155–156
  edit mode, 153, 154, 155
  entering outline, 154–155
  expanding headings, 153, 155–156
  keyboard controls, 156, 157
  mouse, 157
  numbering, 141–143
  organize mode, 153, 154
  outline view, 153
  reorganizing outline, 156–157
  starting outline, 154
  style sheets, 157
  table of contents and, 153
  usefulness of, 152–153
  viewing outline, 155
Overtype mode, 85

Page description language, 168
Page numbers
  changing formatting of, 159
  direct page numbers, 158, 159
  examples of, 159
  Format Character command, 159
  Format Division Page-numbers command, 158, 159
  in running heads, 158, 192
Pages. *See* Division formatting
Pageview, Microsoft Windows, 129–130
Paragraph formatting, 52
  Format Paragraph command, 160–161
  importance of, 159
  indentation, 75–78
  keyboard equivalents, 161
  lists, 110
  style sheets, 77
  types of, 160
  white space, 161
Paragraph placement, 160

Paragraph placement *continued*
  absolute paragraph positioning
    feature, 163, 165–166
  examples of, 166
  side-by-side paragraphs, 162,
    163–164, 166, 168
Path list, creating, 88
Paths, retrieving documents,
  184–185, 186
Pleading numbering. *See* Line
  numbering
PostScript language, 168
PostScript printers, 149, 168–169
  style sheet, 169
  viewing commands, 168
Power failures
  Autosave, 7–8, 9
  recovery, steps for, 9
Predefined variants, style sheet,
  222–223
Preview mode, 97, 99–100
  commands used, 99
  example of, 101
  graphics, 59
  selection of, 98
  use of, 98, 99–100, 101
Print command, subcommands of,
  172
Print Direct, function of, 174
Printer drivers
  cautions about, 171
  conversion to text format, 170
  fonts, 33, 34
  Format Division Margins, 171
  generic drivers, listing of, 170
  indexes, 81
  installation of Word, 89
  installing, 170–171
  MAKEPRD, 170–171
  MERGEPRD, 170–171
  SETUP program, 34, 169
  tips about, 171
Printers, compatibility with Word,
  169
Print File command, function of,
  174, 175
Print File command, importing/
  exporting files, 71, 72, 73

Printing
  borders and boxes, 14
  character formatting and, 17, 18
  columns, 21
  fonts, 32–35
  footnotes, 37–38
  graphics, 59, 61, 63
  margins and, 127
  running heads, 192
  side-by-side paragraphs, 166, 168
  special characters, 87
Print Merge command, form letters,
  40, 42, 43, 47, 48
Print Merge Document command,
  form letters, 40, 42
Print Merge Options command,
  form letters, 40, 42, 43
Print Merge Printer command, form
  letters, 40, 42, 43
Print Options command, 143
  choices for, 172
  fields, listing of, 173–174
  graphics, 61
  keeps, 91, 92
Print preView command, running
  heads, 196
Print preview. *See* Layout
Print Queue commands, 174
Print Repaginate command,
  repagination, 178
Program, 170
Program information file (PIF),
  Microsoft Windows, 129
Proportional fonts, tabs and, 229
Punctuation checking, 211–212

Queue, Print Queue, 174
Quit command, commands
  preserved by Word, 175–176

RAM disk, 10
RAM-resident programs, 140
R-Doc/X, 75
RDONLY command, networks, 141
RDWRITE command, networks,
  141
Reading from disk, Transfer
  command, 237–239

README.DOC, 89
Read-only files, creating, 141
Ready!, 140
Record numbers field, form letters,
  40
Records, form letters, 40
Redlining. *See* Revision marks
Repagination
  automatic repagination, problems
    related to, 177
  from beginning of document,
    actions related to, 178–179
  Print Repaginate command, 178
  time factors, 178
Repeat action key (F4) method,
  copying formats, 22
Replacing text
  case of characters, 180
  caution about, 181
  Format repLace command, 181
  formats, replacing, 181
  macros, 181
  Replace command, 179, 181
  search, 179–180
  special characters, 180–181
  styles, replacing, 181
  toggling case, 181
Retrieving documents
  caution about, 186
  characters allowed in search, 185,
    186
  Library Document-retrieval
    command, 183 184
  Library Document-retrieval
    Query command, 182,
    184–185
  paths, 184–185, 186
  search criteria, 184
  summary sheet and, 182–183
  tips about, 186
Revision marks
  actions of Word and, 187
  cautions about, 188–189
  Format revision-Marks
    accept-Revisions command,
    188, 189
  Format revision-Marks
    command, 187

Format revision-Marks Option command, 188

Format revision-Marks Search command, 188

Format revision-Marks Undo-revisions command, 189

strikethrough and, 17, 189

Revision marks *continued*
style options for inserted text, 189

use of, 188

RFT (Revisable Form Text), importing/exporting files, 72, 73–74

Rightwriter, 150

Ruler
display of, 190

Format Paragraph command, 189

Format Tabs command, 189

macro, 191

marks, listing of, 189

sliding and scaling rulers, 189–190

Window Options command, 190

Running heads
caution about, 195

and division of document, 191, 196

even/odd pages printing and, 192, 194

F4 key, use of, 196

Format Division Margins command, 191, 193

Format Division Page-numbers command, 192

Format Paragraph command, 193, 195

Format Running-head command, 191, 192, 195

multi-line heads, 192

page numbers in, 158, 192

paragraph as, 192–193

printing, 192

Print preView command, 196

sample report, 193–195

styles for, 193

tips about, 195–196

two-sided printing and, 192, 193

vertical/horizontal positioning, 193

Saving, Autosave, 7–10 *See also* Transfer command

Scrap
cautions about, 197

display of, 197

emptying scrap, 197

moving text, 137, 138

special characters, display of, 197

tips for use, 197

Transfer Clear All command, 197

usefulness of, 196

Screen display
character formats, viewing, 17

columns, 18–19

screen display modes, 59

Screenplay word processing, programs used with Word, 151

SCREEN.VID file, 64

Scriptor from Screenplay Systems, 151

Scrolling
with keyboard, 198

macro, 199

with mouse, 199

mouse, 134–135

Searching
cautions about, 201

documents, 185–186

formats, 201

Format sEarch command, 200, 201

hyphens and, 201

options for, 200

replacing text and, 179–180

special characters, 201

styles, 201

summary sheets, 182–185

Selecting
with keyboard, 198

with mouse, 199

Sequences
cross-referencing and, 24, 202

sequence holders, 202, 203

skipping numbers, 202

for tables/figures in same document, 203

SET instruction, merging, 47–48

SETUP program
printer drivers, 34, 169

use for installation, 87–89

Shading
ASCII characters for, 205

examples of, 204

Format Border command, 204

printer type and, 204–205

Sheet-feed labels, 123–125

Side-by-side paragraphs
example of, 162

indentation, 163, 165

printing, 166, 168

style sheets, 168

Sidekick, 140

SKIP instruction, merging, 46–47

Sliding and scaling rulers, 189–190

Sorting
annotations, 5

Library Autosort command, 206, 207

options, 205

procedures, 206–207

Transfer Clear All command, 207

Spaces, nonbreaking spaces, 85

Special characters
ASCII code list of, 86

form letters, 50

indexes, 81

nonbreaking spaces, 85

printing, 87

replacing text and, 180–181

Scrap, display of, 197

searching, 201

Speed move, mouse, 23, 135, 137–138

Speller
cautions about, 212

commands/actions of spell mode, 210–211

deleting words from, 212

document dictionary, 208, 212

Library Spell command, 208

Library Spelling Options command, 212

limitations of, 207–208

mispunctuation, 211–212

misspelled words, options for, 211

other programs used with Word, 151
standard dictionary, 208, 212
startup/use of, 208–209
tips about, 212
usefulness of, 207
and versions of Word, 208
Splitting screen, mouse, 135
Spreadsheets
cautions about, 214
character formatting and, 215
currency values, 215
data used by Word, 213
Library Link Spreadsheet command, 213
macro, 215
procedure for integration, 213–214
specifying data for integration, 213
tag next, 214
unlinking, 214
updating, 214–215
Windows Option command, 214
Standard dictionary, 208, 212
Strikethrough
character formatting, 15–18
revision marks, 189
Styles
versus direct formatting, 215, 216, 217
document review and, 217–218
elements/uses, listing of, 216
function of, 215
replacing, 181
searching, 201
storage of, 216
used with direct formatting, 221
usefulness of, 216, 217
Style sheets
annotations, 6–7
attaching to document, 221–222
cautions about, 224
character formatting, 16, 17–18
commands, gallery mod, 218–219
creation of, 218–221
editing, 222
fields, listing of, 220
footnotes, 36

Format Stylesheet Attach command, 218, 221
Format Stylesheet Record command, 221
formatting, 53
freezing styles, 223–224
Gallery command, 218
indexes, 83
Insert command, 219, 222
macros, 225
Name command, 222
outline, 157
paragraph formatting, 77
PostScript printers, 169
predefined variants, 222–223
printing, 222
saving, 221
side-by-side paragraphs, 168
source book on, 224
"standard" paragraph/division variants, use of, 224
style bar, showing, 224–225
tips about, 224–225
Transfer Load command, 222
Transfer Merge command, 222
Transfer Save command, 221, 222
Subscripts and superscripts, 160
character formatting, 15–18
Format Character command, 225
procedure, 225
tips about, 225
Summary sheet
fields/uses in, 182–183
function of, 182
search criteria, 184
Superscript. See Subscripts and superscripts
Symbols
fonts, 33
in macros, 118, 120
Synonyms, thesaurus, 235–237

Tables
borders, 14
columns, moving, 229
numbering of, sequences, 202–203
side-by-side paragraphs, 230
tab stops, 226–229

tips about, 230
viewing all characters on screen, 230
Tables of contents
cautions about, 235
compiling, 233–234
formatting, 231, 234–235
heading, 234
hidden text, 231, 232, 233, 235
Library Table command, 230, 231, 233, 235
macros, 232
marking entries for, 231–233
moving, 235
page sizes, 233
with styles, 2231
table of figures, 235
text in, 230–231
tips about, 235
Tabs
default tab width field, 226
deleting, 228
examples of, 227
Format Tabs Set, 227–228
leader characters and, 227
mouse, 228
proportional fonts and, 229
setting tabs, 227–228
tabs/actions, listing of, 226
tab character, separation in form letters, 42, 50
vertical tables, 227
Tag next, spreadsheets, 214
Telecommunications, conversion programs, 75
TexDCA, 75
Text selection
keys for, 93–94
mouse, 134
Thesaurus
options with, 236–237
tips about, 237
usefulness of, 235–236, 237
Thumbing, mouse, 135
Toggling case, 181
Transfer Allsave command, 239
Transfer Clear All command
macros and, 120
Scrap, 197

Transfer Clear All *continued*
   Sorting, 207
Transfer command
   cautions about, 239
   loading file, 238
   low memory and, 238
   saving file, 238
   subcommands of, 237–238
   Transfer Allsave command, 239
   Transfer Delete command, 239
   Transfer Options command, 239
Transfer Delete command, 139, 239
Transfer Glossary Clear command
   glossaries, 56
   macros and, 120
Transfer Glossary Load command,
   4
   glossaries, 56–57
   macros, 111
Transfer Glossary Merge command,
   54, 56
Transfer Glossary Save command,
   56, 57
Transfer Load command, 30
   importing/exporting files, 72
   networks, 140
   style sheet, 222
Transfer Merge command
   importing/exporting files, 72
   networks, 140
   style sheet, 222
Transfer Options command, 30, 185,
   239
Transfer Save command, 8

importing/exporting files, 71, 73, 74
style sheet, 221, 222
Tutorial, help and, 67

Underline, character formatting,
   15–18
Undo command
   cautions about, 241
   checking results of, 241
   commands affected by, 240
   commands unaffected by, 240
   Library Spell command, 241
   purposes of, 239
Unlinking, spreadsheets, 214

Variable operator expression, 117
Variable operator value, 116
Variable operator variable, 116
Variables, macros, 114, 115–117
Vertical frame position, absolute
   paragraph positioning
   feature, 165, 166

White space, determining, 161
Widows, 91 *See also* Keeps
Window Options command, 143
   fields/uses of, 245
   Ruler, 190
   spreadsheets, 214
Windows
   cautions about, 245
   closing window, 244
   macro, 245–246
   mouse, 135

moving between windows, 243
moving lower-right corner of, 244
tips about, 245–246
Window Split Horizontal
   command, 243
Window Split Vertical command,
   243
zooming, 244–245
Window Split Footnote command
   annotations, 3
   footnotes, 36–37
Windows Write, Microsoft
   Windows, 130
Word
   features of version 5, 241–242
   importing/exporting files, 72, 73
   Microsoft customer service
      number, 242
   modes, listing of, 133
   OS/2 and, 148
   programs available for
      editing program, 152
      fonts/graphics, 149–150
      legal word processing, 151
      *Microsoft Word Companion
         Products*, 152
      screenplay word processing, 151
      writing tools, 150–151
Word Exchange, 75
Wrapping text, columns, 19
Writing to disk, Transfer command,
   237–239

Zooming, windows, 244–245

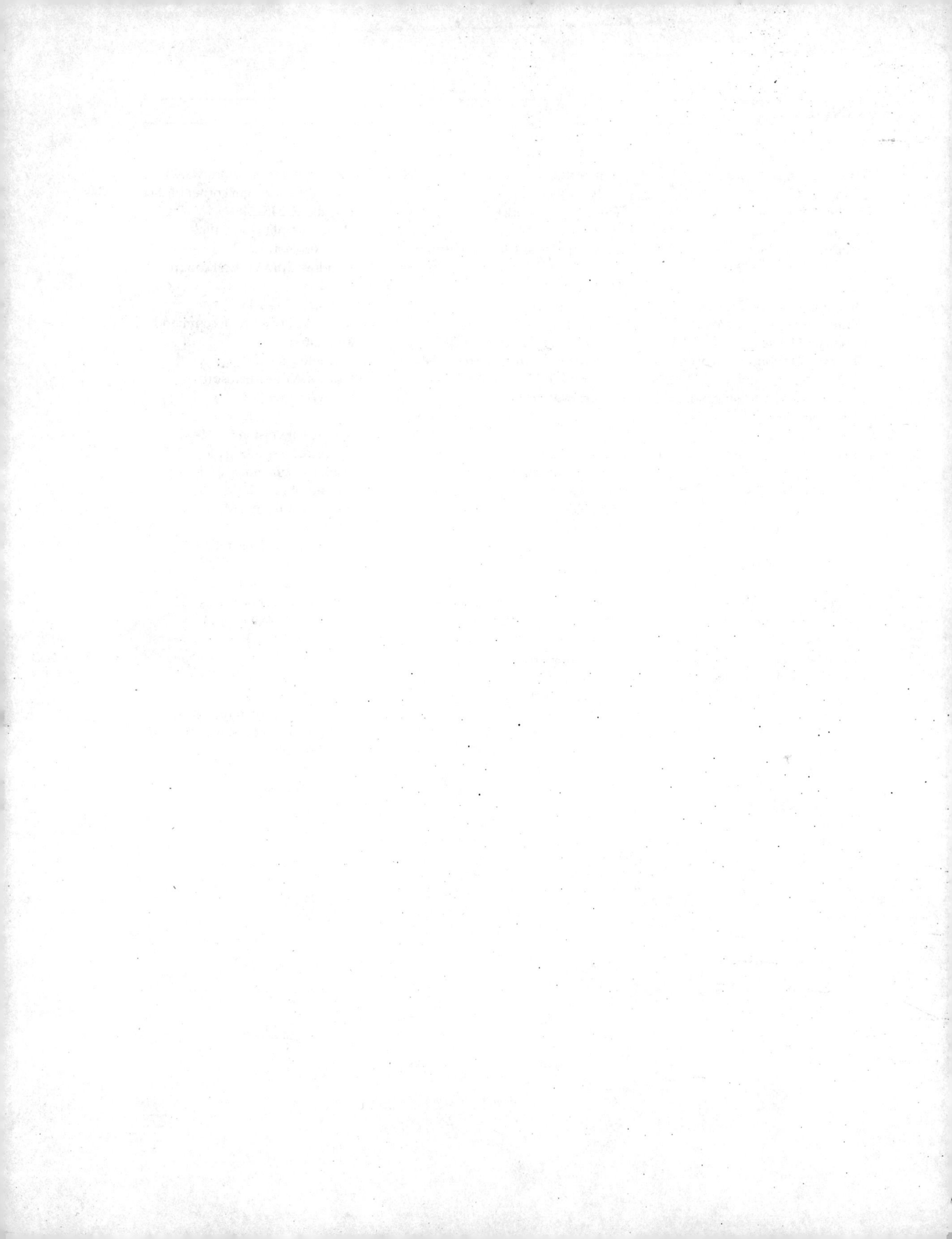

EXPERT ADVISOR

Microsoft® Word™ 5.0 for the IBM® PC

QUICK REFERENCE

EXPERT ADVISOR

Microsoft® Word™ 5.0 for the IBM® PC

Paul E. Hoffman

QUICK REFERENCE

Addison-Wesley Publishing Company, Inc.

Reading, Massachusetts Menlo Park, California New York
Don Mills, Ontario Wokingham, England Amsterdam Bonn
Sydney Singapore Tokyo Madrid San Juan

Project Manager: Rachel Guichard
Text Design: Grafica Multimedia, Inc.

ISBN: 0-201-51765-5
ABCDEFGHIJ-AL-89
First printing, September 1989

Contents

Introduction v

Alphabetical Entries 1

Appendix A 70

Introduction

This quick reference is a guide to all of the commands in Microsoft Word, version 5 for the IBM PC. Both the beginning user new to Word and the advanced Word user will find this book a convenient reference. Novices will find brief yet thorough descriptions of all of the program's commands, and advanced users can refresh their memories of the program's features. The alphabetical arrangement of all entries from **CAPTURE PROGRAM** to **WINDOWS COMMANDS** will allow you to find the information you want quickly and easily.

Every command included in this reference is explained in an *Overview* section which provides in clear and simple terms a summary of essential information. Here you can refresh your knowledge of commands you already use and understand as well as learn how to use commands unfamiliar to you. Since Word uses specific capital letter combinations to invoke commands, this quick reference denotes those letter combinations in boldface capital letters whenever referencing a Word command, for example, **F**ormat rep**L**ace command.

This quick reference is a complement to *Expert Advisor: Microsoft Word 5.0 for the IBM PC*. When you need a more detailed and comprehensive discussion of a command or feature, you can refer to the Expert Advisor volume for more information. By using this quick reference, either by itself or in conjunction with the Expert Advisor book, you will increase your knowledge of and expertise in Microsoft Word, version 5 for the IBM PC.

Capture Program
Overview
The Capture program included in Word allows you to capture graphics screens from other programs and to include them in your Word documents.

To use Capture you must first load it into memory. Capture is a TSR program, which means that it takes up memory space in your computer. You load it by giving the CAPTURE command at the MS-DOS prompt. A message tells you that the program is loaded.

Once Capture is loaded, run the application you want to get a screen dump from, get the program to show what you want in the screen shot, and press Shift Print Screen. When Capture prompts you for the name of the file you want to save the screen as, type in a file name and press Enter to save the screen.

The screens created with Capture can be used in Word just like any other graphics screens. When you use the Library Link Graphics command, enter the name of the file you saved.

Copy Command
Overview
The Copy command puts a copy of the selected text in the scrap or creates a glossary entry. If you use the Copy command to put text in the scrap when there is already text in the scrap, the new text replaces whatever was there.

To put text in the scrap, select the text you want, give the Copy command, and press Enter at the prompt; or, press Alt F3.

1

To make a glossary entry, select the text, give the Copy command, enter the name for the glossary entry, and press Enter.

Delete Command
Overview
The **D**elete command removes the selected text from your document and puts a copy of it in the scrap or creates a glossary entry. If you use the **D**elete command to put text in the scrap when there is already text in the scrap, the new text replaces whatever was there.

To remove text from your document and put it in the scrap, select the text you want, give the **D**elete command, and press Enter at the prompt; or, press the Delete key. To remove the text and make a glossary entry, select the text, give the **D**elete command, enter the name for the glossary entry, and press Enter.

Format Annotation Command
Overview
To add an annotation in your text, select the character to which you want to anchor the annotation and give the **F**ormat Annotation command. Enter the annotation type in the *mark* field (the annotation type can be up to 28 characters) and press Enter. Word automatically jumps to the end of the document where the footnote and annotation text is kept. For instance, if many people are annotating a document, each one may use his or her name as an annotation mark. To remove an annotation, delete its annotation mark; Word deletes the associated annotation text.

Annotations are marked in the text with a number in the footnote numbering sequence and with the specified annotation mark. The annotation text is preceded by the same number and mark. You can also include the date of the creation of the annotation. These items can be edited or removed if desired.

Format bookmarK Command
Overview

You can use the **F**ormat bookmar**K** command to place markers throughout a document so that you can flip to them at a later time. These bookmarks are more convenient than standard physical bookmarks since they mark a range of text, not just a page. You can also assign a name to each bookmark to easily locate specific sections of text. The **F**ormat bookmar**K** command is also used to create cross references, as described later in this section.

To create a bookmark, select the text you want to mark and give the **F**ormat bookmar**K** command. Enter the desired name in the *name* field. Bookmark names can be up to 31 characters and can include letters, numbers, periods, hyphens, and underscores, but not spaces.

The bookmark is "anchored" to the first and last characters in the range. As long as that first character is in your document, the bookmark will be valid. If you move the text in that range, the bookmark will refer correctly to the range wherever you move it. If you delete some of the text in the range (but keep the first character), the bookmark will still be valid but it will include the same number of characters as you originally specified. For example, if your range was 90 characters long, the bookmark continues to refer to the same first character and to the 89 characters after it even if you delete 50 characters from the middle of the original range.

To change a bookmark name, select the first character and give the Format bookmarK command. Word fills in the *name* field with the current name; delete this and enter the new name. To remove a bookmark without deleting the anchor character, select the anchor character, give the Format bookmarK command, clear the bookmark name from the entry field, and press Enter. When Word prompts you to confirm the loss of the bookmark, press Y.

The Format bookmarK command is also used for cross referencing. Word's cross referencing feature allows you to imbed the page number with the reference (such as "See *Financial Standing* on page 54 for more detail"). Using cross referencing for pages removes the necessity of keeping track of all the page numbers which might change as you edit your document or as you change printers. Cross referencing becomes very convenient with Word's "sequence" feature. That is, instead of cross referencing to a figure or table by its number, you can refer to it by name. Thus, if the sequence number changes due to the addition of a figure or table, the printed output will still refer to the correct number.

To cross reference an item on a page, you must first mark the item with a bookmark. Select the beginning of what you want to refer to (such as the first letter of a title), give the Format bookmarK command, and enter a bookmark name in the *name* field. To refer to the page of that bookmark in your document, type `page:` followed by the bookmark name and press F3. Word displays the bookmark name in parentheses to indicate that it is a special mark, similar to the special glossary marks.

To refer to a sequence holder, that holder must be immediately followed by a bookmark. To refer to that holder, type
the sequence name, a colon, and the bookmark name, then
press F3.

Format Border Command

Overview

You can use the **F**ormat **B**order command to insert various
boxes and borders around paragraphs in your documents. This
command is also used to add shading over a paragraph.

Boxes surround an entire paragraph while borders are lines
that only go along one side of the paragraph. You can specify
more than one border for a paragraph (for example, the left and
top border together). Boxes and borders are formats associated
with paragraphs, so they automatically shrink and expand if
you change other paragraph indents. If you add text to a paragraph in a box, the bottom of the box automatically moves
down.

Boxes and borders go from the left indent to the right
indent; however, if you have a negative measurement for the
first line (such as for an outdented paragraph) the box or border aligns with the first line in the paragraph. There are four
line styles for boxes and borders: normal, bold, double, and
thick.

If you have two adjacent paragraphs with boxes, the bottom of the upper box is joined with the top of the lower box.
However, if the line styles are different (for example, if the
upper box is normal and the lower box is double), the boxes are
not joined. If you have two side-by-side paragraphs with boxes,
and the right indent of the first box is at the same position as
the left indent of the second box, the common border is joined.

Use the **F**ormat **B**order command to add lines above, below, to the left, or to the right of a paragraph. To add lines above and below a paragraph, for example, give the **F**ormat **B**order command, change the *type* to *Lines*, and select *Yes* for both *above* and *below*.

The **F**ormat **B**order command also allows you to add shading over a paragraph. A shaded paragraph is printed with an overlay of dots. You specify the density of the dots as a percentage of black: 0 indicates no shading, 50 indicates half gray, and 100 indicates completely black.

Format Character Command

Overview

You can apply character formats to any text or graphics in Word using the **F**ormat **C**haracter command. Word's wide variety of character formats allows you to give your documents a distinctive style by adding flair and embellishment. Character styles are also used to add emphasis and clarity to specific words in your documents.

To format a group of characters or a style, select the characters or style and give the **F**ormat **C**haracter command. Select *Yes* or *No* for each character display type. You can format any character with as many character formats as you want.

Although most character formatting involves changing the appearance of the characters, you can also change their position on a line with the *position* field of the **F**ormat **C**haracter command. Superscripts are often used in reports for footnote references. Subscripts are used most often in formulae in scientific papers.

The faster method of adding character formats to selected characters is with the Alt key. The following table shows the keys that you can use.

FORMAT	KEY
Bold	Alt B
Double underline	Alt D
Hidden	Alt E
Italic	Alt I
Small caps	Alt K
Strikethrough	Alt S
Subscript	Alt -
Superscript	Alt +
Underline	Alt U

There are two ways to remove a character format from a character after you have selected it. You can give the Format Character command and select *No* for the format, or you can press Alt Space Bar to remove all character formatting from the selected characters.

In addition to formats, you can also change the character fonts. Most advanced printers allow selection of fonts for printing. Some dot matrix printers use different font cartridges, and most letter-quality printers have different print wheels for different fonts. Almost every laser printer has built-in fonts and accepts font cartridges, downloadable fonts, or both.

Word has two types of font names: specific names and generic names. Word's generic font names provide printing flexibility. If you specify a generic name and the printer on which you are printing has a font that falls in that family, Word uses that printer font. Even if you use a specific name, Word can determine the family of the font from the font number associated with its name and use a similar font. If you are using a daisywheel printer, Word prompts you *Enter Y after mounting font* for each font change and waits for you to type Y.

Format Division Commands

Overview

Word uses divisions as a method for breaking up a document into sections. You add a division mark to separate two parts of your text if you want to have different division formatting in the two sections. If you also work with Microsoft Word on the Macintosh, note that divisions in that program are called "sections."

Division formatting includes margins, headers and footers, page numbers, placement of footnotes, number of columns, and line numbers. This formatting can be applied to any division in a document.

Each new document starts off as a single division. To split a division into two divisions, move the cursor where you want to split and press Ctrl Enter. The two divisions will have the same division formatting as the previous single division.

The initial division formatting is the same as the formatting that is applied in the style sheet to the style entry that contains the "Standard" division variant. If you change the settings in that style, documents will use those settings as the base division formatting.

Format Division Layout Command
Overview
The Format Division Layout command lets you choose among
several kinds of division breaks. Your choices are:

CHOICE	ACTION
Page	Starts the division on a new page
Continuous	Continues the layout directly after the previous division
Column	Starts the division at the top of the next column
Even	Starts the division at the top of the next even-numbered page
Odd	Starts the division at the top of the next odd-numbered page

Format Division Layout is also used to create multi-column
documents, such as newsletters and brochures. This feature is
sometimes referred to as *newspaper columns*.

You can specify the number of columns for each division.
If your document has only one division, the number you specify will be valid for the entire document. Use the Format
Division Layout command to tell Word how many columns
you want and how much space you want between the columns.
To force Word to go to a new column, enter a column break by
pressing Alt Ctrl Enter.

Finally, the Format Division Layout command lets you tell
Word where you want the footnotes to appear when printed.
Unfortunately, you cannot specify the characters that are used

to make the line between the body text and the footnotes at the bottom of the page; Word just uses a line. When you print, Word makes sure that both the footnotes that are referenced in the body text and the text itself appear on the same page. This is not always possible if the footnote appears near the bottom of the page and the associated text is long.

Format Division line-Numbers Command
Overview
Lawyers preparing pleadings and motions often need to have the lines of their documents numbered. This is often called *pleading numbering* since it is rarely used for any other purpose. In Word you print out divisions with pleading numbering with the **F**ormat **D**ivision line-**N**umbers command.

Word gives you a great deal of flexibility in determining the look of divisions that have numbered lines. You can choose to number each line or only by increments, such as every fifth line. You can place the numbers close to or far away from your text, and you can even change the formatting for the line numbers.

Select the division you want to number and give the **F**ormat **D**ivision line-**N**umbers command. Change the first field to *Yes* to turn line numbering on for this division. Set *from text* to the amount of space you want between the left margin and the right side of the numbers; be sure not to set this value too high or the numbers will run off the left side of the page.

Set the *increments* field to the frequency you want the line numbers. Set *restart at* to either *Division* or *Continuous* if you want the line numbers to not be reset to 1 at the top of each page.

You can set the style for the line numbers separate from the style of the text in your document. In the gallery, there is a predefined character style called *Line Number* for the line numbers that are applied by the Format Division line-Numbers command. Specify the character formatting you want for the line numbers in this style.

Format Division Margins Command
Overview

If you are going to copy your document onto both sides of a piece of paper and bind it, you need to determine how much space to leave for the *gutter*. The gutter is extra space that you leave for the binding. It is added to the right margin of even-numbered pages and to the left margin of odd-numbered pages.

To set the margins, use the Format Division Margins command. Set the *top*, *bottom*, *left*, and *right* fields to the amount you wish. If you are going to copy your document on both sides of a page, set the *gutter margin* field to the amount you want to leave.

You also use the Format Division Margins command to set the page length and width and to position the running heads.

You specify how far from the top and bottom of the paper you want the running heads. Thus, the position of the running heads remains the same if you change the top and bottom margin of the page. You can specify the horizontal position of the running heads from either the edge of the page or from the left margin.

Format Division Page-numbers Command
Overview

This command is used to add direct page numbers to a division. You may want to use direct page numbers if you are sure that you want the page number to appear in the same position on each page and that you do not want any text before the page number. Direct page numbering conforms to the way that many other word processors handle page numbers.

To add page numbers to a division, select any text in that division and give the **F**ormat **D**ivision **P**age-numbers command. Select *Yes* in the first field, then fill in the other fields to specify the position and format of the page number.

The choices for this command are:

FIELD	MEANING
from top	Distance from the top of the paper
from left	Distance from the left side of the paper
numbering, at	*Continuous* indicates that the page numbering should continue from the previous division; *Start* indicate that you want to start the numbering at the number in the *at* field.
number format	Format for the page number. The choices are: 1　Arabic numerals (1, 2, 3, ...) I　Uppercase Roman numerals (I, II, III, ...) i　Lowercase Roman numerals (i, ii, iii, ...) A　Uppercase letters (A, B, C, ...) a　Lowercase letters (a, b, c, ...)

If you want to change the formatting of the page number, such as the font or character format, you must have a style sheet

F

attached to the document. In the gallery, give the **I**nsert command, choose *Character* in the *usage* field, select the *variant* field, and press F1. In the list, select *Page number* and press Enter. Give the **F**ormat **C**haracter command to set the format you wish and save this as part of your style sheet.

Format Footnote Command

Overview

This command lets you create and place footnotes in your document. Word automatically numbers footnotes for you, so adding and deleting footnotes in the middle of a document is as easy as adding them at the end. Word makes sure that the footnote number in your text (the *footnote reference*) always matches the numbers on the footnote text.

Word lets you view your footnotes as you scroll through your text. If you open the footnote window, Word shows the footnote for the text in the main window. The footnote window always shows the footnote for the text currently on the screen.

There are two types of footnotes: numbered (or *enumerated*) and simple marks (such as asterisks). Most people use numbered footnotes since there is less ambiguity about which footnote reference is associated with each footnote. Also, few printers can produce any standard footnote marks other than the asterisk.

To create a footnote, use the **F**ormat **F**ootnote command. Word prompts you for the *reference mark*. For numbered footnotes, simply press Enter; if you are using footnote symbols, type the symbol (such as an asterisk) at the prompt. Word figures out the correct number for the footnote mark and inserts it in your text. Note that this mark is special, because the footnote is associated with the mark. If you delete the footnote mark, Word also deletes the corresponding footnote. When Word adds a footnote in the middle of a document, it also renumbers any footnotes that follow the new one. Word then opens the footnote window unless you already have it open or are near the end of the file where the footnotes are shown.

Format Paragraph Command
Overview

Each paragraph in a document has three types of indentation: left, first line, and right. The left and right indentations of a paragraph are always measured from the margins, not from the edge of the page; the first line indentation is always measured from the left indentation. If you change the margins in a division, the indentations will move with them.

You cannot enter a negative number for the *left indent* field. You can enter a negative number for the *first line* field, but this cannot move the first line further to the left than the margin.

Word has a few keyboard equivalents to make direct formatting easier. They are:

KEY	ACTION
Alt F	Increases *first line* by one tab stop
Alt M	Decreases *left indent* by one tab stop
Alt N	Increases *left indent* by one tab stop
Alt P	Sets *left indent* to 0, *first line* to 0, and *right indent* to 0
Alt T	Increases *left indent* by one tab stop and decreases *first line* by one tab stop (hanging indent)

Use the **F**ormat **P**aragraph command to choose between keeping a paragraph together or with the following paragraph. Set the *together* field to *Yes* to ensure that the paragraph is never split. Set the *keep follow* field to *Yes* to ensure that at least the last two lines of the selected paragraph appear on the same page with at least the first two lines of the following paragraph (assuming that you have widow and orphan control set on).

Try not to have too many paragraphs in a row formatted with *keep follow* set to *Yes*. If the aggregate length of the paragraphs becomes too long, Word may leave large blank spaces at the bottom of the pages as it determines pagination. If you find that your document has many short pages, check that you don't have more *keep follow*'s than you expected in the paragraphs after the gap.

The **F**ormat **P**aragraph command's choices for *alignment* are *Left*, *Centered*, *Right*, and *Justified*. These refer to how the left and right end of the lines align with the margins.

The four fields indicate:

CHOICE	ALIGNED WITH LEFT MARGIN	ALIGNED WITH RIGHT MARGIN
Left	Yes	No
Centered	No	No
Right	No	Yes
Justified	Yes	Yes

In the *line spacing* field you specify the amount of space occupied by each line on the page. You can specify the number of lines taken by each line (such as 2 li for double-spacing) or auto to set the spacing correctly for the largest font size on the line. You can also use `auto` in paragraphs that have super-script or subscript characters.

The *space before* and *space after* fields let you specify a fixed amount of white space to include before and after a paragraph.

The keyboard equivalents for paragraph formatting are:

KEY	FORMAT
Alt C	Centered
Alt F	First line indentation increased by one tab stop
Alt J	Justified
Alt L	Left flush
Alt M	Left indentation reduced by one tab stop
Alt N	Left indentation increased by one tab stop
Alt O	One line after
Alt P	Normal paragraph
Alt R	Right flush
Alt T	Hanging indentation increased by one tab stop
Alt 2	Double space

You can use as many side-by-side paragraphs as you want on a line. To create two or more side-by-side paragraphs, you must set the left and right indents of each paragraph so that the indents do not overlap, then set the *side by side* field in the Format Paragraph command to *Yes*. If any paragraph has the *side by side* field set to *Yes*, Word checks whether it can fit that paragraph on the same line with the previous paragraph. You do not have to order the side-by-side paragraphs; simply have them appear before and after one another in the document.

Format pOsition Command
Overview

The Format pOsition command marks a paragraph as an absolutely positioned paragraph which consists of a frame and of the text that goes in that frame. The frame's definition includes the width of the frame (but not the height, since that is adjusted depending on the amount of text in the paragraph), the frame's horizontal position, and the frame's vertical position. The frame is like a miniature page into which the text fits: all indents for the paragraph are relative to the frame border. All normal paragraphs flow around absolutely positioned paragraphs.

A frame can be horizontally aligned with the column, the margin, or the page, or it can be an absolute value from the left edge of the page; it can be vertically aligned with the current paragraph, margin, page, or be an absolute value from the top edge of the page. Note that these are the alignments of the frame borders, not of the text within the borders. That text can still be aligned and have indents just as normal paragraphs can. Word automatically resolves conflicts in absolutely positioned paragraphs.

To position a paragraph, first format its text with the Format Paragraph command, then give the Format pOsition command. The fields *frame position horizontal, vertical*, and *frame width* take many values. To see the options in any of these three fields, select the field and press F1.

The *frame width* field specifies the width of the field. The two choices are *Same as column* and an absolute value. Setting *frame width* to *Same as column* on a single-column page is the same as specifying the entire page for the width. If you enter an absolute value, you can enter any amount. If you specify a column wider than the page, Word will truncate your text. For

F — Format repLace Commands

divisions with more than one column, you can also specify *Double Column* or *Between Margins*.

The choices for the *horizontal frame position* field are *Left*, *Centered*, *Right*, *Inside*, and *Outside*. These are relative to the column, margins, or to the page edges, as specified in the first *relative to* field. The choices for the *vertical frame position* field are *In line*, *Top*, *Centered*, and *Bottom*. These are relative to the margins or to the page edges, as specified in the second *relative to* field. *Inside* indicates that the left edge of the frame is aligned with the left edge of the *relative to* item on odd pages and that the right edge of the frame is aligned with the right edge of the *relative to* item on even pages. *Outside* indicates that the left edge of the frame is aligned with the left edge of the *relative to* item on even pages and that the right edge of the frame is aligned with the right edge of the *relative to* item on odd pages.

You can also enter an absolute value for the *horizontal frame position* and *vertical frame position* fields. The absolute positions are measured from the left and top edges of the paper, respectively.

Format repLace Commands

Overview

The Format repLace command lets you replace the formatting and styles of the characters in your document. It has three subcommands (Character, Paragraph, and Style), and each subcommand has a *confirm* option. With the Character and Paragraph subcommands, choose any format or combination of formats you want to search for, press Enter, and select the format or combination of formats you want to apply. With the Style subcommand, enter keycodes of the styles you want to search and replace.

Format revision-Marks Commands

Overview

The **F**ormat revision-**M**arks **O**ptions command lets you turn on revision marks. Select *Yes* for the *add revision marks* field to begin using revision marks. You can also select the format in which the added text is shown and whether you want to see revision bars. Word displays *MR* at the bottom of the screen to indicate that you are adding revision marks. After you turn on revision marks, Word stores the choices you make for the **F**ormat revision-**M**arks **O**ptions command in the file. Deleted text is always displayed with struckthrough characters unless you are using a color adapter, in which case it is shown in red.

The choices for the *inserted text* field are *Normal, Bold, Underlined, upperCase,* and *Double-underlined.* To make the additions stand out, choose a style that you do not use in your document.

Generally, it is useful to see revision bars, and you can specify their position: *None, Left, Right,* and *Alternate* (outside of the page for even and odd pages).

After you are finished with the revision process, you can either accept your changes or reject them. To accept the changes, select the portion of the document for which you want to make the changes permanent and give the **F**ormat revision-**M**arks **R**emove-marks command. "Removing marks" indicates that the changes are made permanent and thus the marks are removed. To make the changes permanent for the whole document, select the entire document with Shift F10 before giving the **F**ormat revision-**M**arks **R**emove-marks command. To reverse your changes, select the changed text and give the **F**ormat revision-**M**arks **U**ndo-revisions command.

You can search for revised text with the **F**ormat revision-**M**arks **S**earch command. This command moves the selection to the next revised text in your document. Word keeps the **F**ormat revision-**M**arks command selected, so you can repeat the search by pressing S again.

Format Running-Head Command
Overview

The **F**ormat **R**unning-head command is used to mark a paragraph as a running head and to specify its position on the page as well as the type of page on which it should appear (even, odd, first in the division, or a combination of these three). If this is the first text on the current page, Word begins using that running head immediately; if not, the running head takes effect beginning on the next page.

Enter the text you want in the running head and give the **F**ormat **R**unning-head command. Select either *Top* or *Bottom* for the *position*, and set the *odd pages*, *even pages*, and *first page* fields. You can use Ctrl F2 to make a paragraph a header and Alt F2 to make a paragraph a footer, but Word will use the last settings you used for the options, which may not be what you want. You will generally want at least one of your running heads to contain the page number. To include the page number, type page and press F3 (the page number is a special glossary entry). If you want to include the date that the document was printed, use the "dateprint" special glossary entry.

When you format a paragraph as a running head, Word puts a caret (^) in the selection bar. If you want to see exactly what type of running head a paragraph is, you have to display the style bar. If the style bar is not showing, give the **W**indow

Options command and set *style bar* to *Yes*. You will see the following styles for running heads:

CODE	TYPE OF RUNNING HEAD
b	Bottom, odd, and even pages
be	Bottom, even pages
bf	Bottom, first page of the division
bo	Bottom, odd pages
t	Top, odd, and even pages
te	Top, even pages
tf	Top, first page of the division
to	Top, odd pages

If you have made a paragraph a running head and want to change it back to a normal paragraph, give the **F**ormat **R**unning-head command and select *None* in the *position* field.

Format sEarch Commands
Overview
The **F**ormat s**E**arch command lets you search for text based on the character formatting and styles used in your document. It has three subcommands: **C**haracter, **P**aragraph, and **S**tyle. With the **C**haracter and **P**aragraph subcommands, you choose any format or combination of formats you want to search for. With the **S**tyle subcommand, you enter the keycode of the styles for which you want to search.

Format Stylesheet Commands
Overview

You can add styles to a document with the **F**ormat **S**tylesheet **C**haracter, **F**ormat **S**tylesheet **P**aragraph, and **F**ormat **S**tylesheet **D**ivision commands. When you are finished editing a style sheet, be sure to save your changes to the style sheet with the **T**ransfer **S**ave command.

In regular edit mode, you can add styles using Alt key combinations. First use the **F**ormat **S**tylesheet **A**ttach command to be sure the desired style sheet is attached to your document. Select each item to which you want to attach a style, hold down Alt, and type the key code. To attach a character style, select only the characters you want with that style, hold down Alt, and type the key code.

If you are editing a document with direct formatting and want to turn some formatting into a style, select the formatted text and give the **F**ormat **S**tylesheet **R**ecord command or press Alt F10. Enter the style information in the dialog box and press Enter; Word adds the style to the attached style sheet. This method is not used much, however, since you usually do not use styles in a document with much direct formatting.

Format Tabs Commands
Overview

The **F**ormat **T**abs commands let you set and reset the tabs for paragraphs. The four types of tabs are left-aligned, right-aligned, center-aligned, and decimal-aligned (there are also vertical tabs, which act differently and are described later). Each type of tab affects the text that follows it. The actions of the tabs are:

TYPE	ACTION
Left	Aligns the left side of the following text to the right of the tab stop
Right	Aligns the right side of the following text to the left of the tab stop
Centered	Aligns the middle of the following text with the tab stop
Decimal	Aligns the decimal point of the following text with the tab stop; if there is no decimal point, this tab acts the same as a right-aligned tab

If you do not set your own tabs, you can still use tab stops. Word has preset tab left-aligned stops set at regular intervals (you can change the interval with the *default tab width* field in the **O**ptions command). Even if you set tab stops, Word uses the preset tab stops for the area to the right of your rightmost tab stop.

Vertical tabs do not act like other tabs, because they do not affect placement of text. A vertical tab simply causes Word to draw a vertical line at the position indicated. Vertical tabs are very useful for creating boxes and for making columns in tables more distinct.

Word inserts special characters in the blank space before a tab stop. These characters are called leader characters, and are most useful in tables of contents or in widely-spaced tables. You can use periods, dashes, or underscores for leader characters.

If you are using the keyboard with the Format Tabs Set command, enter the desired location for the tab stop in the *position* field and make selections in the *alignment* and *leader char* fields. If you want to select from a position on the ruler, move the selection to the *position* field and press F1. You can then move back and forth on the ruler with the Left Arrow and Right Arrow keys. When you have set the tab stop you want, press Insert. Set each tab stop in this fashion and press Enter when finished.

To delete a tab stop that you have placed, give the Format Tabs Set command and enter its position in the *position* field (or move around the ruler by pressing F1 and the Left Arrow and Right Arrow keys) and press Delete. If you are using the mouse, you can point at the tab stop on the ruler and press both mouse buttons. To clear all the tabs at once, use the Format Tabs Reset-all command.

When you give the Format Tabs Set command and press F1 in the *position* field, you have more power as you move back and forth along the ruler. To set a tab at the current position, press L, R, C, D, or V to set left-, right-, center-, decimal-aligned, or vertical tabs. To make a leader character, move to the desired tab and press the period, hyphen, or underscore keys.

To move tabs, put the cursor over the desired tab stop and press Ctrl Left Arrow or Ctrl Right Arrow. To delete all the tab stops to the right of your current position, press Ctrl Delete.

Numbers in decimal-aligned tabs always align on the tab stop, even if there are punctuation marks such as parentheses at the right side of the number.

You can move a tab around on the ruler with the mouse. In the Format Tabs Set command, point at the tab stop you want to move, hold down the right mouse button, move to the new location, and release the button. You cannot move tabs with the keyboard: you must remove the tab and place a new one.

To place tabs on the ruler with the mouse, specify the *alignment* and *leader char* fields, point at the desired position, and press the left mouse button. Be sure to make the settings before placing the tab, or Word will use the default settings (left-aligned tab with no leader).

Gallery Commands

Overview

Use the **G**allery command to create or modify a style sheet. This command takes you to gallery mode in which you can edit and change style sheets, but not document them. A style is a description of a repeating element and its format. Repeating elements can be bulleted lists, book titles, or warning paragraphs. The list of styles for a document is called a *style sheet*.

Styles are stored in files separate from documents. A style sheet file (which has the extension .STY) holds a group of styles, and can be attached to any Word document. One style sheet can be shared by many documents; in fact, it is likely that you will use only a few style sheets for all your work. Any changes made to the style sheet are immediately reflected in any document to which the style sheet is attached.

Each style in a style sheet has four elements:

ELEMENT	USE
Key code	A two-letter code that identifies the style in the document. When you format your document with styles, you select the text to which you want to apply a style, hold down Alt, and type the key code. If you have set *style bar* to *Yes* in the **W**indow **O**ptions command, you will see each paragraph and division key code listed in the style bar.
Usage	The type of style. A style may have either character, paragraph, or division usage. Styles with character usage can have any set of character formatting; styles with division usage can have any type of division formatting. Styles with paragraph usage can have both character and paragraph formatting. You will find that the majority of styles you define are paragraph styles.
Variant	Each usage type has many variants; that is, you can have many different character styles, paragraph styles, and division styles. Each variant within a usage is unique.
Remark	An optional comment. You should fill in the remark for each style you create so that later you can remember the use for that style.

Each style has a set of formatting instruction associated with it. You set the formatting just like you do with direct formatting. All the formatting options that you can perform with direct formatting are also available in the styles.

When you first start out, Word loads the style sheet called NORMAL.STY. If there are styles which you want to use often, you should store them in NORMAL.STY. You can create as many style sheets as you want, and you can merge styles from one style sheet into another.

You can also add a style to the current style sheet with the **F**ormat **S**tylesheet **R**ecord command. You can add and modify styles any time you want. To attach a style sheet to a document, use the **F**ormat **S**tylesheet **A**ttach command.

Enter gallery mode by giving the **G**allery command. The commands that you can give in gallery mode are very similar to the commands in normal mode. They are:

COMMAND	USE
Copy	Copies the selected style to the gallery scrap
Delete	Deletes the selected style from the gallery scrap
Exit	Leaves gallery mode
Format	Adds or changes formatting to the selected style
Help	Gives help on gallery commands
Insert	Adds a new style to the style sheet or copies the style from the gallery scrap
Name	Changes the information in the selected style
Print	Prints the style sheet
Transfer	Loads, merges, and saves style sheets
Undo	Undoes the last **C**opy, **D**elete, **F**ormat, **I**nsert, **N**ame, **T**ransfer **M**erge, or **U**ndo command.

To start a style sheet, give the **I**nsert command, fill in the fields, and press Enter. The fields are:

FIELD	COMMENTS
key code	A one- or two-character code. The first letter should not be "X" for reasons described below. Use key codes which might be mnemonic such as "LI" for "list item." Generally, two-letter key codes are preferable so that you have a wider range of possible key codes. If you have a two-letter code such as "LI," you cannot later name a style with the one-letter code "L."
usage	Either *Character*, *Paragraph*, or *Division*. Once you assign a usage to a style, you cannot change the usage with the **N**ame command.
variant	The name or number for the style. Choose either one of Word's defined variants or an unused variant number; you can press F1 to see a list of choices of the variants for the usage you choose.
remark	A comment. Enter a meaningful comment, up to 28 characters long.

To change the formatting of a style from the default, select the style and give the **F**ormat command. If the style is a character style, Word brings up the character formatting dialog. If the style is a paragraph style, you can add character formatting, paragraph formatting, tabs, border, or absolute positioning. If the style is a division style, you can add margins, page numbers, layout, or line numbers. Each time you add formatting, Word shows that formatting in the gallery window.

Save your style sheet with the **T**ransfer **S**ave command. If you are editing your NORMAL.STY file or another style sheet, Word will prompt you with the file's name. For convenience, you should save the style sheet in the same directory as your document or in the directory in which you store Word.

To edit a style sheet, simply enter gallery mode. To edit a style sheet other than the one that is attached to the current document, use the gallery **T**ransfer **L**oad command in gallery mode.

To read in styles from another style sheet, use the **T**ransfer **M**erge command. This may bring in styles with the same key codes or variants; you must change them with the **N**ame command before saving the merged style sheet. You can change the order of the styles in the style sheet by deleting styles from the scrap with the **D**elete command and inserting them in other positions with the **I**nsert command. This change is only cosmetic, but it can help make a style sheet easier to read. You can print a style sheet with the **P**rint command.

Help Command
Overview
The **H**elp command brings up a help screen giving information on whichever command is currently highlighted. To get help on a particular command with a mouse, give that command, point at the question mark in the middle of the bottom of the screen, and click the left button of the mouse. If you are using the keyboard, select the command and press Alt H. (If any styles attached to your document begin with the letter H, you must press Alt X H instead of Alt H.) If you want help on a particular field in a dialog, you can select that field and ask for help; if Word has specific help it will give it, otherwise it will show the help screen for the dialog.

Most help screens include information on which tutorial in the Learning Word program and which chapter in the Word manual have more information on the subject. If you did not install the Learning Word program during installation, you will not be able to use the tutorials. To get out of the Help system, select **E**xit.

Your choices for navigating through the **H**elp command are:

COMMAND	ACTION
Exit	Returns you to where you were in Word. If you started Help while giving a command, you will be able to complete that command.
Next	Shows the next screen
Previous	Shows the previous screen
Basics	Shows basic information on using Word
Index	Shows an index of the **H**elp command. This index contains the same information as Word's Quick Reference Card.
Tutorial	Runs the Learning Microsoft Word application and starts at the section that relates to this topic
Keyboard	Lists Word's keyboard actions
Mouse	Lists Word's mouse actions

Insert Command

Overview

The **I**nsert command has two distinct uses: it inserts a copy of the scrap or a glossary entry into your document, and it runs macros by name. Its most common use is in moving text. You use the **D**elete command to cut some text to the scrap, move the cursor to where you want the text to be in your document, and give the **I**nsert command.

To insert the text in the scrap into your document at the current cursor location, give the **I**nsert command and press Enter or Insert. If you are using a mouse, click on the **I**nsert command with the right button.

To insert text from a glossary into your document at the current cursor location, give the **I**nsert command, type the name of the glossary at the prompt, and press Enter. If you are running Word under Microsoft Windows, you can include the contents of the Windows Clipboard by typing `CLIPBOARD` for the glossary name.

To run a macro, give the **I**nsert command, enter the name of the macro at the prompt, and press Enter.

Jump Annotation Command

Overview

The **J**ump **A**nnotation command jumps to annotation marks and annotation text. The rules for the **J**ump **F**ootnote and **J**ump **A**nnotation commands are:

SELECTION	JUMPS TO
Reference mark	Text associated with reference
Text in document	Next reference mark
Text in footnote window	Reference associated with the text

Jump Bookmark Command
Overview
The Jump Bookmark command lets you go to the bookmark you name. A bookmark is associated with a range of characters. When you give the Jump Bookmark command, Word selects the entire range. The Jump Bookmark command prompts you for the name of the bookmark you want to find. Type in the name and press Enter; Word selects the entire bookmark.

Jump Footnote Command
Overview
Give the Jump Footnote command to go to the next footnote or annotation. Once you have found the reference mark, you can open the footnote window and select the text associated with the reference mark by giving the Jump Footnote command again. To jump back to the mark from the footnote, give the Jump Footnote command one more time.

Jump Page Command
Overview
To jump to a specific page, give the Jump Page command and type the page number you want. If your document has more than one division and the divisions have repeating page numbers (for example, each chapter starts the page numbering at 1), type the desired page number, the letter "D," and the division number. For example, to find page 7 in the fourth division, enter 7D4.

Library Autosort Command

Overview

Use the **Library A**utosort command to sort selected text. Select
the type of sort you want to perform in the *by* field and the
order you want for the list in the *sequence* field. Setting *case* to
No tells Word to ignore case when it sorts. You can use this
option if you have mixed-case words but you do not want
Word to differentiate them based on case (such as a list that
contains some proper names together with uncapitalized
words).

If you select entire paragraphs, Word will sort based on the
first letter of the paragraphs. If you select a column, Word will
base the sort on that column. If you set *column only* to *Yes*,
Word will sort the column without moving the other rows. This
is rarely what you want, since it changes the contents of each
line of the table.

To sort a table by two columns, you must select the less
important column, give the **Library A**utosort command, select
the more important column, then give the **Library A**utosort
command again.

Library Document-retrieval Commands

Overview

Word documents can have a *summary sheet* attached to them
that lists pertinent information about the contents of the document. The information in the summary sheets can then be
scanned by the **Library D**ocument-retrieval commands to find
documents that meet certain criteria or contain particular
words. To find all documents with specific key words, give the

Library **D**ocument-retrieval **Q**uery command and specify the key words in the command's dialog. Word presents a list of all files whose summary sheets include those key words.

The **L**ibrary **D**ocument-retrieval command has eight subcommands. When you give the **L**ibrary **D**ocument-retrieval command, you are put in document retrieval mode, indicated by *DOCUMENT-RETRIEVAL* in the lower left corner of the screen. Once a document or a group of documents has been selected, you can use the **C**opy, **D**elete, **L**oad, and **P**rint subcommands to perform the indicated actions. The **E**xit subcommand leaves the document retrieval mode.

Your first step is to use the **Q**uery subcommand to find the files with which you want to work. After stating the file searching criteria, you are presented a list of files which meet those criteria; you can then select from that list and the selection is used by the other subcommands. After you have selected a file or files, four of the subcommands can act on them. They are:

SUBCOMMAND	USE
Load	Loads the documents as if you had given the **T**ransfer **L**oad command
Print	Prints the documents, the summary sheets, or both
Copy	Copies the selected files to a different drive or directory
Delete	Deletes the selected files

The **V**iew subcommand lets you change the way that the selected files are listed. You can specify a sort order and how much information is given in the list of the selected files. You can sort by directory, author, operator, revision date, creation date, or file size. You can choose among three views:

VIEW	MEANING
Short	Shows only the file and path names
Long	Shows the file and path name, as well as the sort key in a one-column format
Full	Shows a list like *Short*, with the addition of a window containing the summary sheets in the middle of the screen

The **U**pdate subcommand lets you update the information in the selected summary sheets.

The **E**xit subcommand leaves the document-retrieval mode.

When you give the **L**ibrary **D**ocument-retrieval **Q**uery command, Word prompts you for the search criteria. These include the *author, operator, keywords, creation date,* and *revision date* fields from the summary sheets, as well as a path, text from the documents, and consideration of case-sensitivity. The path is all the paths you want Word to search for documents. You must state the paths exactly, with each path separated by a comma.

You can enter up to 256 characters for each of the *author, operator,* and *keywords* fields. You can use wildcard characters (* and ?) in the text for which you are searching.

You can use logical operators in all fields (including the *creation date* and *revision date* fields) to make your search more specific. The logical operators must be used without spaces around them.

The logical operators are:

ACTION	CHARACTER
AND	& (ampersand) or a space
greater than	>
less than	<
NOT	~ (tilde)
OR	, (comma)

Library Hyphenate Command
Overview
To add optional hyphens in your text, select the region you want to hyphenate and give the **Library H**yphenate command. If you want to hyphenate from a particular part of the document to the end, put the cursor at the beginning of where you want to hyphenate. You can stop hyphenating at any time by pressing Escape.

Word adds hyphens only to words that are at the ends of lines. If you edit the lines, change the margins, or change fonts in such a way that the lines change, you will probably want to rehyphenate the lines.

Note that the **Library H**yphenate command does not remove unneeded optional hyphens; it simply adds new ones where needed at the time that the command is given. Also, the **Library H**yphenate command doesn't add optional hyphens to a word that already has hyphens in it. Thus, if you have added normal or nonbreaking hyphens, or have added optional hyphens by hand, the command will not add optional hyphens to the word.

In the *confirm* field, select *No* if you want Word to hyphenate without prompting you for each word, or select *Yes* if you want to check each hyphenation. Unless your document is very long, it is probably a good idea to select *Yes* and follow along as Word hyphenates.

The *hyphenate caps* option lets you tell Word whether to hyphenate words that start with a capital letter, such as proper names or the first letter in a sentence.

Word switches to printer display and scrolls the screen horizontally if necessary. As the command is running, Word selects any word at the end of a line that can be hyphenated to make the line break closer to the end. Word prompts *Enter Y to insert hyphen, N to skip, or use direction keys*. Press Y to accept the hyphenation or N if you do not want to hyphenate the word. If you want to hyphenate the word at a different syllable, press the Down Arrow or Up Arrow keys to move back and forth. If you don't agree with Word's choice of where to break the syllables, use the Left Arrow or Right Arrow keys to move the hyphenation point back and forth character-by-character. When you have the hyphen in the place you want, press Y. You can't add a hyphen to the left of the second character or to the right beyond the point at which the word would be moved to the next line.

Library Index Command
Overview
Creating an index in Word is similar to creating a table of contents. As you edit your document, you flag words that you want in the index with special codes that are in hidden character format. When you are finished marking index entries, you

give the **Library Index** command and Word compiles the index
and places it at the end of your document in its own division.
Word also adds hidden text at the beginning and end of the
index so that it can replace the current index if you give the
Library Index command a second time.

To mark an entry, add the *index code* before the entry and
the *endmark* after the entry. For most entries, the index code is
".i." and the endmark is ";." Both are formatted as hidden text.
To mark a subentry, type . i . followed by the name of the main
entry and a colon, and format everything as hidden text. Add
the endmark (a hidden semicolon) at the end of the subentry.

Entries that include a colon, a semicolon, or a quotation
mark (Word's special characters for indexes), require particular attention. If the entry contains a colon, a semicolon, or a
quotation mark, enclose the entire entry in hidden quotation
marks.

Once your document is completely marked, you can
compile the index. First make sure that hidden text is not shown
(use the **Window Options** command); showing hidden text is
included in the repagination, which will throw off the page
numbers in the index. You should also be sure that you have
specified a printer driver in the **Print Options** command so that
Word knows how to determine the page sizes.

The choices for the **Library Index** command are:

FIELD	MEANING
entry/page # separated by	The character(s) you want to use to sepa-rate the entry and the page number. Word's default is two spaces; other com-mon choices are a comma and one space or a Tab character (type ^t to enter a tab).

L

FIELD	MEANING
cap main entries	Word normally capitalizes the first letter of an entry in the index. If you want it to leave the entries in the case in which they appear in the text, select *No*. Note that if two entries only differ in capitalization, Word will treat them as one and the same and include both page numbers in one entry, regardless of how you set this field. If you specify *No* here and there are both capitalized and uncapitalized entries, Word will use the first entry for the index.
indent each level	For direct formatting, this field tells Word how much to indent subentries from the preceding level.
use style sheet	It is often convenient to use a style sheet for the index entries. If you select *Yes* for this field, Word formats each entry as "Index level 1," "Index level 2," and so on instead of using direct formatting. You can then change the appearance of the lines of the index in the gallery.

When you execute the command, Word compiles the entries, sorts them, and places them at end of the document. It also inserts a division mark and the hiddent text *.Begin Index.* before the index, and the hidden text *.End Index.* after the index. This operation can take quite a while, depending on the size of your document and on the number of index entries you have specified.

Library Link Document Command
Overview

This command lets you bring part or all of another Word document or ASCII file into your document when you print. The command prompts you for a file name and a bookmark in that file. If you do not include a bookmark name (for an ASCII file, for example), Word links in the entire file.

Library Link Graphics Command
Overview

The **Library Link Graphics** command prompts you for the name of the graphic file you want to include in your document. There are many formats of graphics files that Word can read. These include:

- Lotus graphics files (.PIC format)
- PC Paintbrush files (.PCX format)
- HPGL files
- Files of PostScript commands
- Encapsulated PostScript files
- Windows Clipboard format
- Microsoft Pageview documents (unfortunately, the size and clipping information is lost)
- Some TIFF documents (there are many variants on the TIFF standard)
- Files already formatted with the printer codes for the printer on which you are printing
- Files created with Word's Capture program (.SCR files)

Give the **Library Link Graphics** command and type the name of the graphics file for *filename*. If the file is not in the same directory as the current document, Word will make the name an absolute reference from the root directory of the disk. After you type the file name and select another field in the dialog, Word attempts to determine the graphics format of the file. If it is successful, Word places it in the *format* field; if it can't determine it, you must fill in the format yourself.

When you execute the **Library Link Graphics** command, Word creates the tags for the paragraph with the graphic. The paragraph can be treated like any other paragraph in your document, and can moved in the scrap.

The other choices in the dialog let you specify the width of the frame for the graphic, the alignment of the graphic within its frame, and any space above and below the graphic. The *graphics width* and *graphics height* refer to the desired size of the picture; if the file contains information that can be used to determine it, Word fills in these fields. You can also select *Same as column* for the *graphics width* to make the graphic as wide as the column or the page (if there is only one column). If Word can't determine the suggested height of the graphic but knows the preferred ratio of the height to the width, it will attempt to keep the ratio when you enter a size for *graphics width*. You can also enter any value you want for either field.

The choices for *alignment* are *Centered*, *Left*, *Right*, or a measurement from the left side of the frame. The *space before* and *space after* fields are similar to their functions in the **Format Paragraph** command. If you don't specify any amounts for *space before* and *space after*, Word will still put a small amount of space so that the objects don't touch the surrounding text.

To resize or reposition a graphic, select the tag and give the **Library Link Graphics** command. Word displays the current settings for that paragraph, for you to change as desired.

Library Link Spreadsheet Command

Overview

The methods you use for specifying the data you want to integrate differ for different spreadsheets, but they are similar in nature. Basically, you name the spreadsheet and the area of the spreadsheet you want to include in your document. Word reads the current values for the data when you first integrate the spreadsheet with the **Library Link** command; you can update the data any time by selecting the data and giving the **Library Link** command again.

Put the cursor where you want the spreadsheet data and give the **Library Link** command. In the *filename* field, type the name of the spreadsheet file from which you want to read. You should specify the full path name for the file, although you can use a relative path name if you wish. However, Word uses relative path names in reference to the path in the **Transfer Options** command. You can see the names of all the files in the default path by typing * . * in the *filename* field and pressing F1.

Enter the range that you want to use in the *area* field. You can enter a range name or a range of cells; if you want the entire spreadsheet, leave this field blank. To see a list of named ranges in the spreadsheet, select this field and press F1.

To update the information in an integrated spreadsheet, select the entire paragraph in which the data resides and give the **Library Link** command again. Don't fill in the fields; simply press Enter.

To unlink an integrated spreadsheet from the spreadsheet file, simply delete the header and trailer tags. Word then views the data just like data you entered manually. To relink it, delete the data and give the **Library Link** command again, specifying the spreadsheet name and desired range.

Library Number Command

Overview

The Library Number command gives you a great deal of flexibility in numbering a document. Word determines what kind of numbering you want by example. That is, if you have a report and want the primary headings numbered with capital Roman numerals and the secondary headings numbered with lowercase letters, you simply put the first number of each style at the beginning of the first paragraphs of that style, and Word will take those as cues for how to number the rest of your document.

For Word to recognize a number when you renumber your document, it must begin with the first character in the paragraph unless you begin it with a left parenthesis. Each number must end with a period or right parenthesis; however, legal format numbers cannot end with any punctuation. The period or right parenthesis must be followed by a space or Tab character. When you first number your document, Word formats the new numbers according to the character format of the first letter after the number.

You can number a section of your document by selecting it and giving the command. If you select only one character, the entire document is numbered. The *number* field lets you specify whether to update the numbers in the document or remove the current numbering. The *restart sequence* field tells Word whether or not you want to restart the numbering for the selected text.

Always save a copy of your document before you give the Library Number command the first time. You can sometimes get unexpected results from the first time you number, such as if some of your headings start with numbers and Word mistakes them for heading numbering. Immediately go through your document after numbering it. If there are large errors, you can reverse the effects of the numbering with the **U**ndo command.

Library Run Command
Overview
The **L**ibrary **R**un command lets you give standard MS-DOS commands (such as COPY and TYPE, batch files, and small application programs) from within Word without having to quit the application.

After saving all open files, give the **L**ibrary **R**un command. Word prompts you for the name of the command you want to run. Type in the command just as you would on the MS-DOS command line and press Enter; Word clears the screen, displays any output from the command, and displays the message *Press a key to resume Word*. To get back into Word, press any key.

You may want to run more than one MS-DOS command before returning to Word. If so, enter COMMAND at Word's prompt and press Enter. This loads a copy of the MS-DOS command processor so that you can enter as many commands as you wish. You will see the MS-DOS prompt after you give each command. When you are finished, type EXIT at the MS-DOS prompt and press Enter. When Word prompts *Press a key to resume Word*, press any key.

Library Spell Command

Overview

To start Word's speller, give the **L**ibrary **S**pell command or press Alt F6. If you are on a floppy-based system, you may have to shuffle disks in order to get the spelling program and data into Word.

If you have only a single character selected, Word starts checking from the word on which the selection resides, or the word immediately preceding it if the selection is on a space, tab, paragraph mark, or end mark. If more than one character is selected, the speller only checks the selected words.

When you enter spell mode, Word zooms the document window and puts the spell window at the bottom of the screen. The spell window has two parts: the top is used for suggesting alternatives to misspelled words, and the bottom is used for messages.

The speller immediately begins looking for suspect words. When it finds one, it scrolls the document and highlights the word; this lets you see the word in context so that you can remember what you were trying to say. Like in gallery mode, the commands change to only spell commands and can be selected by pressing their first letters, or pressing Esc first. To stop the speller during the search, press Escape and give the **E**xit command.

The commands in spell mode are:

COMMAND	USE
Add	Adds a word to one of the three dictionaries (*Standard*, *User*, and *Document*). This tells Word that the selected word is in fact spelled correctly and that you want it remembered for use in the future.
Correct	Corrects the misspelled word
Exit	Exits from the speller and unzooms the document if necessary
Ignore	Ignores the highlighted word. Use this when you want Word to ignore other instances of the word during the current session, but not to add the word to a permanent dictionary.
Options	Sets spelling options. The fields are:

Field	Meaning
user dictionary	Gives the name of the user dictionary
lookup	Sets the amount of checking Word does when looking for alternatives
ignore all caps	Specifies whether to stop for suspect words in all caps
check punctuation	Specifies whether to look for improper punctuation

Field	Meaning
alternatives	Sets whether or not Word should look immediately for alternatives when it finds a suspect word

COMMAND	USE
Undo	Reverses the last spelling change or dictionary addition and lets you specify again what action to take

When you reach the bottom of a document, Word prompts *Enter Y to continue spelling from top of document, N to exit, or Esc to cancel.* This allows you to continue checking if you did not begin at the top of the document. If you enter N, Word will go back to the place from which you started the speller.

Library Table Command

Overview

If you use Word's outlining feature to create the headings in your document, you do not need to do anything else before creating a table of contents. Word uses the automatic styles "Heading level 1," "Heading level 2," and so on when you create an outline. The **L**ibrary **T**able command uses these styles to create the table of contents.

If you do not use styles, each heading you want in your table of contents must be marked. All marks are entered in hidden text, so it is likely that you will want to make hidden text visible when you are adding your table of contents entries. (To do so, set the *show hidden text* field to *Yes* in the **W**indow **O**ptions command.)

To mark an entry for one-level tables, you add the *table code* before the entry and the *endmark* after the entry. If the end of the entry is the end of the paragraph, you do not need to include the endmark, although doing so does not hurt. For first-level entries, the table code is ".c." and the endmark is ";." Both must be formatted as hidden text. You can use a letter other than "c" if you wish.

Most table of contents in longer works generally have two or three levels. The table of contents might have the first-level entry aligned with the left margin, the second-level entries indented slightly, and so on. Another common practice is to have all entries left-aligned, with first-level entries in a larger font and bold face. To mark a second-level heading, you enter the table code . C . : before the entry and the endmark (a hidden semicolon) after the entry. Third-level headings are marked with . C . : : , and so on. If you want some of the entries in your table of contents to not have page numbers, add a colon before the endmark.

Once your document has the styles attached or is marked, you can compile the table of contents. First make sure that hidden text is not shown (use the **W**indow **O**ptions command); showing hidden text is included in the repagination, which will throw off the page numbers in the table of contents. You should also be sure that you have specified a printer driver in the **P**rint **O**ptions command so that Word knows how to determine the page sizes.

Give the **L**ibrary **T**able command and, after selecting the options, press Enter. If the document already has a table of contents, Word asks if you want to replace the existing table of contents; press Y to create the new table of contents. The choices for the **Library** **T**able command are:

FIELD	MEANING
from	You must specify whether Word should create the table of contents from styles (*Outline*) or from your hidden text markings (*Codes*).
index code	If you did not use "c" for the code, you must specify the letter you used here.
page numbers	You can prevent Word from including page numbers in the table by setting *page numbers* to *No*.
entry/page number separated by	The character(s) that you want to use to separate the entry and the page number.
indent each level	For direct formatting, this field tells Word how much to indent subentries from the preceding level.
use style sheet	It is often convenient to use a style sheet for the table of contents entries. If you select *Yes* for this field, Word formats each entry as "Table level 1," "Table level 2," and so on instead of using direct formatting.

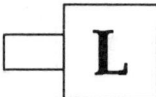

When you execute the command, Word compiles the entries and places them at end of the document. It also inserts a division mark and the hidden text *.Begin Table C.* before the table of contents and the hidden text *.End Table C.* after the table of contents.

Library thEsaurus Command

Overview

Select the word you want to look up and give the **L**ibrary th**E**saurus command or press Ctrl F6. If you have a floppy-based system, you may have to shuffle disks in order to get the thesaurus program and data into Word. Word opens up the thesaurus window, and you are in thesaurus mode.

Your choices are:

KEY	ACTION
Ctrl F6	Looks up a synonym for the word selected in the thesaurus window
Direction	Moves the selection over the words in the thesaurus window. Use this to select words you wish to insert in your document or to continue your search.
Enter	Replaces the selected word in your document with the word selected in the thesaurus
Esc	Leaves the thesaurus

Options
Overview

The **O**ptions command lets you configure your Word environment. Some options are for the currently active window while others are for the whole program. The options are:

FIELD	USE
show hidden text	Specifies whether hidden text is shown. If you choose *Yes*, Word displays hidden text with a dotted underline. Be sure that you are not showing hidden text when you repaginate, since Word will include the hidden text as it determines where text goes on the page.
show ruler	Shows the ruler at the top of the window
show non-printing symbols	Shows graphic characters for special word processing characters. *None* shows none of the characters. *Partial* shows the paragraphs, newlines, optional hyphens, and hidden text if the *show hidden text* field is set to *No*. *All* shows the same characters as *Partial*, but also shows tabs and spaces.
show layout	Shows your document in layout mode with all paragraphs on the page as they will print. Setting *show layout* to *No* puts Word into galley mode.
show line breaks	Shows lines as they will print. Line breaks change according to the setting for the printer (in the **P**rint **O**ptions command) and the font chosen. This field can also be changed with Alt F7.

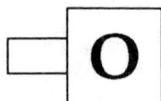

FIELD	USE
show outline	Shows the text in outline view
show style bar	Specifies whether the style bar is shown. The style bar shows the key codes for styles and the type of running head.
mute	Prevents Word from beeping when you get an error message. Setting *mute* to *No* allows normal beeping.
summary sheet	Shows a blank summary sheet each time a file without a filled-in summary sheet is saved. Setting *summary sheet* to *No* causes Word to ignore the summary sheet for new files.
measure	Specifies the unit of measurement Word will use. You can choose *In* (inches), *Cm* (centimeters), *P10* (10-pitch characters, or 10 characters per inch), *P12* (12-pitch characters, or 12 characters per inch), or *Pt* (points, or 1/72 of an inch).
display mode	Selects the mode Word uses to display the screen. The numbers for graphics modes indicate that you have a graphics adapter and want Word to use the graphics mode. Although this can be slower than text mode, the mouse pointer gives more information. Also, if you have a Hercules Graphics Card Plus, you can better see how your text will print since the text is displayed with italicized and boldface words; superscripts and subscripts are shown as smaller characters. This field can also be changed with Alt F9.

FIELD	USE
paginate	Tells Word either to repaginate as you work or only when you give a specific command (such as **P**rint **R**epaginate). *Auto* indicates automatic repagination, which usually slows Word down; *Manual* indicates no automatic repagination.
colors	Sets the color for the menu, background, messages, and character formats. The numbers for colors vary with the type of adapter you use. Pressing F1 in this field shows a list of the items for which you can change the colors.
autosave	Tells Word how often to automatically save your document, in minutes. Setting *autosave* to 0 or leaving the field blank indicates that you do not want to automatically save the file.
autosave confirm	Specifies that the autosave function will prompt you each time it does an automatic save. Setting *confirm* to *No* tells Word to automatically save the file without prompting you.
show menu	Displays the menu at the bottom of the screen. You may want to turn the menu off by setting *show menu* to *No* if you want more space on the screen. As soon as you press Escape to give a command, Word shows the menus again so you can give commands. Turning the menu display off during macro execution can also increase the speed of macros.

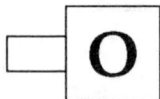

FIELD	USE
show borders	Shows the borders of the window. Setting *show borders* to *No* removes the four borders of the window. If you have more than one window on the screen, setting *show borders* to *No* has no effect until only one window is showing, as is the case in zoom mode.
date format	Specifies the format in which dates are displayed and printed when you use the special glossary entries "date" and "dateprint." *MDY* indicates that Word will print dates with the month first, such as "April 23, 1989." *DMY* indicates that Word will print dates with the day first, such as "23 April, 1989."
decimal character	Specifies the decimal character to be recognized in mathematical calculations and measurements. You can select a period (more common in the United States and Asia) or a comma (more common in many European countries). Note that if you change *decimal character* to a comma, you can no longer separate the fields in form letters with a comma; you must use a semicolon or tab instead.
time format	Specifies the format in which times are displayed and printed when you use the special glossary entries "time" and "timeprint." A *12* indicates that Word will print times in 12-hour format and include "AM" or "PM," and *24* indicates that Word will use 24-hour format.

FIELD	USE
default tab width	Sets distance between tab stops for all tabs to the right of the furthest set tab.
line numbers	Shows line numbers in the lower left corner of the screen. If *line numbers* is set to *No*, only the page and column number are shown. The line numbers are affected by the *count blank space* field.
count blank space	Causes the line numbers displayed by the *line numbers* field to represent each line on the page and not just lines with text in them. Setting *count blank space* to *Yes* causes Word to count blank spaces as well.
cursor speed	Sets the speed of the cursor when using cursor repeat (that is, when you hold down one of the cursor control keys). The range is 0 (slow) to 9 (fast).
linedraw character	Sets graphics character or character set used for line drawing. You can enter a character that will be used in all directions or press F1 to select a character set or character to use.
speller path	Shows the location of your spelling program.

Print Commands

Overview

Word's printing features make it easy to print your documents once you have finished editing them. You set the printing options with the **P**rint **O**ptions command. You can have Word put the files to be printed in a *print queue* so that you can continue to edit while Word prints your document(s). You can also print out Word's special files such as glossaries and style sheets.

The **P**rint command has nine subcommands:

SUBCOMMAND	USE
Printer	Prints the document on the currently selected printer
Direct	Allows you to send keystrokes directly to the printer
File	Causes Word to send the characters that would have gone to the printer into a file
Glossary	Prints the current glossary
Merge	Prints form letters
Options	Sets options such as choosing the printer driver and defining how much of the document should be printed
Queue	Manages Word's print queue
Repaginate	Repaginates the document
pre**V**iew	Shows you how the document will look when printed

Print Merge Commands
Overview

Creating form letters in Word is very similar to creating normal documents. The text of the letter is stored in the *main document*, and the text that varies (such as the names and addresses of each recipient) is stored in the *data document*. When you use the **P**rint **M**erge **P**rinter command, Word prints a version of the main document for each paragraph in the data document. Each paragraph is called a *record*. If you want to save your form letters in a file instead of printing them, use the **P**rint **M**erge **D**ocument command. The files produced by the **P**rint **M**erge **D**ocument command have the merged information, but no printer codes.

The main document has *fields* marked so that Word knows where to put the information from the data document. Each paragraph in the data document has information for the named fields. You can select which records you want to print out of the data document with the **P**rint **M**erge **O**ptions command. To specify the printing of only part of the data document, set the *range* field to *Records* and type the record numbers desired in the *record numbers* field. You can list individual records or ranges of records; a range can be indicated by a colon or hyphen.

As Word processes the document, it displays messages such as *Merging* and *Formatting*. To stop the merging process, press Escape. The **P**rint **M**erge command also has its own error messages for two circumstances:

MESSAGE	MEANING
Not a valid file	The data document named in the DATA instruction is missing. You may have typed the file name incorrectly or the file does not reside in the same directory as the main document.

MESSAGE	MEANING
Unknown field name	The name of a field in the main document does not match the names in the header record of the data document. This is commonly caused by a misspelling or slight difference between the fields in the two documents (such as "address_1" and "address1," which are different to Word) or by an invalid field name.

The DATA instruction is the only required merge instruction. However, the other merge instructions are very useful for creating complex or changing documents. You can use these instructions in your main document to help control the merge process and the text that appears in the merged documents. The additional merge instructions are:

INSTRUCTION	USE
ASK	Prompts you for a field value that will change in each printed document
IF and ELSE	Prints text in merged version based on conditions in the text
INCLUDE	Prints the contents of another document in the current document
NEXT	Prints many records in one merged document
SET	Prompts you for a field value that will appear in all printed documents
SKIP	Skips over the record in the data document if a condition in the text is true

Print Options Command

Overview

Use the **P**rint **O**ptions command to set a variety of options for your printed documents. The fields for the **P**rint **O**ptions command are:

FIELD	USE
printer	Names the printer driver you want to use. To see a list of all printer drivers available, press F1. You should use the SETUP command to copy printer drivers to your disk.
setup	Sets the computer port to which your printer is attached. Your choices are *LPT1:*, *LPT2:*, *LPT3:*, *COM1:*, and *COM2:*.
model	The model of the printer. Use F1 to see the available choices.
graphics resolution	Sets the resolution at which Word will print graphics in the document. Press F1 to see the choices for the printer named in the *printer* field.
copies	Indicates the number of copies you want to print.
draft	Specifies whether to print in draft mode or in final mode. Setting *draft* to *Yes* causes Word to print faster than in final mode since Word will not change fonts or use microjustification.
hidden text	Specifies whether Word will print hidden text in your document. Note that you can print hidden text even if it is not visible on the screen.

59

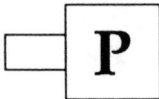

FIELD	USE
summary sheet	Tells Word whether you want to print the document's summary sheet along with the document.
range	Sets the portion of the document you want Word to print.
page numbers	Indicates the ranges of pages you want to print. You can specify the ranges as either a single page or a set of pages with either a colon or a hyphen. Each range is separated by a comma. For instance, to print pages 1 through 7, 12, and 20 through 25, you would type 1-7,12,20-25 or 1:7,12,20:25. If you want to specify specific pages within a division, type the page number followed by "D" and by the division number (for example, type 5D3 for page 5 of the third division).
widow/orphan control	Specifies whether you want widow and orphan control when printing the document.
queued	Causes Word to put the file in the print queue.
paper feed	Controls the printer feed used for the paper. *Manual* indicates that you will insert a piece of paper at the beginning of each page; Word prompts you before printing each page. *Continuous* prints from the main feeder of the printer.
duplex	Tells Word whether you want to print on both sides of a single sheet of paper.

Print preView Command

Overview

The **P**rint pre**V**iew command allows you to see your document as it will appear on the page before you print it.

You cannot edit in preview mode, but you can page through your document quickly to check for page breaks and paragraph positions. When you first enter preview mode, Word displays the page in which the cursor was when you gave the command. Note that the font you see on the screen doesn't match the font or fonts you have specified; instead, it is a single preview font that is scaled to different sizes.

There are a limited number of commands that you can use in preview mode. **E**xit takes you back to the mode in which you were before giving the **P**rint pre**V**iew command. **J**ump allows you to jump to a specific page or bookmark. **O**ptions lets you set whether you want to see one or two pages in preview mode. The **P**rint command works similar to the **P**rint command in the other modes, although the only two options are **P**rinter and **O**ptions. If you change a print option that affects the pagination (such as *hidden text* and *widow/orphan control*), Word will repaginate the document.

If you are using a mouse, you can scroll and thumb like you do in galley mode, although there is no scroll bar. To scroll with the keyboard, press Pg Up and Pg Dn. Ctrl Pg Up and Ctrl Pg Dn move you to the first and last pages of the document respectively. The only other keys you can use are ones to select preview commands, Alt-H to get help, and any macros that you have assigned to Ctrl key combinations.

To speed up scrolling and viewing in preview mode, give the **P**rint **O**ptions command and set *draft* to *Yes*. This prevents the graphics (but not its borders) from being displayed and can give you much faster performance, depending on the speed of your computer and the complexity of the graphics in your document.

Print Queue Commands

Overview

Word's **P**rint **Q**ueue commands let you print files and continue to work. When you print to the queue by setting *queued* field in the **P**rint **O**ptions command to *Yes*, Word sends characters to the printer as you work.

After sending one or more files to Word's queue, you can control the queue with the **P**rint **Q**ueue subcommands. Use the **P**rint **Q**ueue **P**ause command to stop the printer temporarily and the **P**rint **Q**ueue **C**ontinue command to start it again. If you want to get rid of all the print jobs queued, give the **P**rint **Q**ueue **S**top command. If you are printing from the queue and you notice something wrong in the file currently being printed, use the **P**rint **Q**ueue **R**estart command to have Word print the current document again.

The **P**rint **F**ile command lets you store in a file the characters that Word would have sent to the printer. You can then later print the file by using the MS-DOS COPY command to copy the file to the port on which the printer resides. Note that the print output file might be quite large relative to the size of the document file, depending on the type of printer you are using.

The **P**rint **D**irect command sends the characters you're typing directly to the printer and is only useful for putting a short heading on a one-page document without adding it in the file. Give the **P**rint **D**irect command, type the text you want, press Enter, then press Escape. The characters you typed will appear on the printed page but not on the screen. When you print the rest of the page, Word will begin directly after your heading.

Print Repaginate Command
Overview
To force Word to repaginate a document, use the **P**rint **R**epaginate command. The command has an option, *confirm page breaks*, which lets you put your own page breaks in the document on a page-by-page basis. If you set this field to *Yes*, Word shows you each page break and prompts *Enter Y to confirm or use direction keys*. You can change the position of each page break by pressing Up Arrow or Down Arrow. Most of the time, however, you won't want to "tune" Word's page breaks and you will set *confirm page breaks* to *No*.

Quit Command
Overview
The **Q**uit command returns you to MS-DOS or Windows. Before it leaves Word, however, it makes sure that you have saved any changes you have made to documents, glossaries, and any open style sheets. It also saves the current settings for many options in a file called MW.INI so that those settings will be used when you start Word again.

Replace Command

Overview

In simple **R**eplace commands, you enter the text you want to be changed in the *text* field and the replacement text in the *with text* field (you are allowed up to 40 characters for each field). Word always searches forward in the document. If you have only one character selected when you give the **R**eplace command, Word searches and replaces to the end of the document, but not before the selected character. If you have selected more than one character, Word searches and replaces only within that selection.

Setting *confirm* to *Yes* causes Word to prompt *Enter Y to replace, N to ignore, or press Esc to cancel* each time it is about to replace characters. Word shows you the change that it is about to make. If you are sure that you want to do all the replacements throughout the file, set *confirm* to *No*.

The *case* option tells Word whether to search only for characters that match the case of the characters you specified in the *text* field, or to find characters which match the *text* field in either upper- or lowercase letters. The *whole word* option specifies whether or not the text that is searched for must be a whole word. If you are sure that the text you entered in the *text* field is a whole word and that is all you want to replace, set the *whole word* option to *Yes*.

Search Command

Overview

In simple Search commands, you enter the text for which you want to search in the *text* field (you are allowed up to 40 characters). Word lets you choose which direction to search in the *direction* field. The *case* option tells Word whether to search only for characters that match the case of the characters you specified in the *text* field, or to find characters which match the *text* field in either upper- or lowercase letters. Setting *case* to *Yes* indicates that you only want to search for characters that exactly match the case of the characters in the *text* field. Often, you want Word to ignore the case since the word for which you are searching may or may not be at the beginning of a sentence.

The *whole word* option specifies whether or not the text that is searched for must be a whole word. If you are sure that the text you entered in the *text* field is a whole word and that is all you want to find, set the *whole word* option to *Yes.* This also makes the searching process a bit faster.

Transfer Commands

Overview

Word performs all of its reading from and writing to the disk with the Transfer commands. The commands allow you to open, close, and save files, as well as to set the standard directory on which Word looks for documents and style sheets. There is also a Transfer command in the gallery.

The commands are:

COMMAND	USE
Load	Opens files for editing
Save	Saves files to disk
Clear	Clears the current document from the window (**T**ransfer **C**lear **W**indow command). The **T**ransfer **C**lear **A**ll command clears all open windows, glossaries, and style sheets.
Delete	Deletes a file from disk
Merge	Combines a document into the current document after the selection
Options	Sets the default directory for searching
Rename	Renames the current file
Glossary	Loads, merges or clears glossary entries
Allsave	Saves all open documents to disk

Undo Command
Overview
When you give an editing command, you can almost always reverse the action by giving the **U**ndo command. Note that you can only undo the last edit you made. If you delete some text, move the cursor, and start editing again, you can no longer undo the deletion. The **U**ndo command also undoes Word's formatting commands.

The **U**ndo command has a second purpose: you can use it to experiment with some changes and reverse the changes if you don't like them. If you give the **U**ndo command after giving the **U**ndo command, Word redoes the change (that is, it switches back and forth between the edited and unedited state). You can use this to compare the effects of an edit.

The **U**ndo command cannot undo all commands and actions. For instance, it cannot undo moving the cursor, regardless of whether you move the cursor with the mouse, the keyboard, the **J**ump commands, the **F**ormat s**E**arch commands, or the **S**earch command. It also cannot undo changes in the gallery.

Window Commands

Overview

Using many windows at once allows you to move text between documents and between different parts of a Word document. You can also compare the contents of two files easily. You can have up to eight windows open at the same time, but it is unlikely that you will use more than four or five.

Word uses *tiled* windows on its screen. Tiled windows sit next to each other on the screen and share edges. If you are familiar with the Macintosh or Microsoft Windows version 2, you know that these environments use *overlapping* windows.

At any time, only one window is *active*. This means that you cannot edit in two windows at the same time; instead, you have to select the window in which you want to work and make it active.

You can move from window to window by pressing F1. This makes the window with the next higher number active. To move to the window with the next lower number, press Shift F1. You can move between windows with the mouse simply by clicking in the desired window.

To close a window, use the **W**indow **C**lose command. If you are using the mouse, you can close a window by pointing to its right border and pressing both buttons. If there is only one window on the screen and you close it, Word clears the contents of the window but leaves the window itself on the screen.

To move the lower right corner of a window, use the **W**indow **M**ove command. Fill in the *to row* and *to column* fields with the desired locations. To move the corner with the mouse, simply point at the corner, hold down the left button, move to the desired location, and release the button.

If you have a few small windows into different documents on the screen, you may want to enlarge them to full size and be able to flip through them. Microsoft calls enlarging a window *zooming*. To zoom the active window, press Ctrl F1 (Word displays *ZM* at the bottom of the screen when you have zoomed the windows). In effect, this zooms all windows. When you press F1 or Shift F1, the next or previous window will be selected, and will already be zoomed to full height. To return the windows to their previous sizes, press Ctrl F1 again.

To zoom with the mouse, point at the window number and click the right button. To select the next window, point at the window number and click the left button; to select the previous window, point at the window number, hold down the Shift key, and click the left button. To return the windows to their previous sizes, point at the window number and press the right button again.

To split a window, use the **W**indow **S**plit **H**orizontal command. The *at line* field is filled in with the number of the line on which the cursor is on, but you can change this to any number. If you want to open a blank window instead of seeing two views of the current file, set the *clear new window* field to *Yes*. You can also split a window with the mouse by pointing at the right border and pressing the left button (to split and open another window in this document) or the right button (to open a blank window).

If you are using many footnotes, it is generally convenient to leave the footnote window open at the bottom of the screen. To open the footnote window when you are not creating a footnote, use the **W**indow **S**plit **F**ootnote command. Usually, having the footnote window be five or six lines tall is sufficient for most short footnotes. If you are going to be leaving the footnote window open most of the time while you work, you may want to save space by removing the screen borders and even the menu with the **O**ptions command.

Appendix A. Other Tables

Special characters:

TO ENTER	TYPE	COMMENTS
Division mark	Ctrl Enter	
Em dash	Alt Ctrl Hyphen	Long hyphen
New line mark	Shift Enter	
Nonbreaking hyphen	Ctrl Shift Hyphen	Line will not be broken
Nonbreaking space	Ctrl Space Bar	Line will not be broken
Normal hyphen	Hyphen	
Optional hyphen	Ctrl Hyphen	Not shown on screen unless Word breaks a line
Page mark	Ctrl Shift Enter	
Paragraph mark	Enter	
Space	Space Bar	

Types of hyphenation:

TYPE	PRESS	SHOWS ON SCREEN/PRINTOUT	WORD WILL BREAK
Nonbreaking	Ctrl Shift Hyphen	Yes	No
Normal	Hyphen	Yes	Yes
Optional	Ctrl Hyphen	Not unless broken	Yes

Appendix A. Other Tables

Keys for cursor movement:

KEY	MOVEMENT
Ctrl Down Arrow	Beginning of next paragraph
Ctrl End	Bottom of window
Ctrl Home	Top of window
Ctrl Left Arrow	Beginning of previous word
Ctrl Pg Down	Bottom of document
Ctrl Pg Up	Top of document
Ctrl Right Arrow	Beginning of next word
Ctrl Shift Tab	Previous object (in layout mode)
Ctrl Tab	Next object (in layout mode)
Ctrl Up Arrow	Beginning of previous paragraph
Down Arrow	Down
End	End of line
Home	Beginning of line
Left Arrow	Left
Pg Down	Down a windowful
Pg Up	Up a windowful
Right Arrow	Right
Up Arrow	Up

Keys for text selection:

KEY	SELECTION
F7	Previous word
F8	Next word
F9	Previous paragraph
F10	Next paragraph
Shift F7	Previous sentence
Shift F8	Next sentence
Shift F9	Current line
Shift F10	Entire document

Other keyboard commands:

KEY	COMMAND
F1	Next window
F2	Calculate
F3	Expand from glossary
F4	Repeat last editing or inserting command
F5	Overtype on/off
F6	Extend selection on/off
F11	Collapse heading
F12	Expand heading
Shift F1	Undo
Shift F2	Outline view on/off
Shift F3	Record macro on/off

KEY	COMMAND
Shift F4	Repeat last search
Shift F5	Outline edit on/off
Shift F6	Column selection on/off
Shift F11	Collapse body text
Shift F12	Expand body text
Ctrl F1	Zoom window
Ctrl F2	**Format Running**-head *position Top*
Ctrl F3	Step macro
Ctrl F4	Change case
Ctrl F5	Line drawing on/off
Ctrl F6	**Library thEsaurus**
Ctrl F7	**Transfer Load**
Ctrl F8	**Print Printer**
Ctrl F9	**Print preView**
Ctrl F10	**Transfer Save**
Ctrl F12	Expand all
Ctrl Shift \	Redraw the screen (graphics mode only)
Alt F1	**Format Tab Set**
Alt F2	**Format Running**-head *position Bottom*
Alt F3	**Copy** to scrap
Alt F4	Show layout
Alt F5	**Jump Page**

KEY	COMMAND
Alt F6	**Library S**pell
Alt F7	**O**ptions *printer display Yes/No*
Alt F8	**F**ormat **C**haracter *font name*
Alt F9	**O**ptions *display Text/Graphics*
Alt F10	**F**ormat **S**tylesheet **R**ecord

Macro instructions:

COMMAND	USE
«ASK *variable* = ?»	Same as «SET *variable* = ?»
«ASK *variable* = ?*prompt*»	Same as «SET *variable* = ?*prompt*»
«COMMENT *text*»	Places a comment in the macro but does not have any effect. You can also include a comment with «COMMENT»*text*«ENDCOMMENT».
«IF *condition*»	Checks whether the condition is true; if so, Word executes the commands that follow up to the «ENDIF» statement. If the IF command is followed by an «ELSE» statement, it checks whether the condition is true; if so, Word executes the commands that follow up to the «ELSE» statement. If the condition was false, Word executes the commands between the «ELSE» statement and «ENDIF» statement.

COMMAND	USE
«MESSAGE *text*»	Displays a message in the message line near the bottom of the screen. The message can be up to 80 characters. The message will remain there until another MESSAGE command is given or until Word puts a message of its own in that line.
«PAUSE *prompt*»	Suspends the macro so that you can perform actions such as entering text or responses, or selecting text. When you press Enter, Word continues executing the macro.
«QUIT»	Stops a macro. This is usually used as part of an IF command to stop a macro after a condition is no longer true.
«REPEAT *number*»	Repeats all steps between the REPEAT command and the ENDREPEAT command the specified number of times.
«SET *variable* = ?»	Asks you for a value for the named variable. Word displays *Enter text, press Enter when done* in the message area near the bottom of the screen.

COMMAND	USE
«SET *variable = expression*»	Sets a variable to a value. The expression can be the name of another variable, a number, a date, or some text in quotes. If you want to set a variable to be the contents of two or more variables, list them as the expression with spaces between each variable name.
«SET *variable = ?prompt*»	Prompts you for a value for the named variable, displaying the prompt you specify in the message area near the bottom of the screen.
«WHILE *condition*»	Repeats all the instructions after the WHILE command up to the «ENDWHILE» statement as long as the condition is true.

Special macro variables:

VARIABLE	VALUE
echo	Determines whether or not to display updates to the screen from macro actions. If you want to make your macro run faster, you can set the echo variable to "off" with the SET command; Word will not update the screen until the end of the macro or until you set the echo variable to "on."
field	The value of the selected field in a dialog. For example, if your macro gave a Format Character command followed by a Tab character, this variable would be equal to "Yes" if the selected text was italic or "No" if it wasn't.

VARIABLE	VALUE
promptmode	How Word expects prompts to be answered. You can set this to *"user"* if you want the user to respond to prompts, to *"macro"* if you want the macro to respond to the prompts, or to *"ignore"* to have Word ignore any prompts that appear. Unless you specify, Word assumes that the prompts will be responded to by the macro.
scrap	The contents of the scrap. Special characters such as paragraph marks and tab characters are indicated like they are in the Search command.
selection	The contents of the selection. Special characters such as paragraph marks and tab characters are indicated like they are in the Search command. You can test whether you are at the end of the file by seeing if this variable is equal to nothing (that is, "").
window	The number of the window. You can use this in two ways. To move the cursor to a specific window, use the SET command, such as "«SET window = 4»." To determine which window you are in, use the window variable with the IF command: "«IF window = 2»."
wordversion	The version of Word you are running. You can use this to detect if you are running version 5.

Modes in Word:

MODE	CODE	KEY
Caps lock	CL	Caps Lock
Column select	CO	Shift F6
Extend selection	EX	F6
Line draw	LD	Ctrl F5
Numeric lock	NL	Num Lock
Overtype	OT	F5
Record macro	RM	Shift F3
Revision marks	MR	Format revision-Marks command
Scroll lock	SL	Scroll Lock
Step through macro	ST	Ctrl F3
Zoom	ZM	Ctrl F1

Selection of blocks of text with the mouse:

TO SELECT	POINT AT	PRESS
Character	Text	Left button
Entire document	Selection bar	Both buttons
Line	Selection bar	Left button
Paragraph	Selection bar	Right button
Sentence	Text	Both buttons
Word	Text	Right button

To move text quickly with the mouse without affecting the contents of the scrap, select the text you want to move, point to the location you want to move the text, hold down the Ctrl key, and click the left mouse button. You can also tell Word that you want the text to appear before different blocks of text:

TO MOVE IN FRONT OF:	POINT AT:	HOLD DOWN THE CTRL KEY AND CLICK THE MOUSE BUTTON:
Beginning of document	Selection bar	Both
Character	Text	Left
Line	Selection bar	Left
Paragraph	Selection bar	Right
Sentence	Text	Both
Word	Text	Right

Keyboard actions in outline mode:

KEY	USE
Alt 0	Make heading a lower level
Alt 9	Make heading a higher level
Control + n	Expand up to level n
Keypad - or F11	Collapse heading
Shift F2	Switch between document view and outline view
Shift F5	Switch between edit mode and organize mode

KEY	USE
Shift Keypad - or Shift F11	Collapse body text
Shift Keypad + or Shift F12	Expand body text
Keypad *	Expand all headings
Keypad + or F12	Expand heading

Selection with arrow keys in organize mode for outlines:

KEY	SELECTION
Down Arrow	Next heading at the same level, skipping over subordinate headings. If the heading below is a higher level, the selection does not move.
End	Last heading subordinate to this heading.
F6	Extends the selection to all headings and body text subordinate to this one.
Home	Previous heading at higher level.
Left Arrow or F9	Previous heading, regardless of level.
Right Arrow	Next heading, regardless of level. F10 performs the same action.
Up Arrow	Previous heading at the same level, skipping over subordinate headings. If the heading above is a higher level, the selection does not move.

Special characters in the **R**eplace and **S**earch commands:

TO INDICATE	USE
Any white space	^w
Caret mark	^^
Column break	^c
Division mark or forced page break	^d
Newline mark	^n
Nonbreaking space	^s
Optional hyphen	^-
Paragraph mark	^p
Tab character	^t

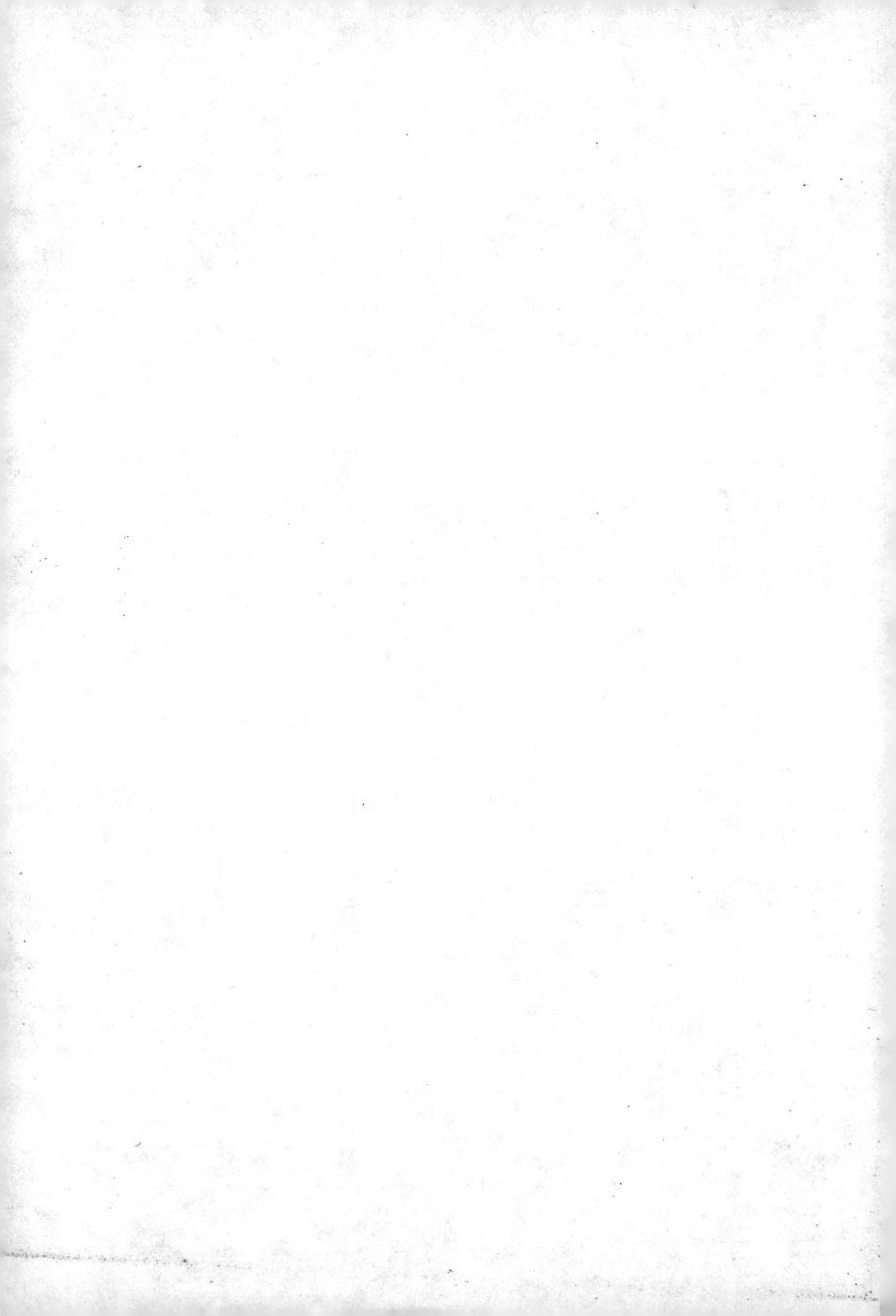